IMAGES
*of America*

# El Camino Real de los Tejas

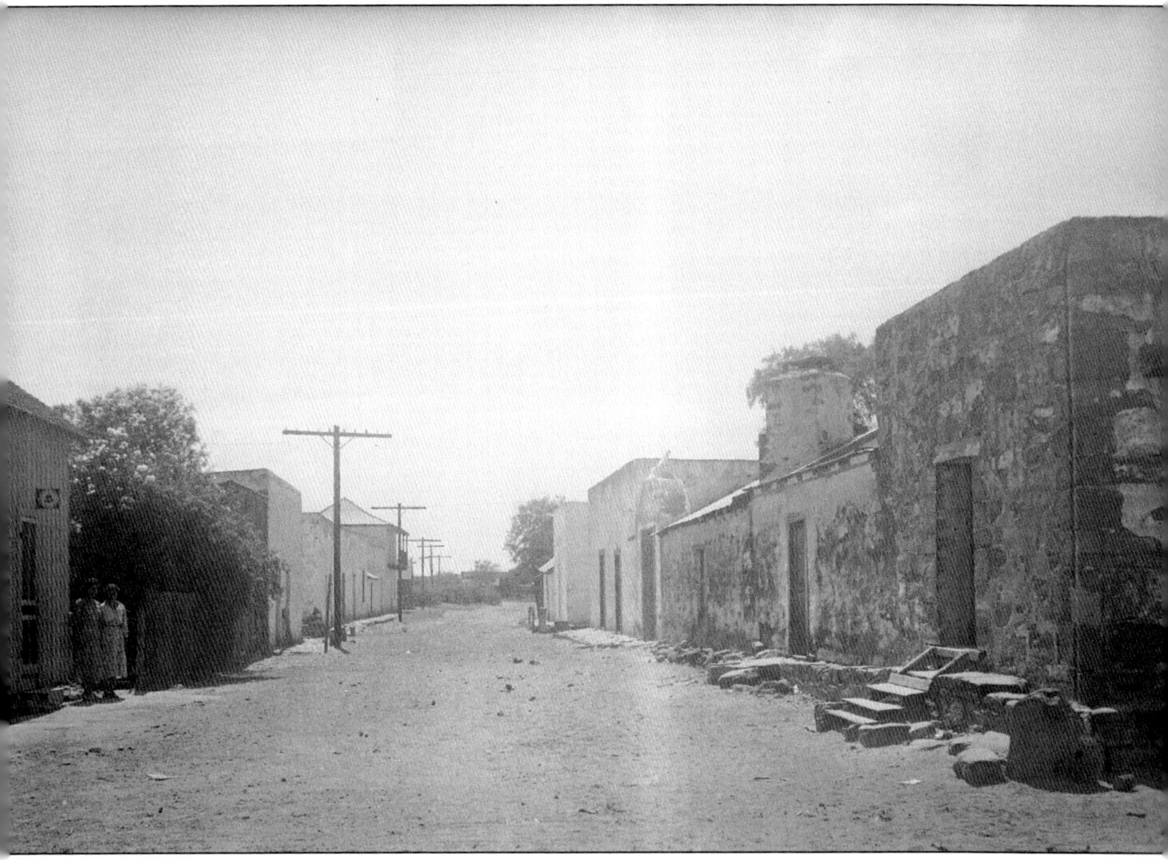

*Caminos* across most of Texas were, in essence, caliche roads. Caliche roads are composed of the subsurface limestone layer of the landscape. This camino can be seen running along the Jesús Treviño Fort y Rancho in San Ygnacio, Texas. (Courtesy of the Library of Congress.)

**On the Cover:** This bird's-eye view shows El Camino Real de los Tejas and the surrounding Texas terrain. The site is Sugarloaf Mountain, located near Gause, Texas. (Courtesy of El Camino Real de los Tejas National Historic Trail Association.)

IMAGES
*of America*

# EL CAMINO REAL DE LOS TEJAS

Steven Gonzales, Mary Joy Graham,
and Dr. Lucile Estell

ARCADIA
PUBLISHING

ISBN 978-1-4671-3194-0

Published by Arcadia Publishing
Charleston, South Carolina

Printed in the United States of America

Library of Congress Control Number: 2014948885

For all general information, please contact Arcadia Publishing:
Telephone 843-853-2070
Fax 843-853-0044
E-mail sales@arcadiapublishing.com
For customer service and orders:
Toll-Free 1-888-313-2665

Visit us on the Internet at www.arcadiapublishing.com

*This book is dedicated to our colleagues at the National Park Service Intermountain Region in Santa Fe, with our sincere thanks for their wonderful and unending encouragement and support in the development of our national treasure: El Camino Real de los Tejas National Historic Trail!*

# Contents

# ACKNOWLEDGMENTS

Presenting the history and significance of this great national treasure, El Camino Real de los Tejas National Historic Trail, has been a labor of love for the authors. Only as we preserve and protect this priceless piece of our heritage can we assure its significance for future generations. We are grateful to those who sponsored the bill that created the trail, Sen. Kay Bailey Hutchison and Rep. Ciro Rodriguez; the Congress who passed the legislation creating the trail; and to Pres. George W. Bush, who signed the legislation into law in October 2004.

Photographs in this book documenting sites deemed to be of high potential by the National Park Service, and showing activities or places of interest, have been gathered by members of the Trail Association Board and by others interested in the trail. The tourism center in Nacogdoches, Texas; Chief Rufus Davis; the Sabine Parish Visitor Center; and the Adai Caddo Cultural Center in Robeline, Louisiana, have also shared photographs with us.

All of the authors' royalties from the sale of this book will go to El Camino Real de los Tejas National Historic Trail Association, based in Austin, Texas. This is done in the hope that the trail will continue to exist for future generations—enriching and educating them as it does people today!

# Introduction

Throughout our history, roads have stood as symbols of progress and growth. It was a road that enabled Paul Revere to make his famous ride, it was a road that took Daniel Boone westward, and it was a road—a royal road—that has historically linked Texas to its neighbors in the south.

El Camino Real de los Tejas, or the Royal Road of the Tejas, has been a part of the history of North America since before the founding of the United States. It has often been presented as a place of history and intrigue, a place that outlaws and ordinary men and women would gravitate to for safety and to further their causes. It was the King's Highway, and one might hope to travel this famous road under a modicum of the crown's protection. There is little doubt that the road originated with the trails of the Native Americans and of the buffalo and other animals. Who better to know the route that would best traverse this land? Its name even includes the word *Tejas*, linking it to the Adai Caddo Indians who still reside along this road in Natchitoches Parish.

El Camino Real evolved slowly as early explorers entered the area now known as Texas and cautiously made their way across this wondrous land. Early records show that the French explorer Robert de La Salle and his men entered Texas by accident, though his landing near Garcitas Creek did not escape the attention of Spanish explorers who had aims on obtaining this fertile land for themselves. Both the French and the Spanish probed the area, traveling on the old game trails, but, according to famed Spanish colonial historian Carlos Castañeda, it was a Spanish expedition—led by Alonso de León—which penetrated all of the way to the Guadalupe River. Castañeda considers this to be the beginnings of Texas. The Spanish then learned of María de Ágreda, sometimes called the "Lady in Blue," a Spanish nun who is said to have visited the Tejas Indians via supernatural means and encouraged them to convert to Christianity. Her stories resulted in the establishment of missions and an influx of people into far east Texas and San Antonio de Béxar. Travel increased, the road became more pronounced, and—as Texas moved toward its revolution—the road became a conduit for people as they explored and settled the land.

In 1918, after much study, the Texas Society Daughters of the American Revolution (TSDAR) used the notes of surveyor V.N. Zivley to place pink granite markers at selected sites along a portion of the trail known as the Old San Antonio Road. These markers are extremely valuable to the history of the trail and will be brought into greater prominence as this historic trail is further developed.

Attention was again focused on the trail in 2004, when—due mostly to the efforts of Sen. Kay Bailey Hutchison and Rep. Ciro Rodriguez—the US Congress designated El Camino Real de los Tejas as a National Historic Trail. The trail extends more than 2,500 miles from near Eagle Pass and Laredo to Natchitoches, Louisiana, and the history of this nation has been strongly influenced by events that occurred upon it. Much of this history has lain hidden by the lack of a way—and perhaps the lack of a desire—to make it known, but now, as the trail develops, so too does awareness of its significance. El Camino Real de los Tejas National Historic Trail has the potential to help us better understand our history and our nation, and it has within it the potential to rewrite—or perhaps write properly for the first time—Texas's colonial history.

Responsibility for the development of this trail lies with a 15-member board of directors, which works directly with the Intermountain Region of the National Park Service and its superintendant, Aaron Mahr Yanez. As the trail is more than 2,500 miles long, one action of the board was to divide it into four geographic regions: South Texas, San Antonio–Goliad, Brazos, and Caddo. The chapters of this book are organized along these same regions. El Camino Real de los Tejas National Historic Trail Association is tasked with the protection of the historical integrity of the trail, and all of the authors' proceeds from the sale of this book will go to the association to help with developing and protecting the trail. This book reflects the love and responsibility each of us feels for this national treasure.

—Steven Gonzales<br>
Executive Director of El Camino Real de los Tejas National Historic Trail

—Joy Graham<br>
Vice President and board member of El Camino Real de los Tejas National Historic Trail

—Dr. Lucile Estell<br>
President and board member of El Camino Real de los Tejas National Historic Trail

# *One*

# Coahuila y (South) Texas

The banks of the Río Grande—dividing the states of Texas and Coahuila, Mexico—are where the history and legends of Spanish Texas run deep. The dusty, semiarid plain that is the backdrop for this area is a transitional zone of the arid desert environments to the west, the hardwood forest to the north and east, and the coastal grasslands to the south.

Coahuila served as the initial Spanish gateway into Texas and contains portions of the Sierra Madre Oriental. East of the Sierra, the land slopes gently toward the Río Grande and is drained by several rivers, including the Salado and its tributary, the Sabinas River. The Tamaulipan Thornscrub, a dry region of scrubland, occupies the eastern portion of the state and extends across the Río Grande into southern Texas.

Culturally, South Texas is often referred to as the "Tejano Homeland" for its deep ties with Mexico and substantial Latino population. The area is also dissected by many rivers, such as the Río Grande, Nueces, and Frio.

The states of Coahuila and Texas have been linked historically for centuries. In the late 1600s and early 1700s, Spanish governors such as Alonso de León and Domingo Terán de los Ríos governed these far northern reaches of Spain's empire. Around 1726, the governance of the two provinces was separated, with Coahuila being governed from Monclova and Texas being governed from Los Adaes.

Nearly 100 years later, the Mexican Constitution of 1824 combined the Mexican provinces of Nuevo León, Coahuila, and Texas as one state. Nuevo León was quickly separated, and by early 1827, the Constitution of Coahuila y Texas was adopted. Over the next several years, due to machinations and much colluding, turmoil enveloped Coahuila y Texas, so that by 1835, Texas was declared a separate state under the Constitution of 1824. The two states would never again be united as one after the Texas Revolution and incorporation of Texas into the United States.

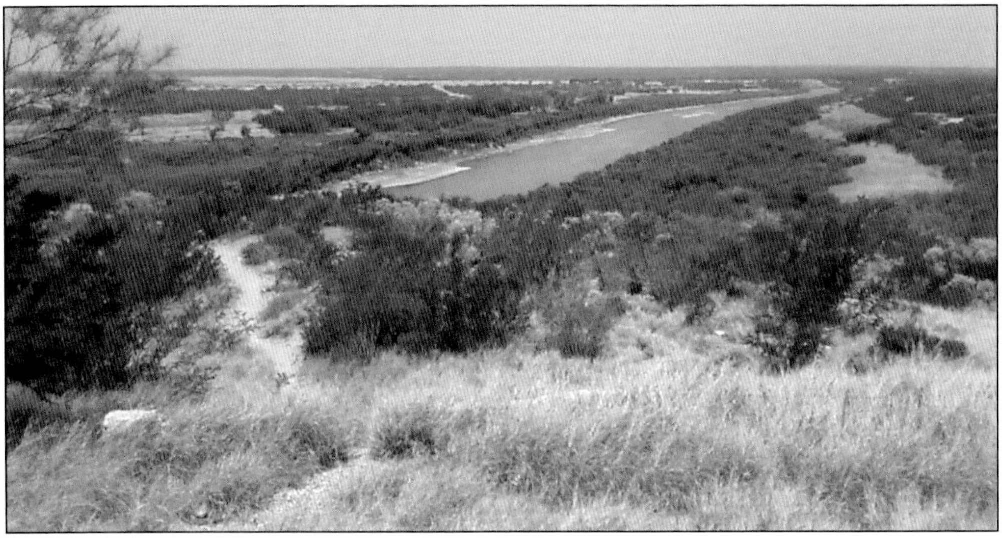

Caminos reales, or "royal roads," originated in the Spanish viceregal capital of Mexico City. El Camino Real de los Tejas headed north into the present-day United States and crossed at points near Eagle Pass, Laredo, and San Ygnacio, Texas. This photograph was taken looking west across the Río Grande and into Mexico from el *parque alto* along US Highway 83, just north of San Ygnacio, Texas. (Courtesy of Steven Gonzales.)

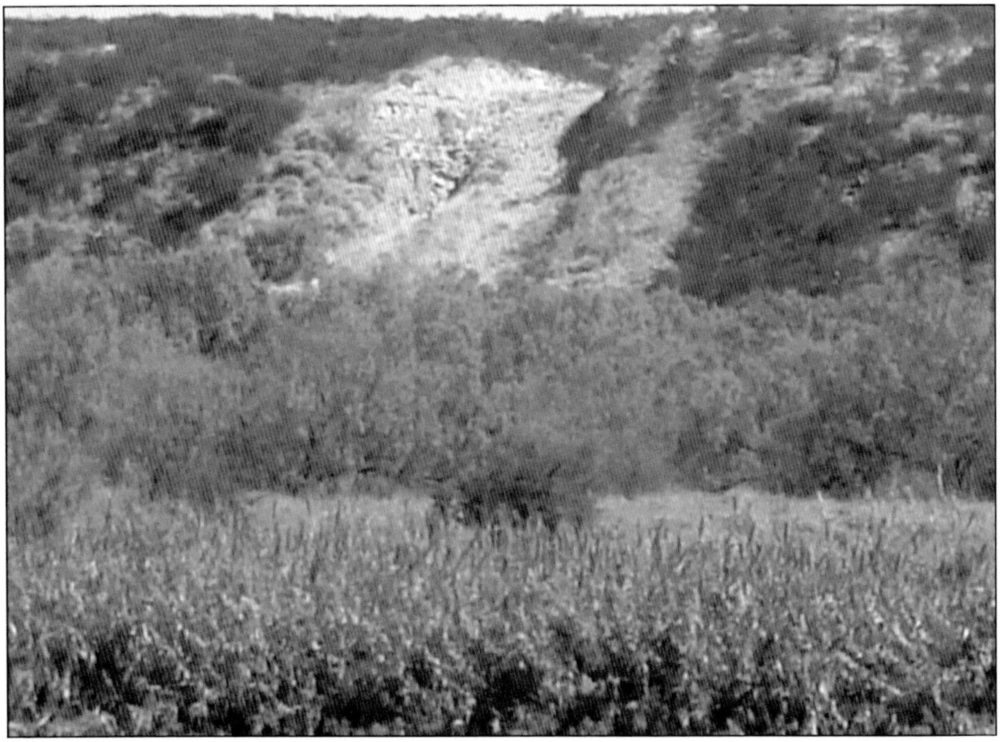

This swale is a physical remnant of El Camino Real and was carved into the landscape by oxcarts and horse travel. It can be seen coming up the east bank of the Río Grande and entering Texas at the Paso de Francia—the Pass of the French—near Guerrero, Coahuila. (Courtesy of Richard Santos.)

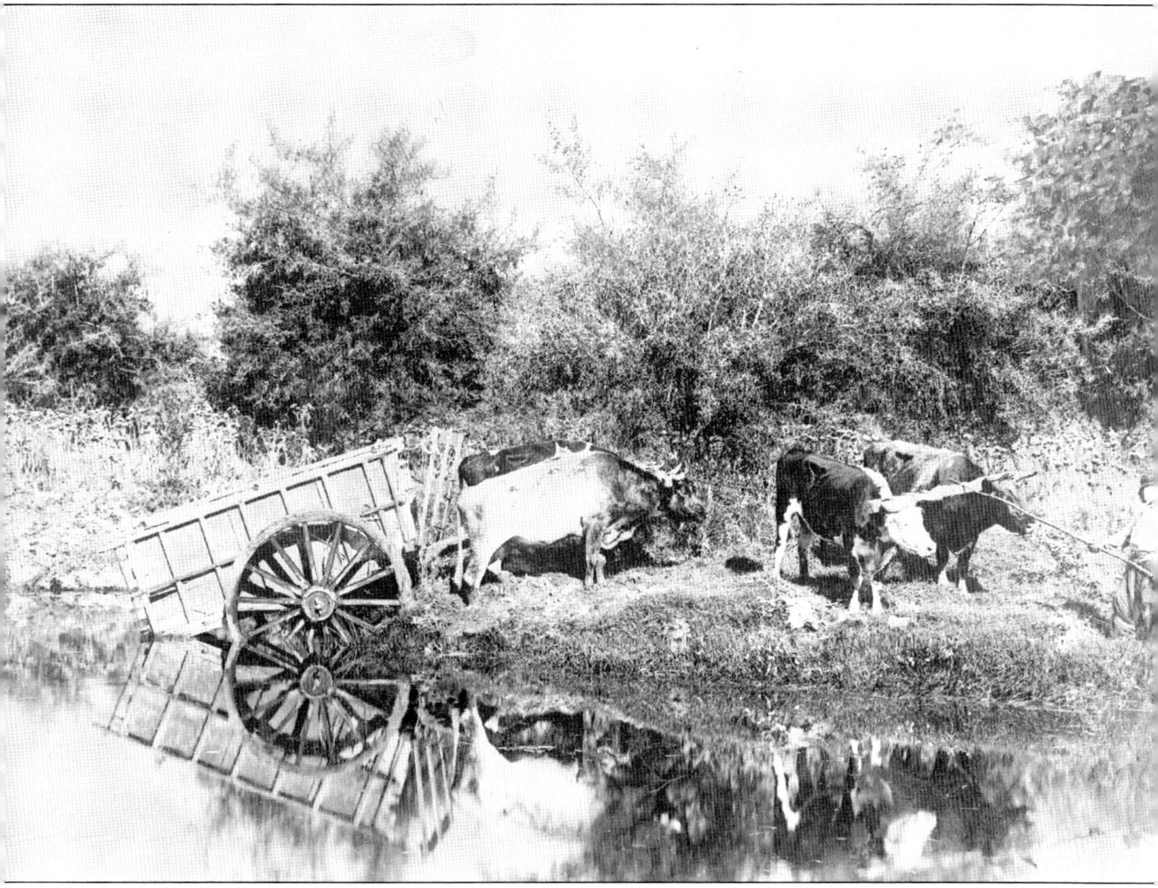

Oxcarts similar to this one traveled the trail from Mexico City to Los Adaes and back for hundreds of years. This photograph illustrates a river crossing being navigated by a team of oxen. It is easy to imagine how this action created swales across the trail, literally carving the road into the landscape as oxen and carts wore away at the land over the centuries. (Courtesy of the Library of Congress.)

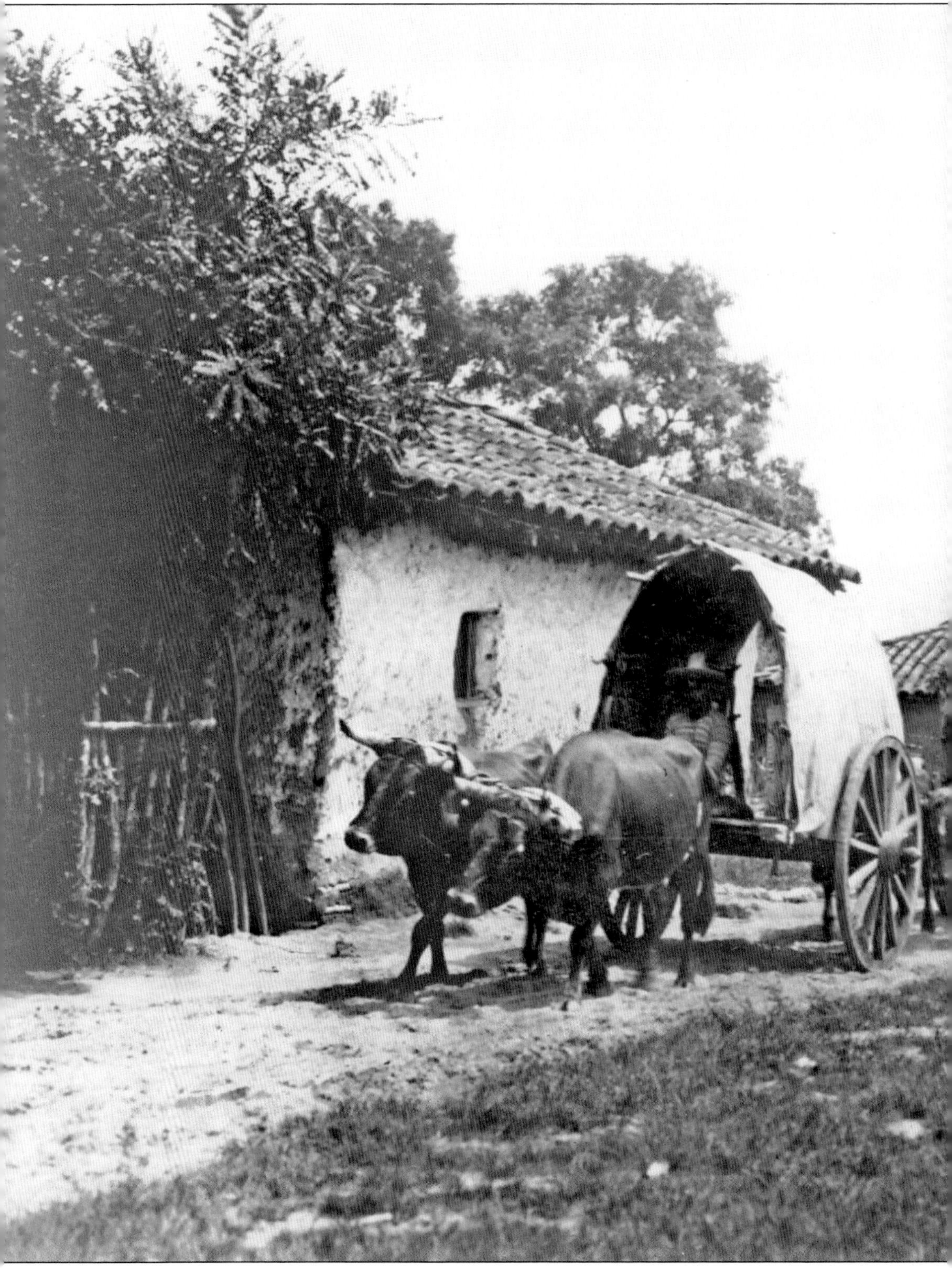

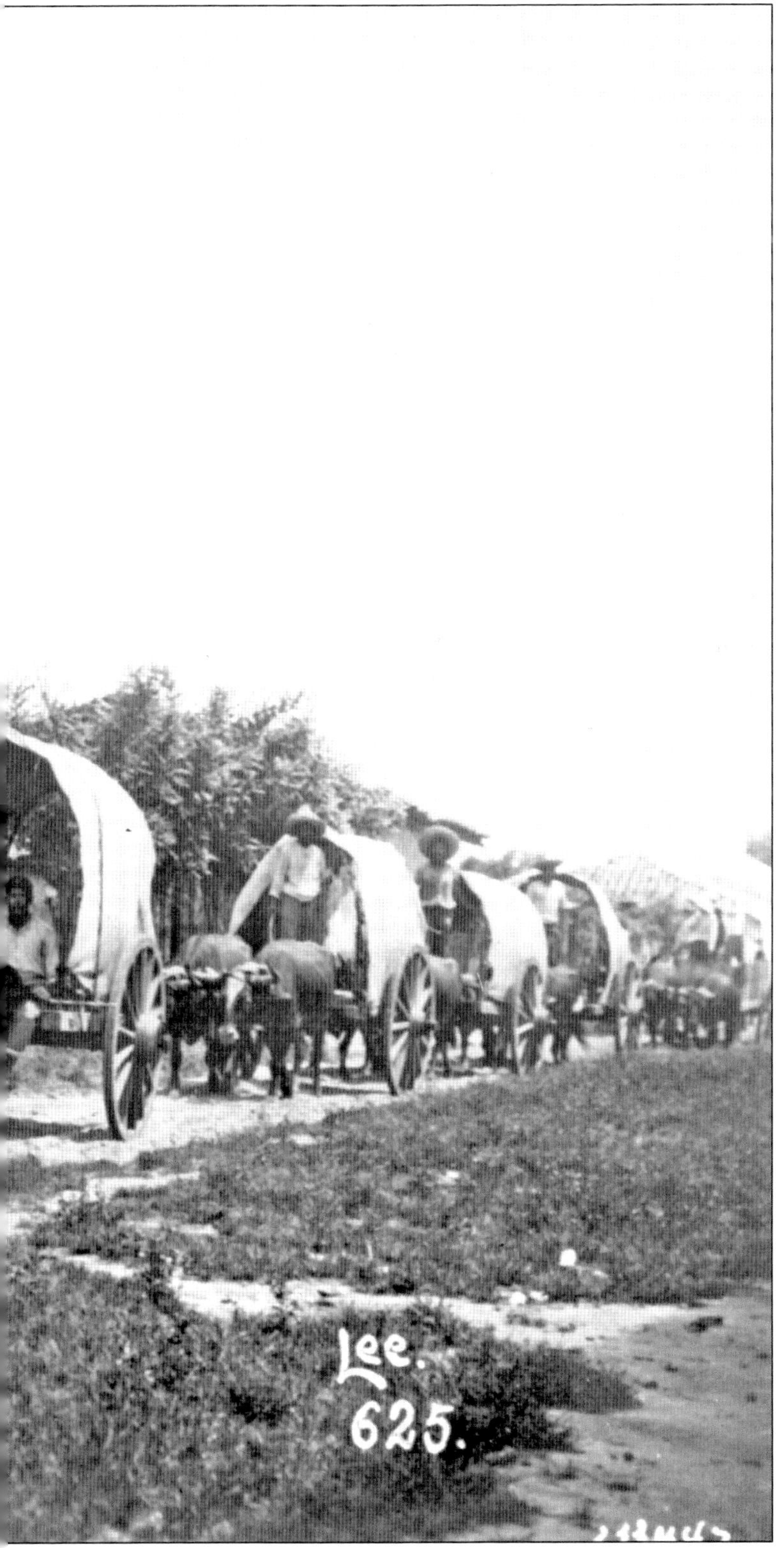


Wagon trains once traveled all throughout Mexico, including what is now the American Southwest. Caravans such as this one carved the Camino Real into the face of the landscape over many years. (Courtesy of the Library of Congress.)

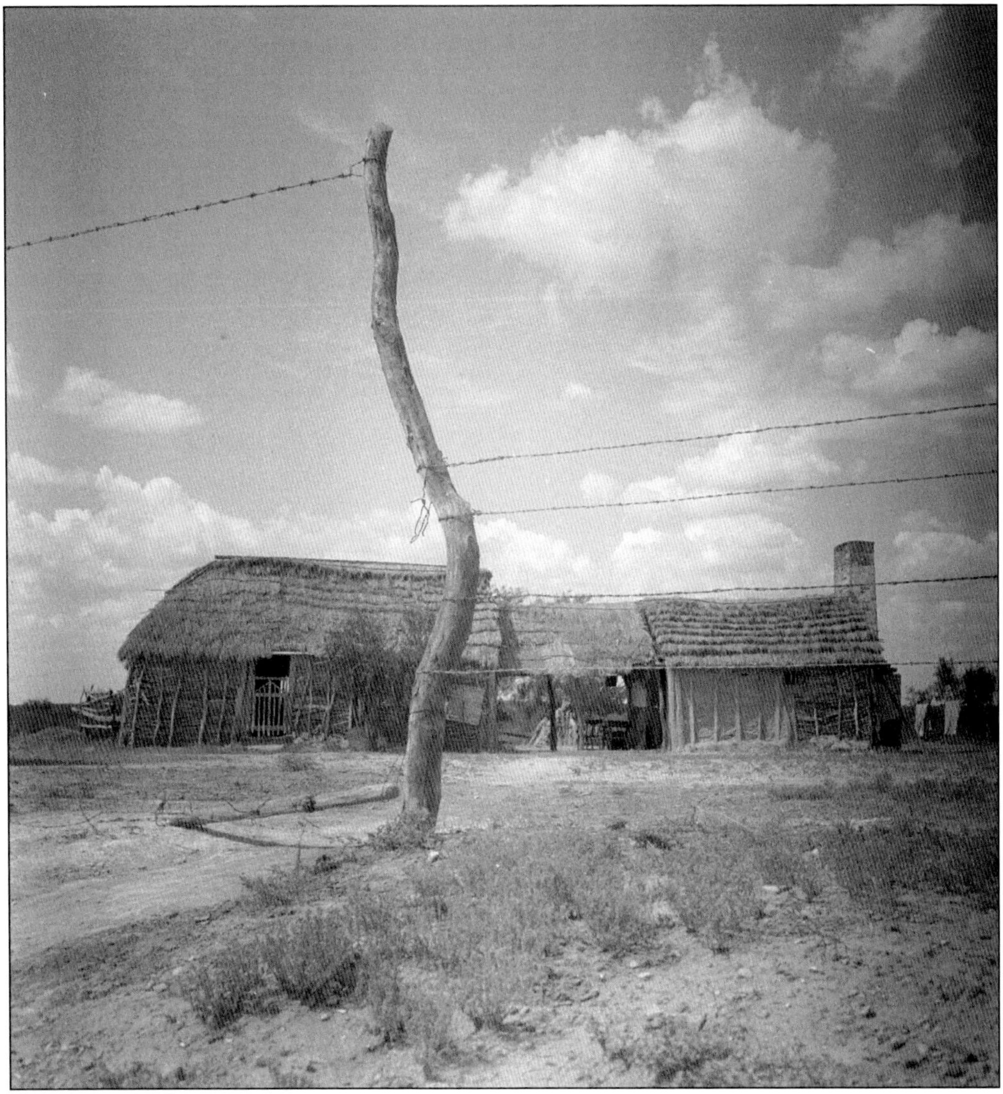

This elaborate jacal was located on the Río Grande in the early 1900s. Jacales were found throughout the American Southwest and Mexico, and many are still in use to this day. A handful can be found on El Camino Real de los Tejas. (Courtesy of the Library of Congress.)

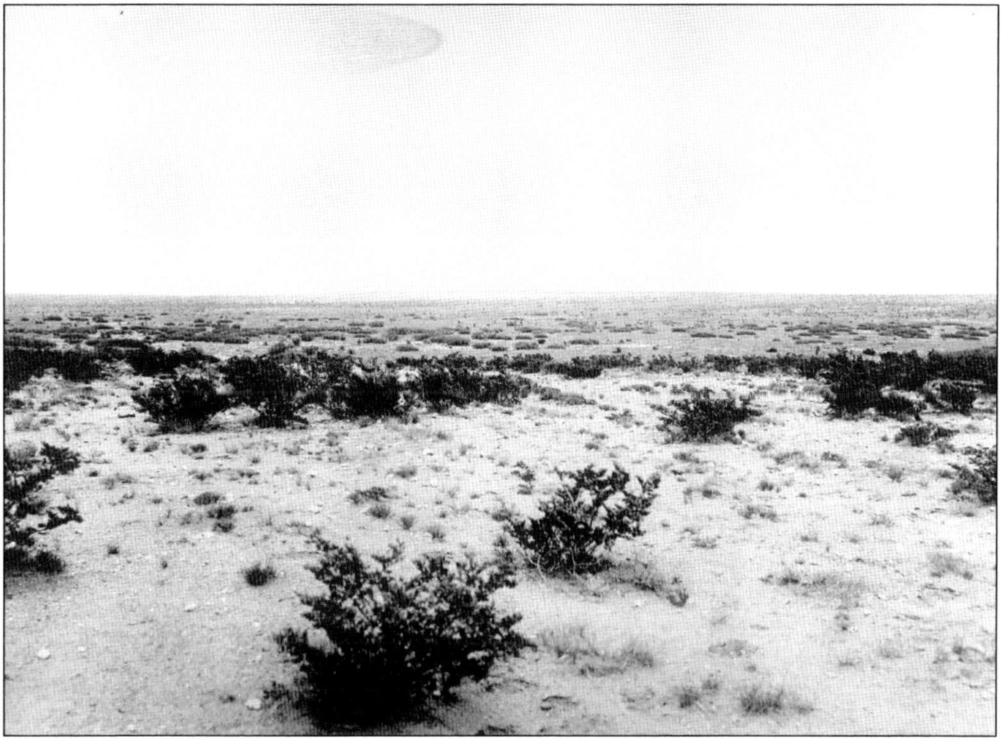

The Río Grande Valley of Texas and New Mexico was a forbidding place that offered the Spanish little in the way of comfort as they crossed its dry, desolate plain. (Courtesy of the Library of Congress.)

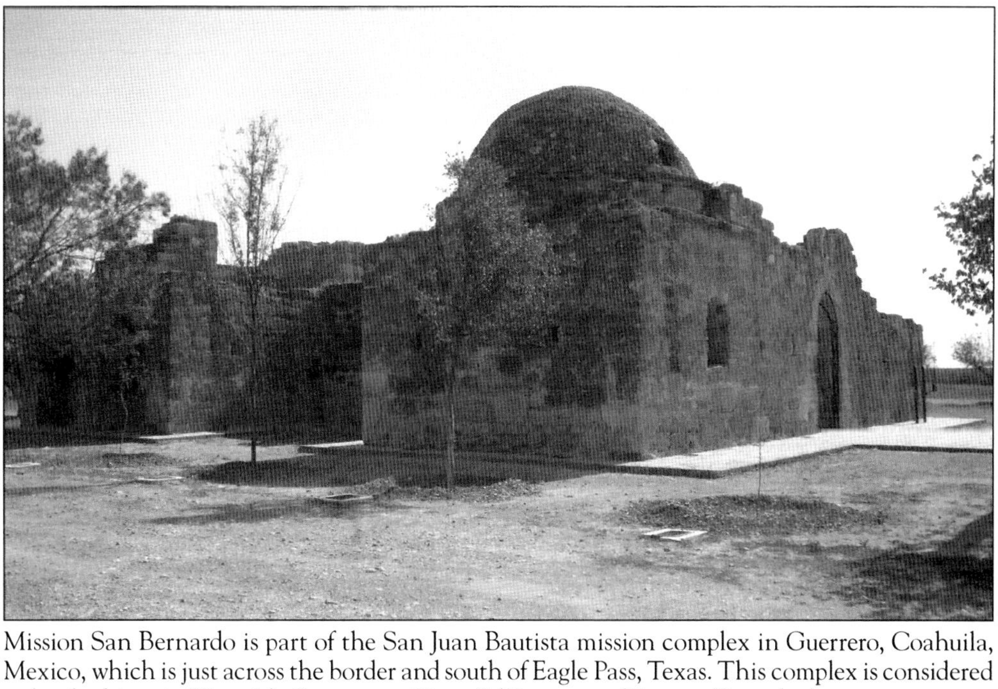

Mission San Bernardo is part of the San Juan Bautista mission complex in Guerrero, Coahuila, Mexico, which is just across the border and south of Eagle Pass, Texas. This complex is considered to be the historic "Spanish Gateway to Texas." (Courtesy of Steven Gonzales.)

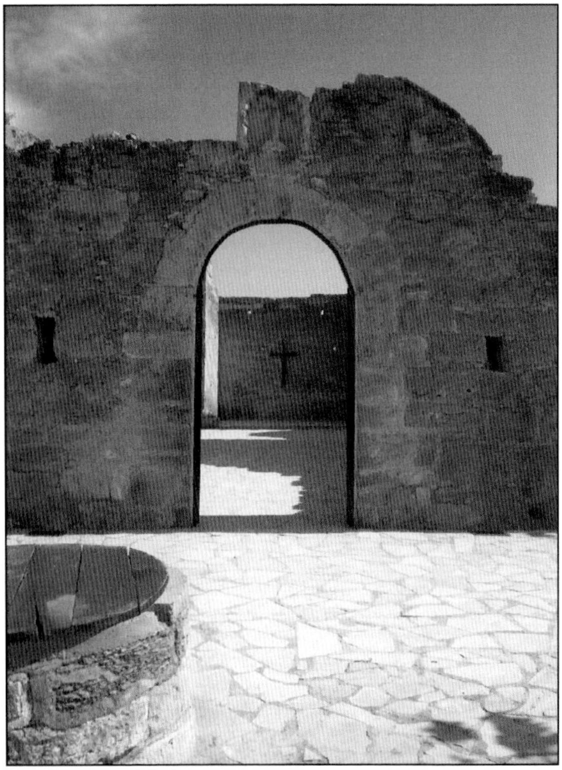

The San Juan Bautista mission complex was first established in 1700 by the Spanish and the Native American peoples along the Río Grande. (Courtesy of Steven Gonzales.)

The Spanish built acequias, or irrigation canals, during the colonial period in order to irrigate mission agricultural fields. This Arabic technology was transferred from Spain to the Americas and, in some instances, the designs incorporated indigenous water transfer methods as well. (Courtesy of Steven Gonzales.)

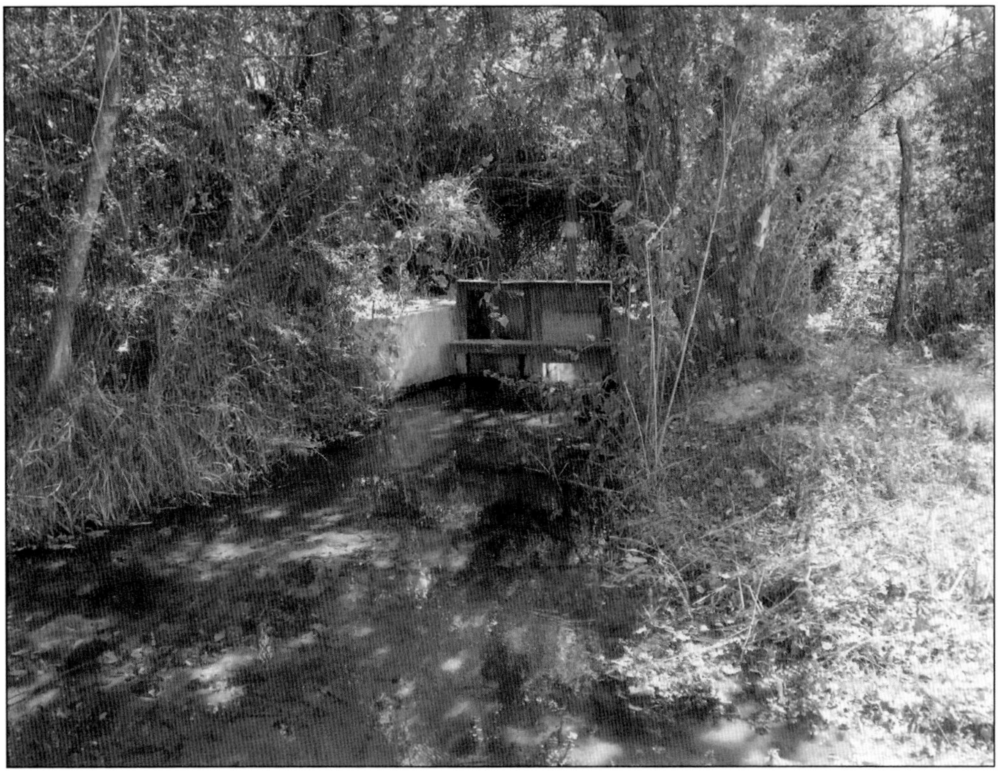

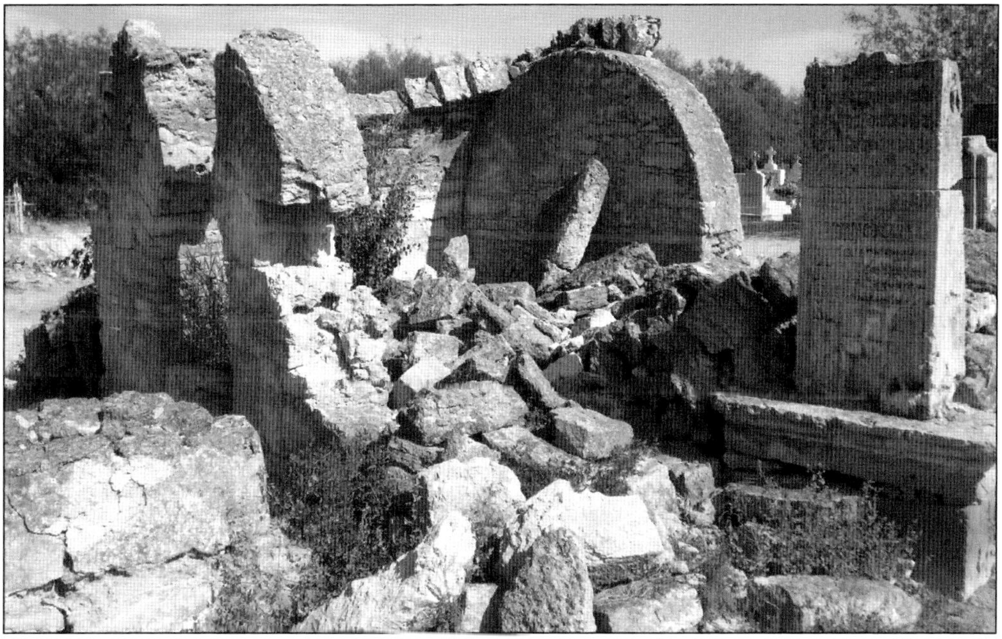

The cemetery, also known as a *campo santo*, in Guerrero, Coahuila, is a very old and beautiful place to visit along El Camino Real. (Courtesy of Steven Gonzales.)

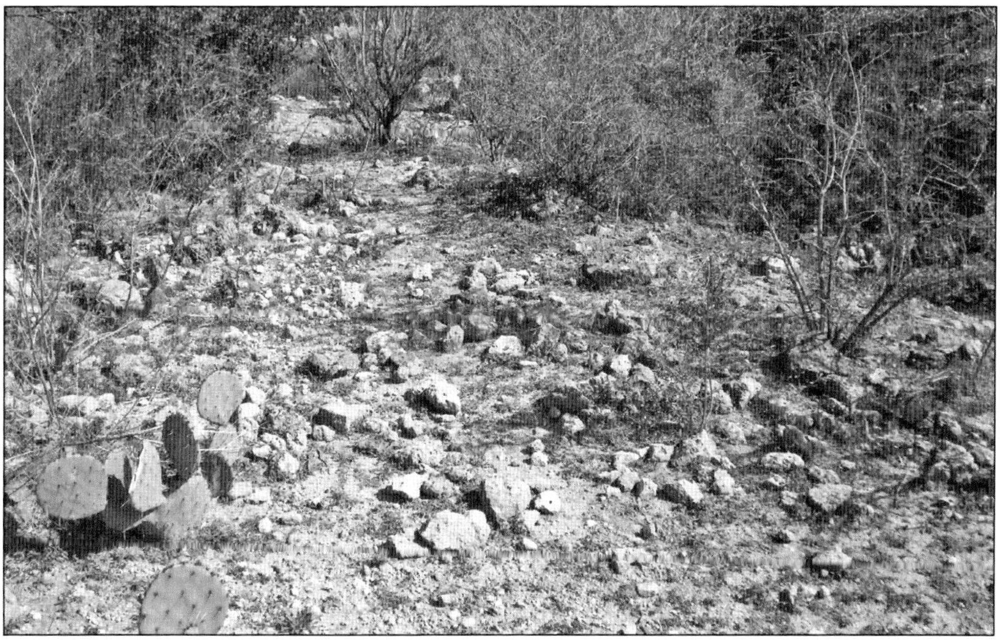

Mission San Juan Bautista was founded on June 24, 1699, on the Río de Sabinas, about 25 miles north of Lampazos, Nuevo León, Mexico. The mission remained at this site for only a short period of time before it was relocated to the site of present-day Guerrero, Coahuila, on January 1, 1700. The new location was at a critical set of river crossings on the Río Grande, such as El Paso de Francia, that were the Spanish gateways into Texas. Though San Juan Bautista was the first mission of the mission complex that bears its name, all that remains of it is the rubble seen in this image. (Courtesy of Steven Gonzales.)

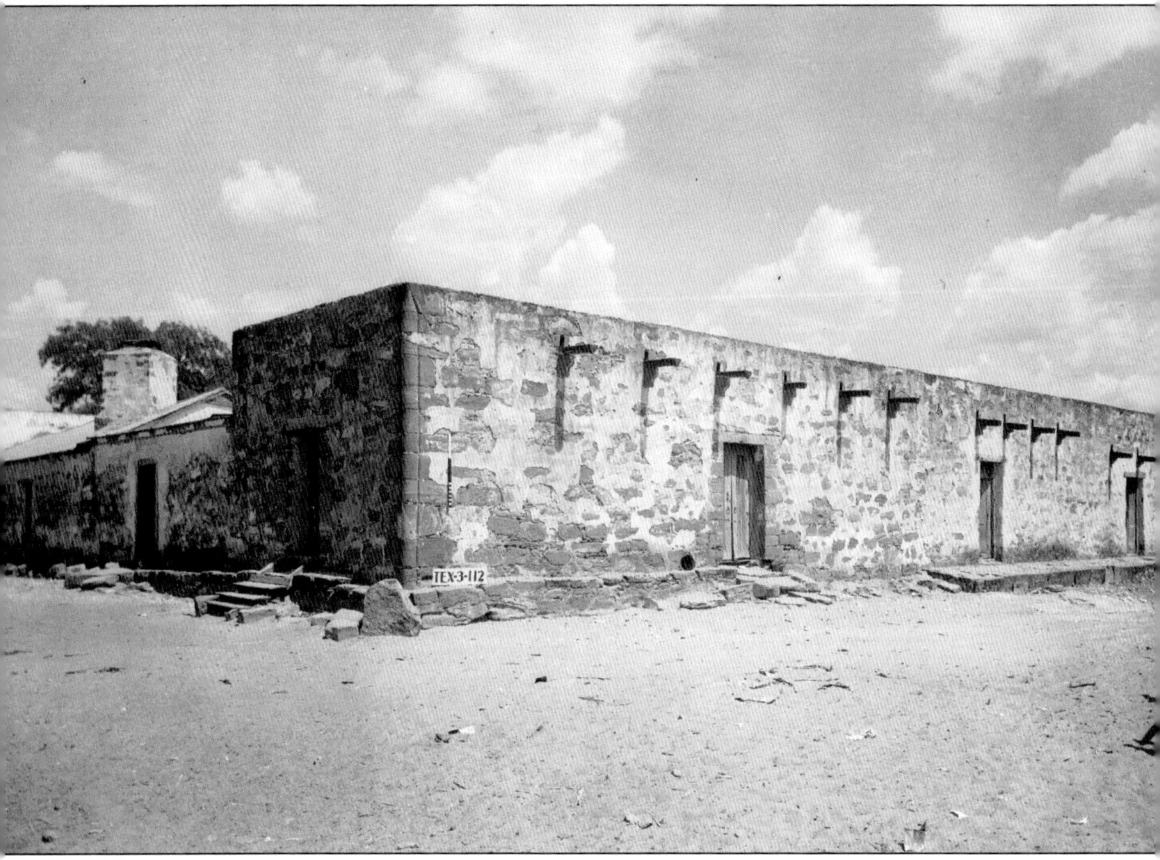


The Jesús Treviño Fort y Rancho was 100 years old when this beautiful photograph was taken in 1936. (Courtesy of the Library of Congress.)

This photograph shows the main courtyard entrance at the Jesús Treviño Fort y Rancho, as seen in 1936. (Courtesy of the Library of Congress.)

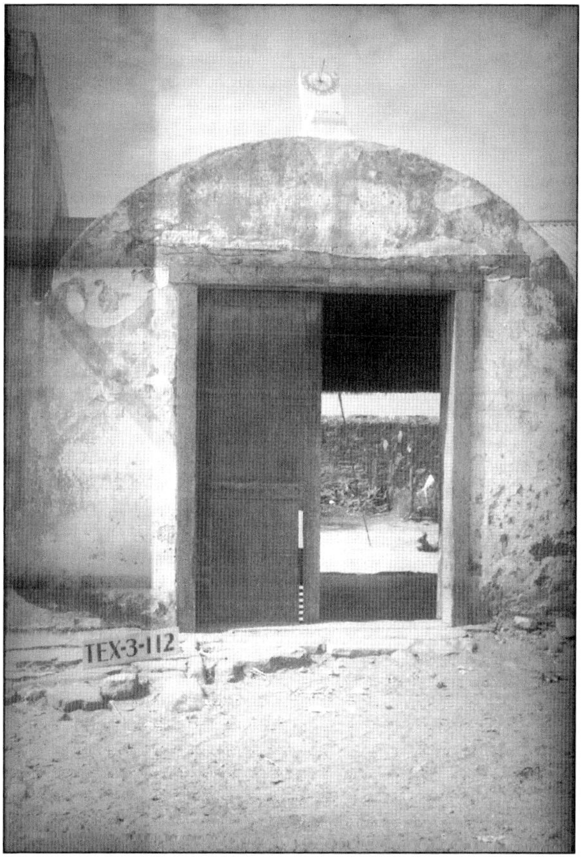


This photograph of the fireplace at the Jesús Treviño Fort y Rancho was taken nearly 80 years ago. Little has changed at the site since this image was taken. (Courtesy of the Library of Congress.)

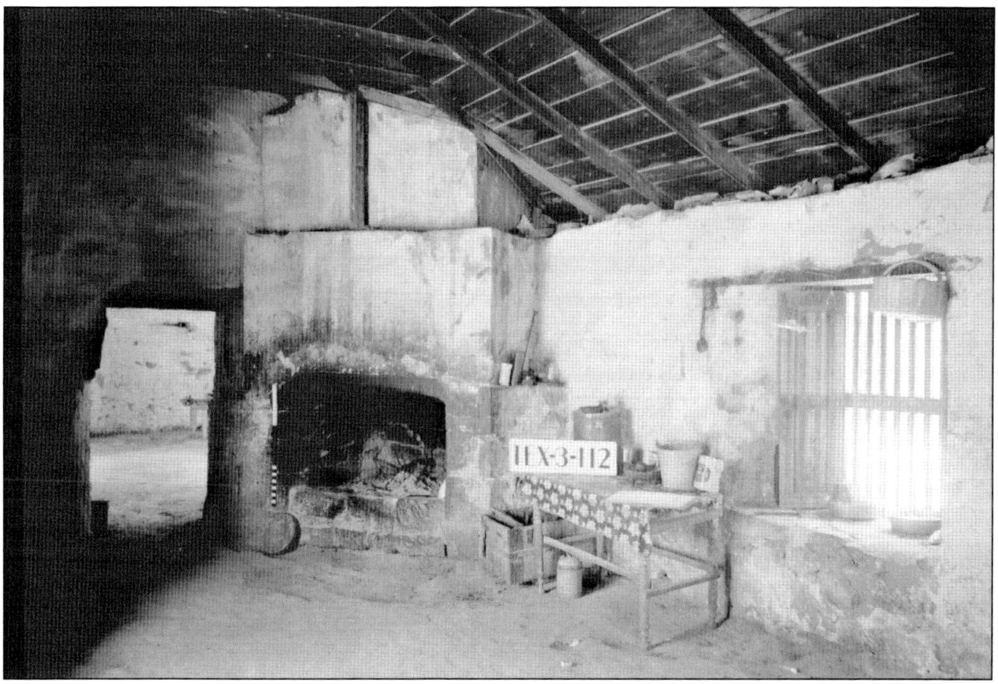

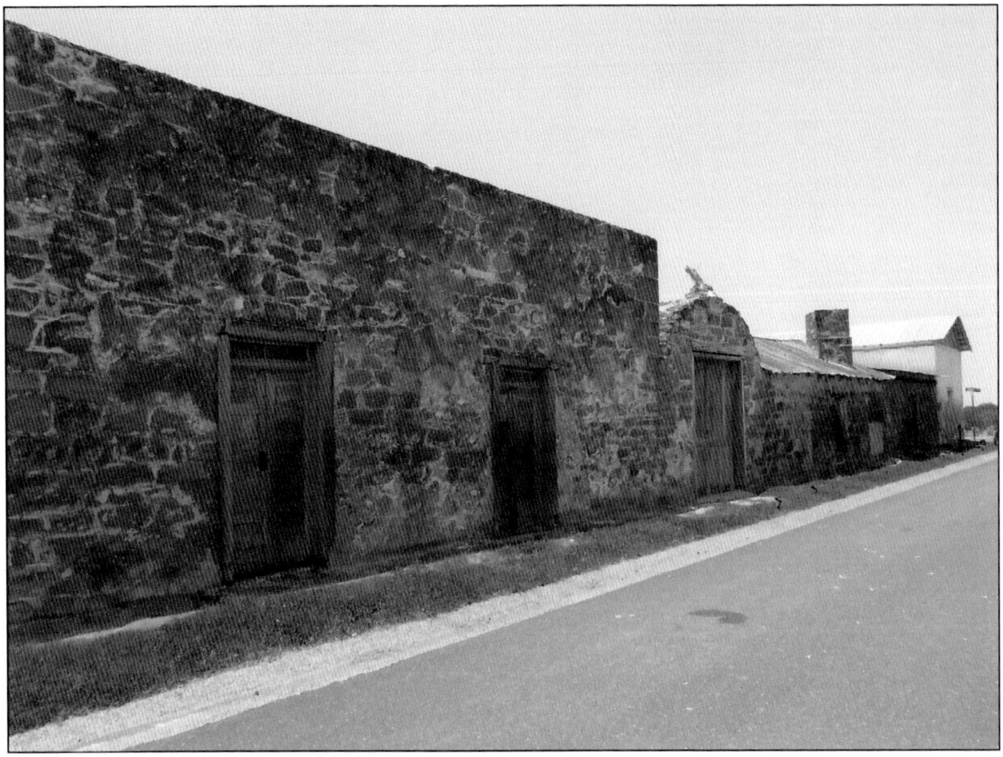

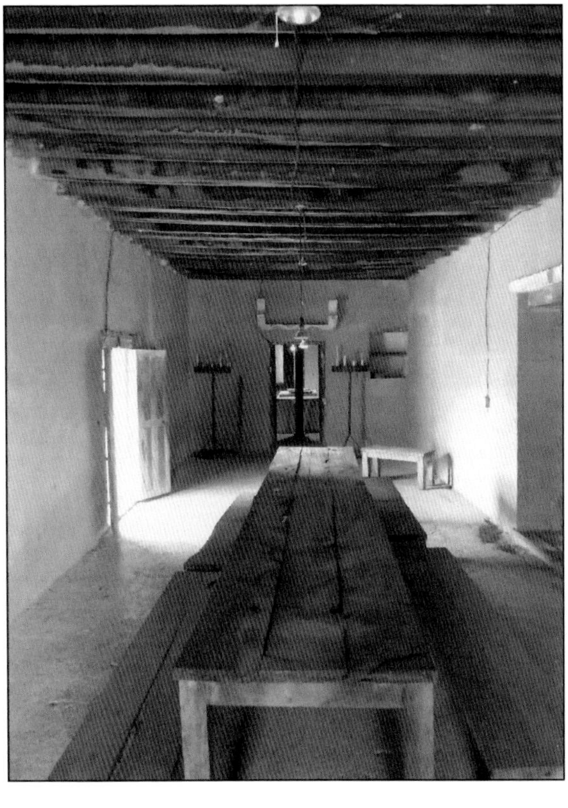

The Jesús Treviño Fort y Rancho was built in San Ygnacio, Texas, in the 1830s. The fort was also the first location along El Camino Real de los Tejas to be certified by the National Park Service as an official site on the trail. (Courtesy of Steven Gonzales.)

The interior of the Treviño Fort demonstrates the simple beauty of Spanish and Mexican architectural design. (Courtesy of Steven Gonzales.)

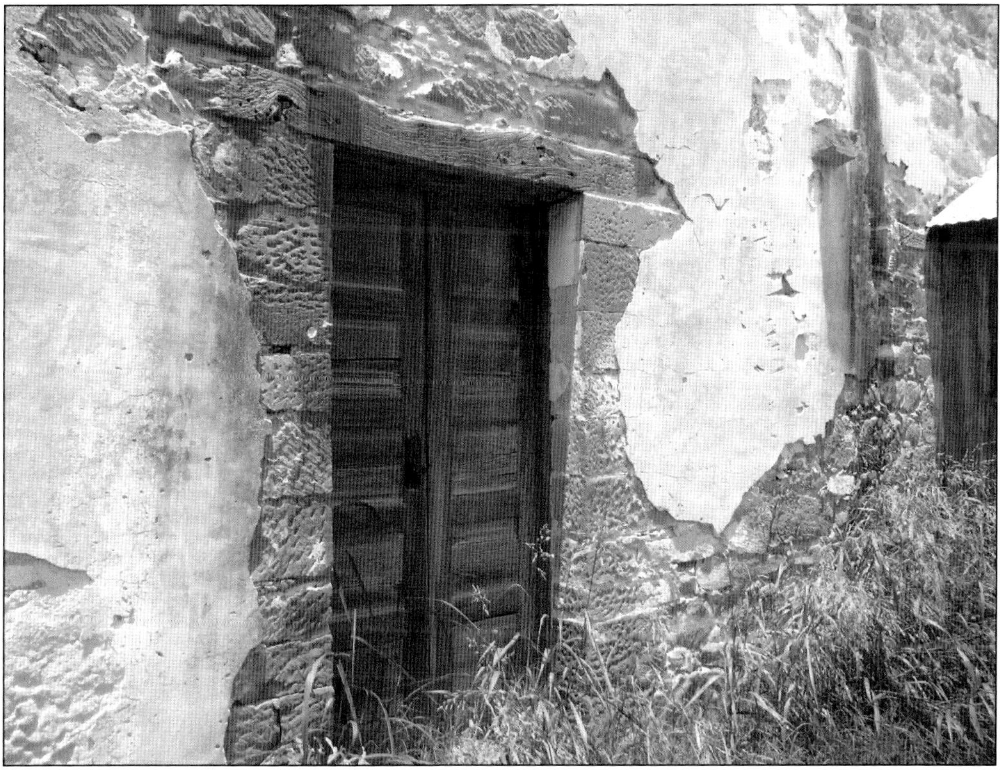

The beautiful wooden doors and stuccoed walls of the interior compound of the Jesús Treviño Fort are a true sight to behold. (Courtesy of Steven Gonzales.)

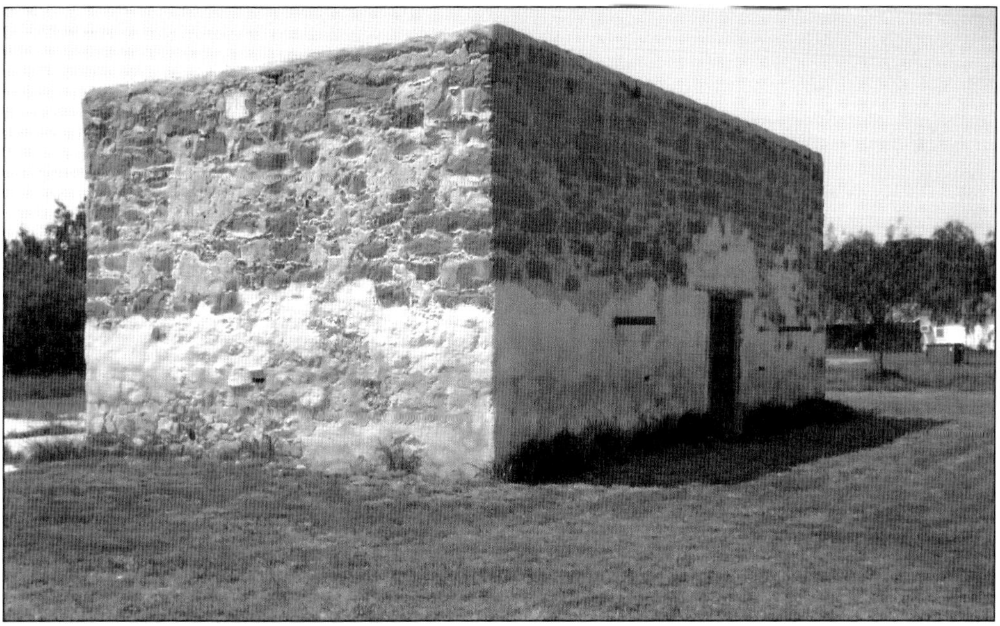

San José de los Corralitos was established in 1753, when José de Escandón donated a 350,000-acre land grant that would eventually become the village of Corralitos. (Courtesy of Steven Gonzales.)

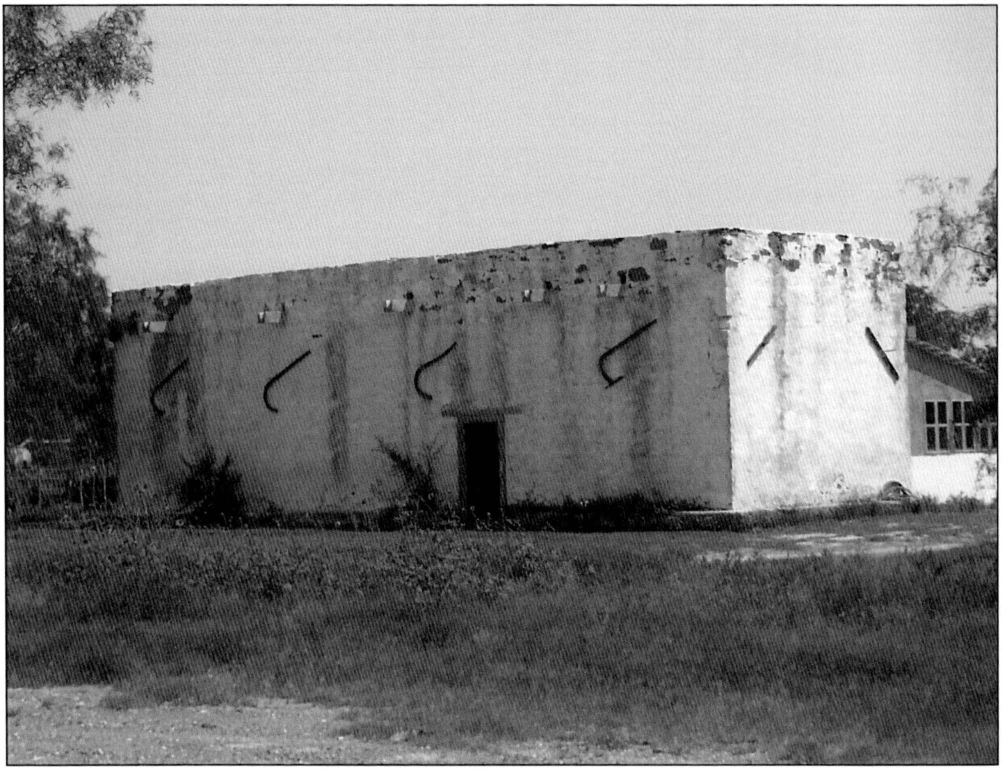

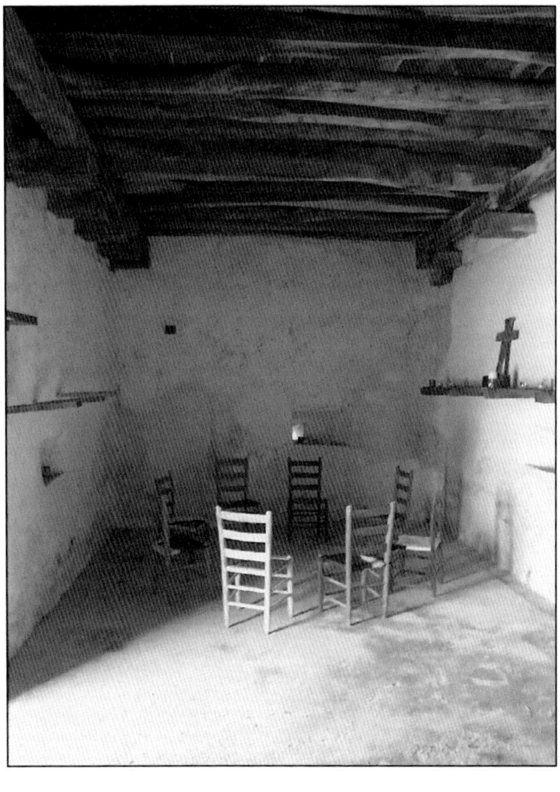

Los Corralitos houses multiple structures that demonstrate life on the northern frontier of New Spain in the 1700s. Los Corralitos was also one of the first places along El Camino Real to receive official National Park Service signage. (Courtesy of Steven Gonzales.)

The interior of Los Corralitos is simple, yet breathtaking. (Courtesy of Steven Gonzales.)

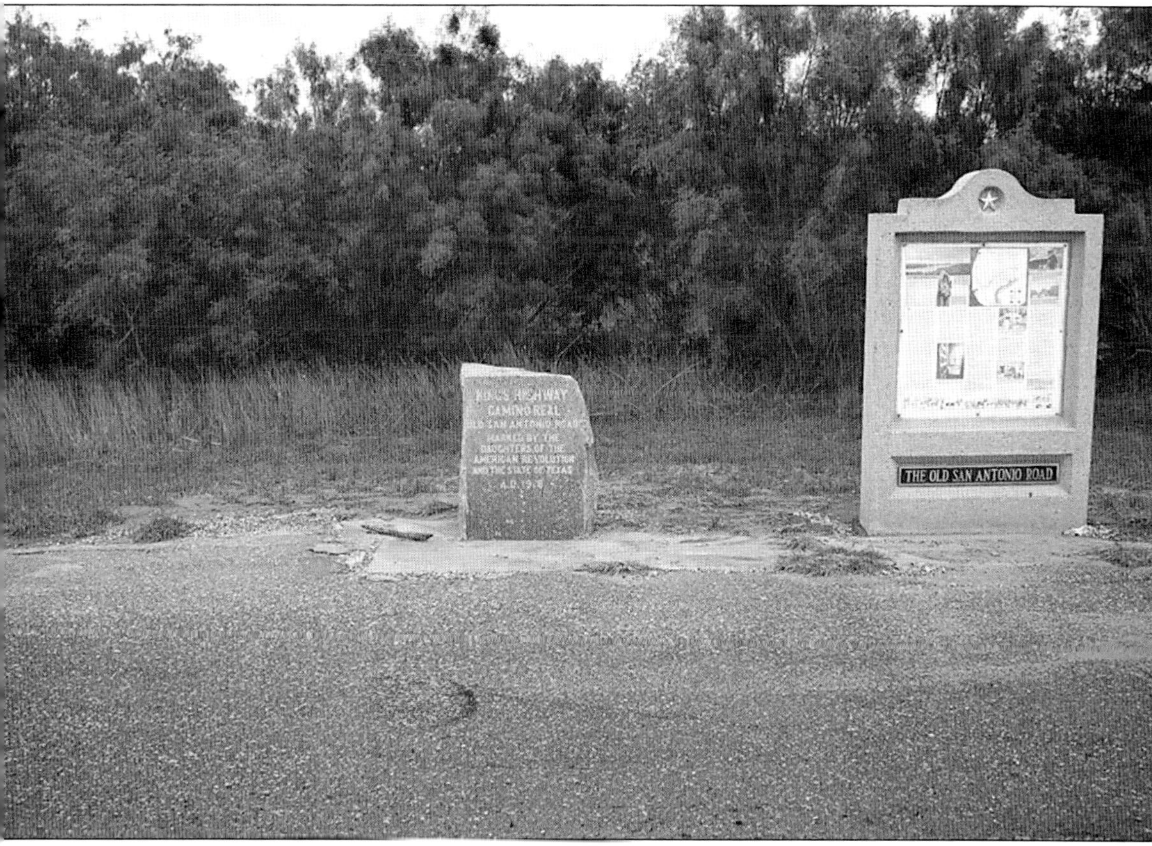


Granite markers, such as these, were placed along one segment of El Camino Real in 1918 by the State of Texas and the Daughters of the American Revolution. Approximately 127 markers were placed at five-mile intervals—generally on the north and west sides of roadways—from the Río Grande to the Sabine River. The markers in this photograph can be found in Catarina, Texas. (Courtesy of Steven Gonzales.)

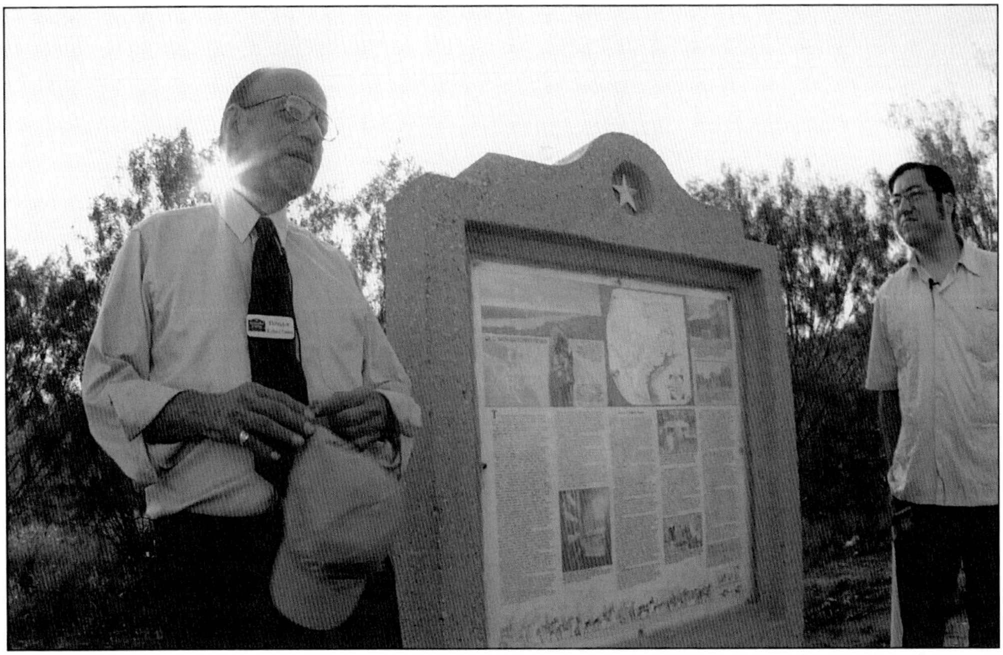

El Camino Real de los Tejas National Historic Trail Association board member Richard Santos (left) and executive director Steven Gonzales (right) give a presentation to a group in Catarina, Texas. (Courtesy of Richard Santos.)

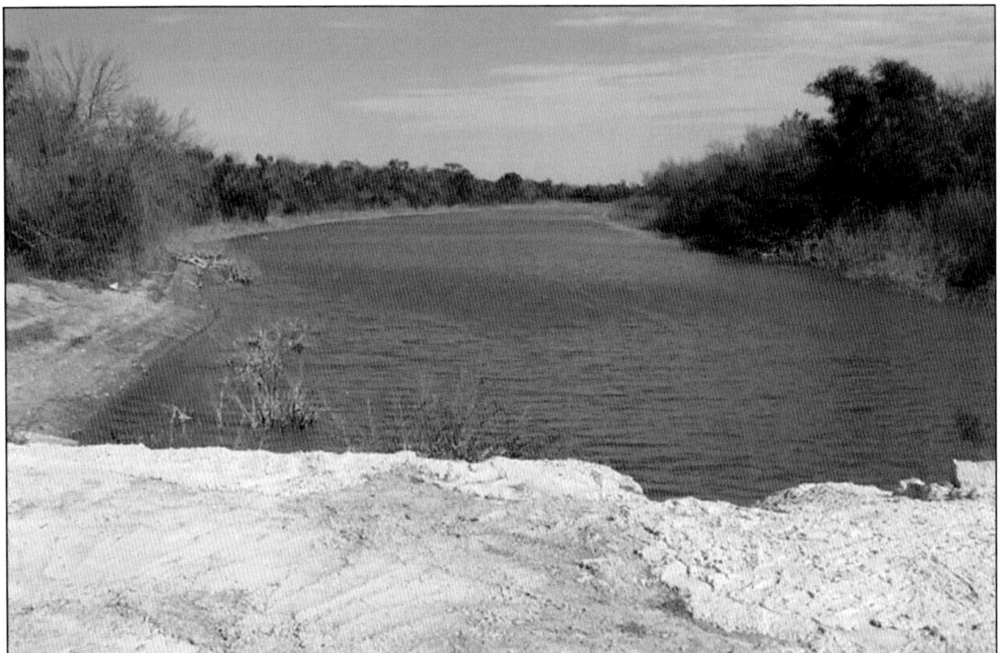

Laguna Espantosa is a former campsite, or *paraje*, in Dimmitt County, along El Camino Real. The translation of Laguna Espantosa is "Frightening Lagoon" or "Amazing Lagoon." The former translation is more often applied to the site, as it was thought to be a haunted place that should be feared. (Courtesy of Richard Santos.)

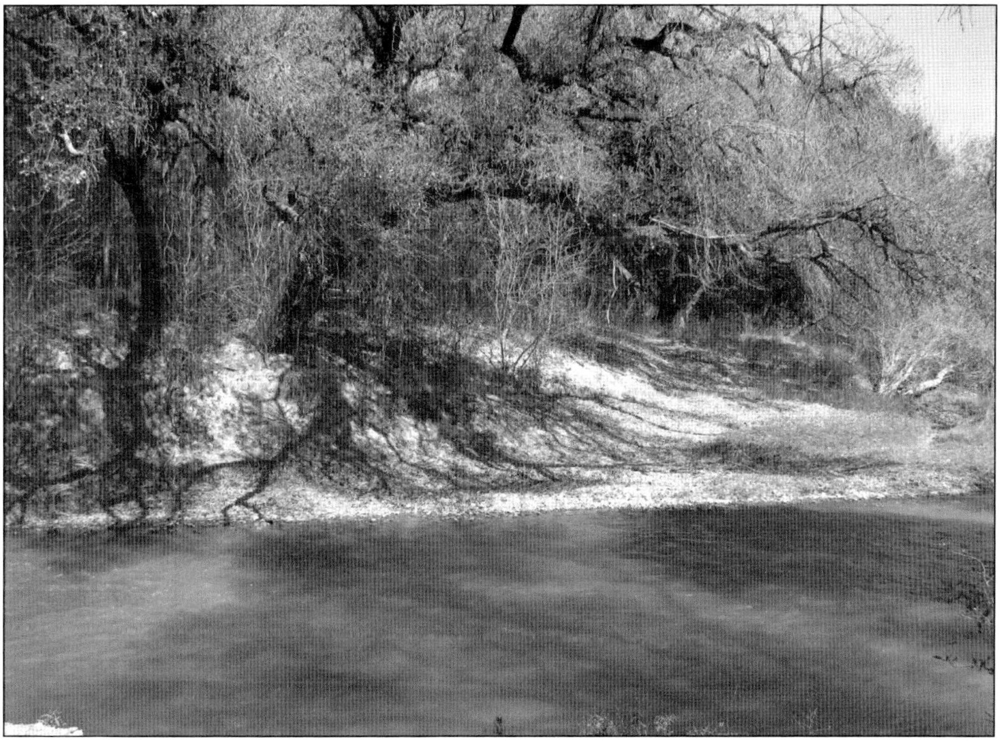

Here, a swale can be seen leaving the bank of the Frio River at El Paso de Piedra in Frio County, Texas. Shallow river fords with solid, rocky bottoms were key crossing points along the entirety of El Camino Real de los Tejas. (Courtesy of Richard Santos.)

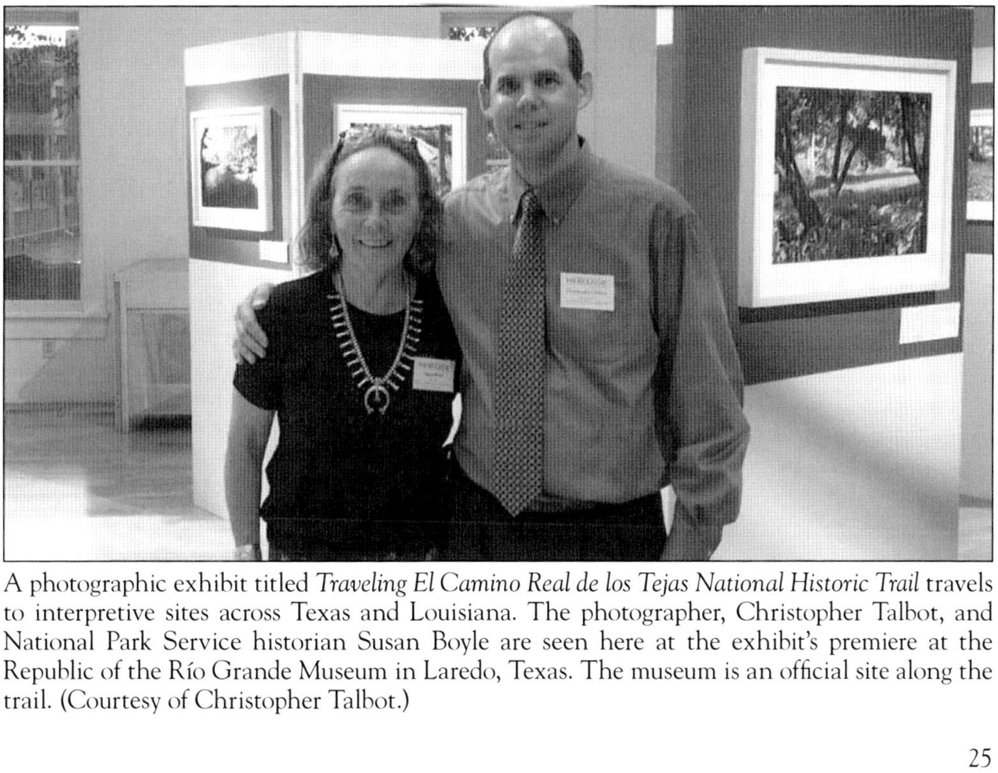

A photographic exhibit titled *Traveling El Camino Real de los Tejas National Historic Trail* travels to interpretive sites across Texas and Louisiana. The photographer, Christopher Talbot, and National Park Service historian Susan Boyle are seen here at the exhibit's premiere at the Republic of the Río Grande Museum in Laredo, Texas. The museum is an official site along the trail. (Courtesy of Christopher Talbot.)

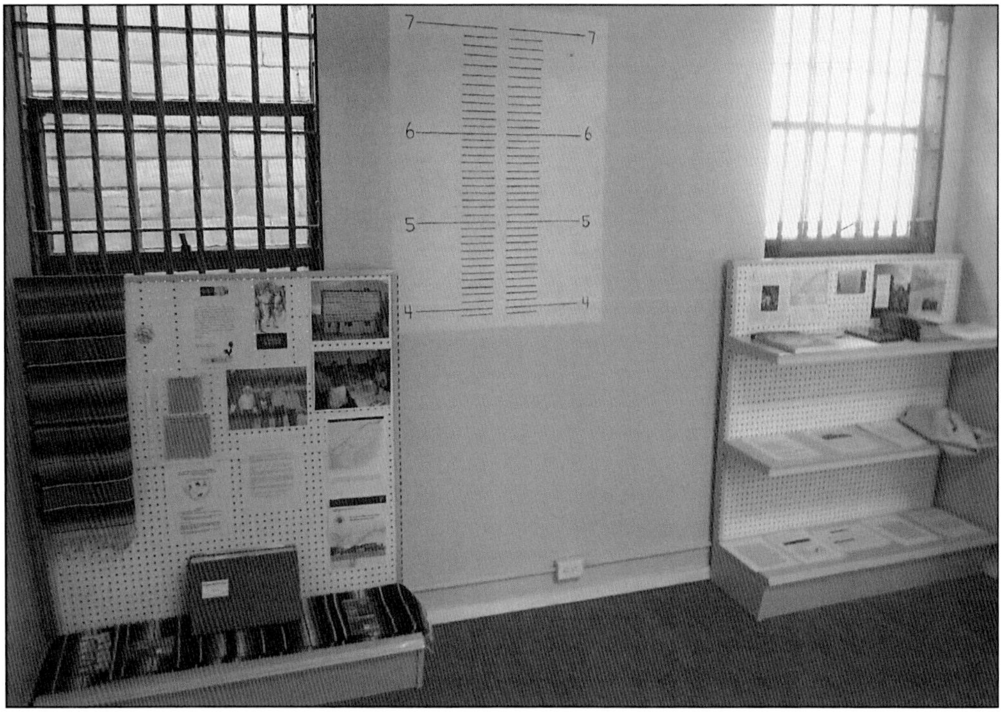

An El Camino Real interpretive center can be found at the former jailhouse in Carrizo Springs, Texas. (Courtesy of Steven Gonzales.)

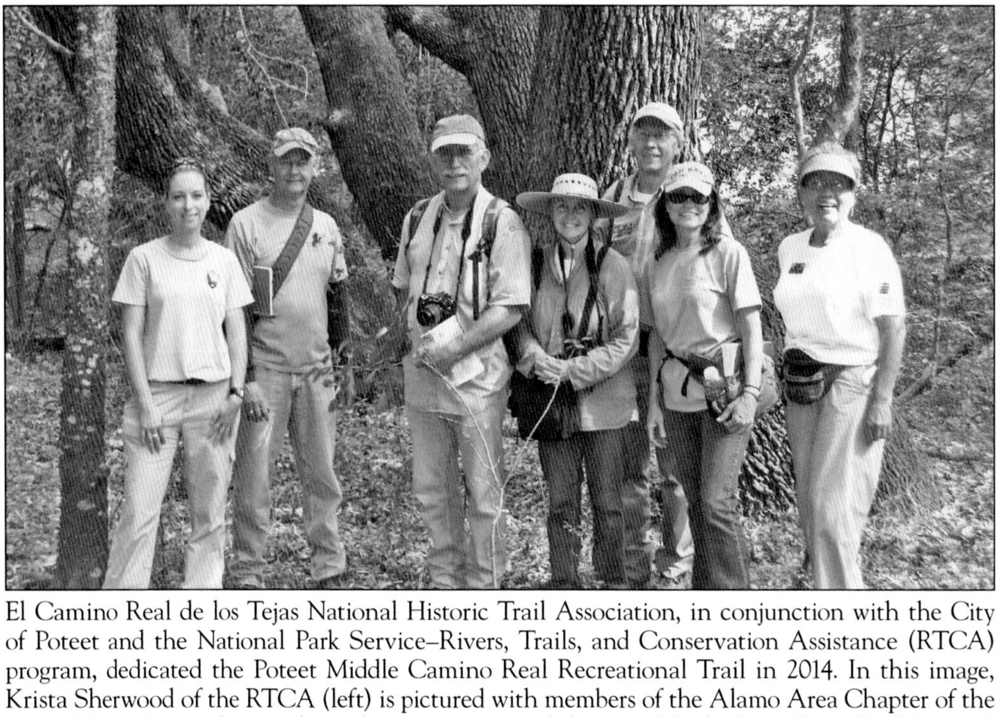

El Camino Real de los Tejas National Historic Trail Association, in conjunction with the City of Poteet and the National Park Service–Rivers, Trails, and Conservation Assistance (RTCA) program, dedicated the Poteet Middle Camino Real Recreational Trail in 2014. In this image, Krista Sherwood of the RTCA (left) is pictured with members of the Alamo Area Chapter of the Texas Master Naturalists as they take an inventory of plants and birds along Phase II of the trail. (Courtesy of Steven Gonzales.)

# *Two*

# San Antonio and Goliad

It is in this region that visitors will find the largest and most enduring structures along El Camino Real: Spanish missions, presidios, and *comandancias*.

As prime examples of Spanish frontier institutions in Texas, the missions and presidios of San Antonio and Goliad are indeed gems of El Camino Real.

Linked by the San Antonio, Guadalupe, and San Marcos Rivers, the region is a combination of the South Texas Plains, Blackland Prairie, Post Oak Savannah, and even a bit of the Edwards Plateau ecological regions.

In the city of San Antonio, the Hispanic population comprises nearly 60 percent of the community. One can find a wide array of cultures in other parts of the region, too, such as German, Polish, and Czech, and that of the Anglo-Americans whose families long ago migrated from the lower south of the United States.

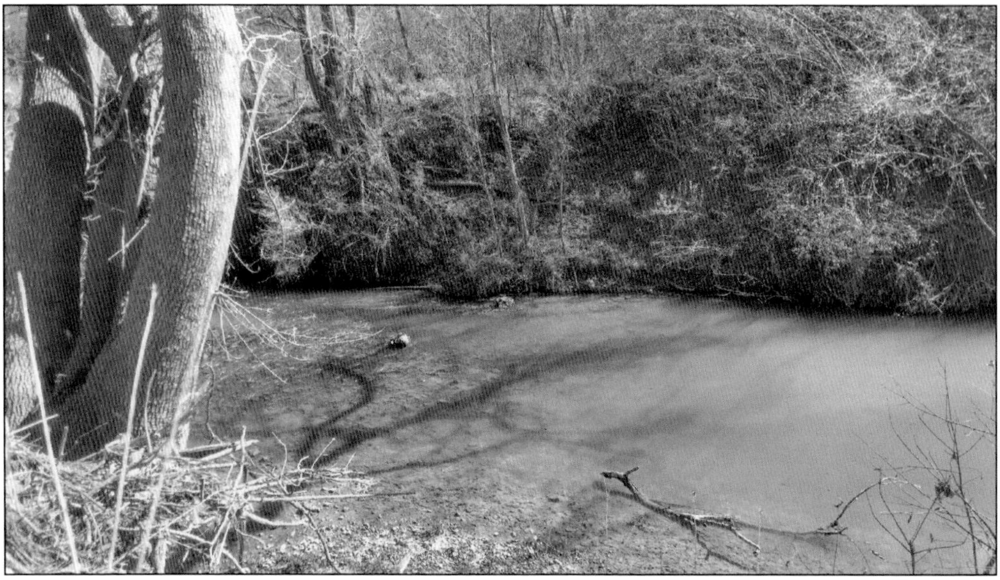

Historically, three segments of the Camino Real crossed the Medina River. The Lower Presidio Road segment had two known crossings of the Medina, including El Paso de Dolores, or the Pass of Sorrows. Today, the crossing is better known as Applewhite Crossing and is associated with a spur of the Lower Presidio Road that led to the ranch of the interim governor of Texas, Juan Ignacio Pérez. In this photograph, El Paso de Dolores can be seen to the right of the tree in the foreground, coming up the opposite bank of the river. It is the U-shaped depression with a relative lack of vegetation in it. (Courtesy of Steven Gonzales.)

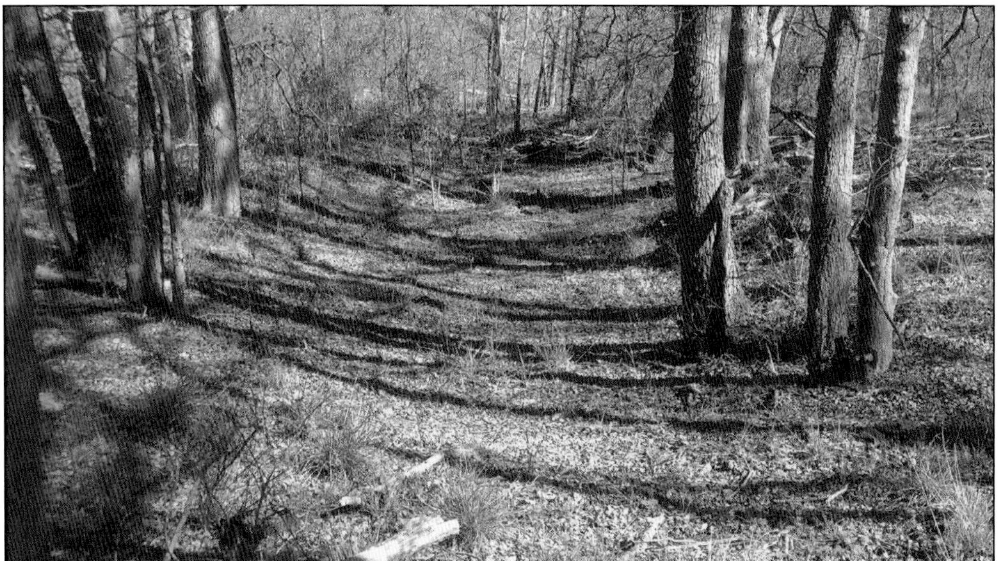

Camino swales are visible at many sites along this stretch of the Medina River Greenway in San Antonio. The swales lead from Applewhite Crossing toward the jacal near the Pérez Rancho in the greenway. (Courtesy of Steven Gonzales.)

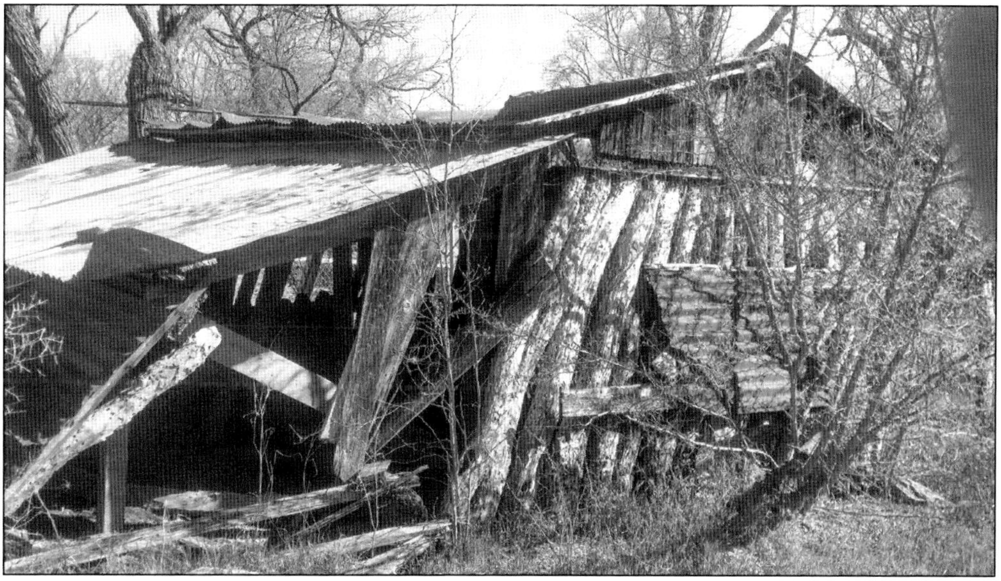

This jacal, or hut, is a true rarity. It is located in the Medina River Greenway, just off of Jett and Applewhite Roads in San Antonio. Jacales such as this were once common at many sites along El Camino Real de los Tejas. (Courtesy of Steven Gonzales.)

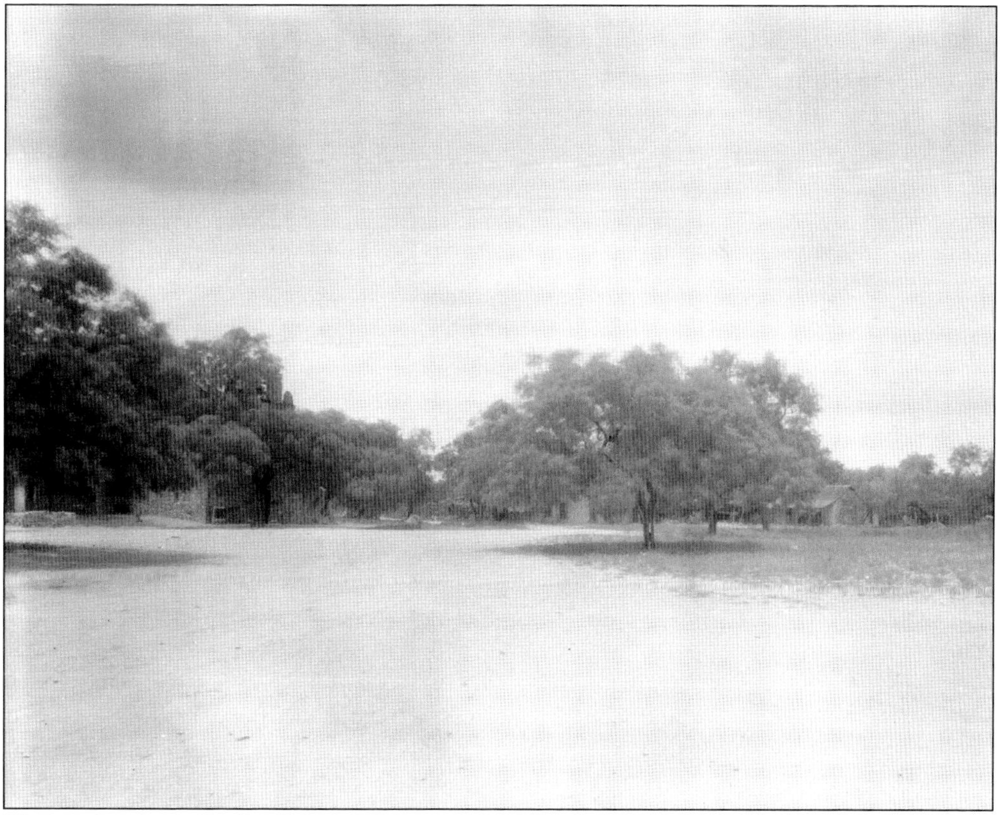

The road passing by the Indian quarters at Mission Espada can be seen in this photograph. (Courtesy of the Library of Congress.)

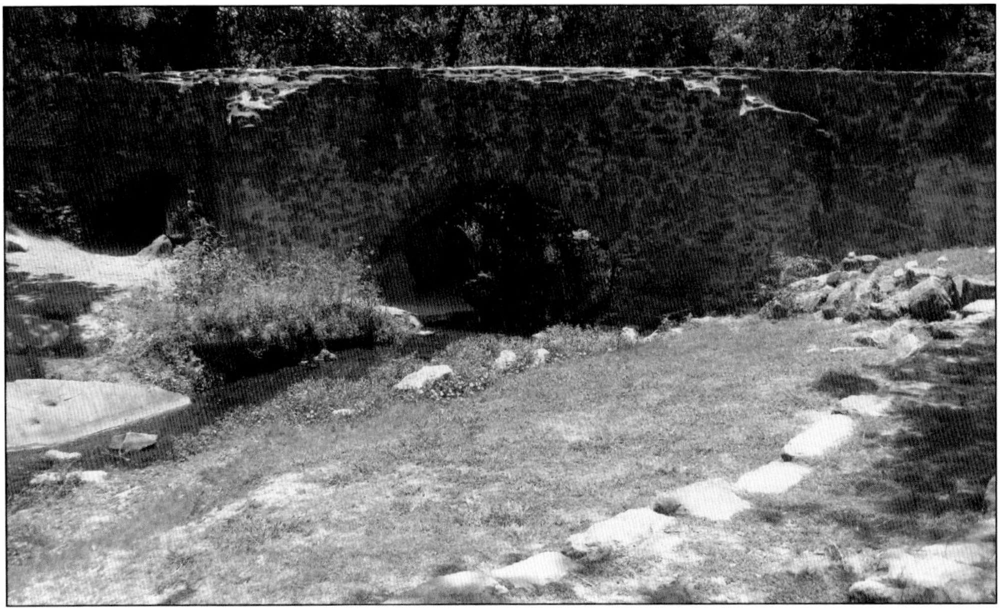

The Espada Aqueduct is located on Espada Road near Mission Espada in San Antonio. Franciscan missionaries constructed the Espada Aqueduct in 1745 to serve the mission lands of Espada. It is the only functioning Spanish aqueduct in the United States. (Courtesy of Steven Gonzales.)

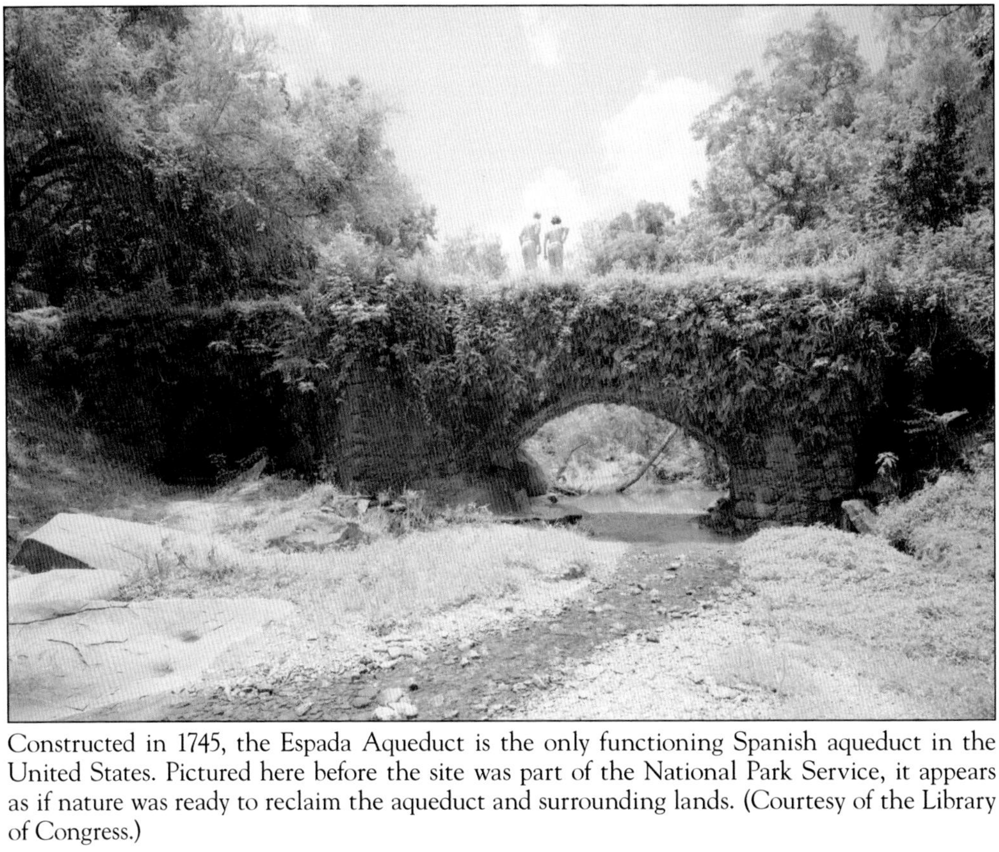

Constructed in 1745, the Espada Aqueduct is the only functioning Spanish aqueduct in the United States. Pictured here before the site was part of the National Park Service, it appears as if nature was ready to reclaim the aqueduct and surrounding lands. (Courtesy of the Library of Congress.)

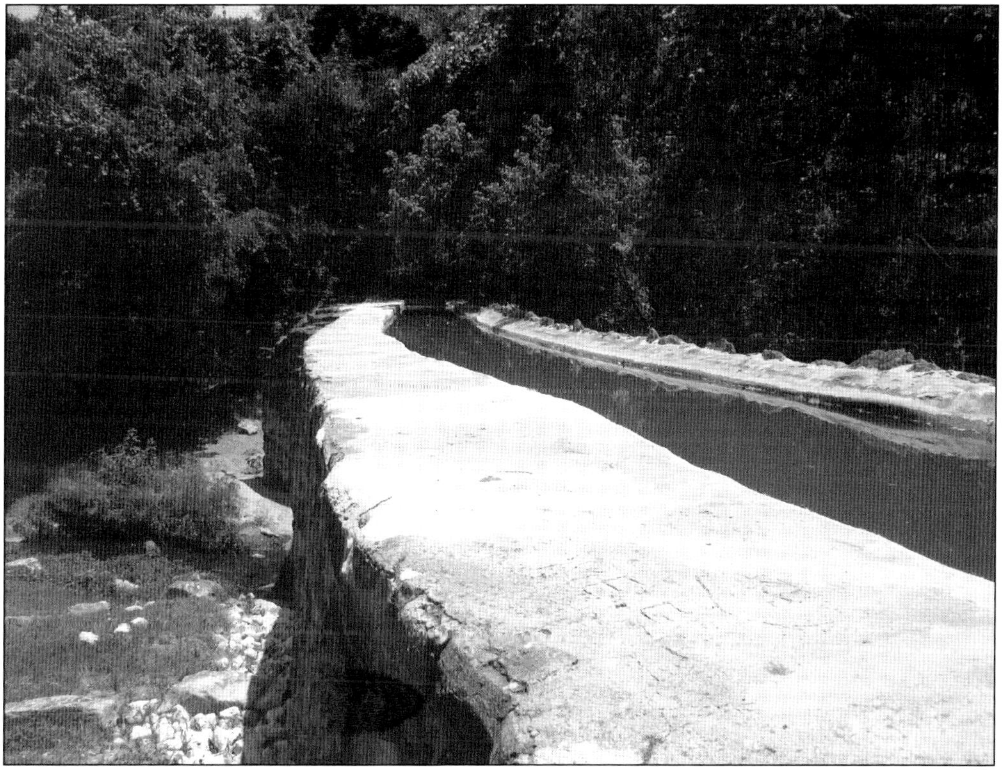

Waters have flowed from the San Antonio River, through the aqueduct, and into the fields around Mission Espada for over 260 years. (Courtesy of Steven Gonzales.)

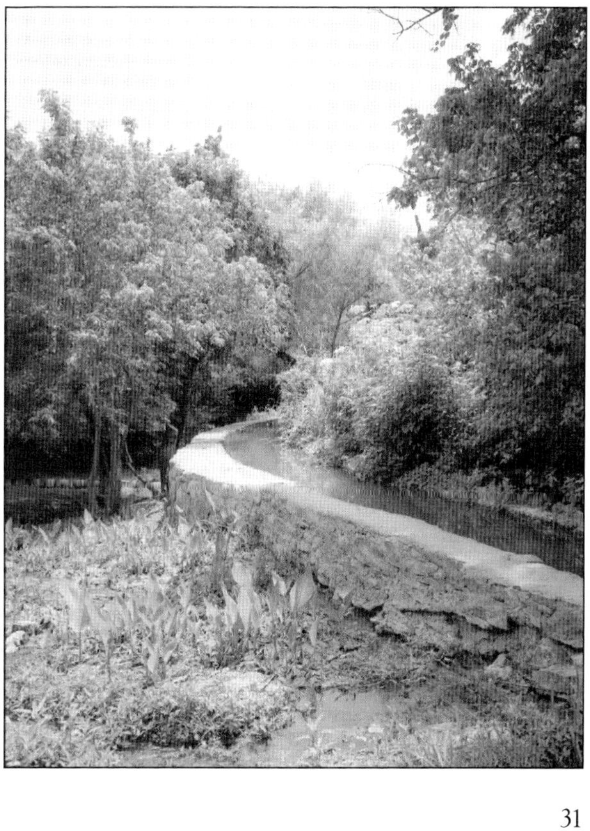

Seen here approaching Piedras Creek, the Espada acequia has irrigated crops and given life to the San Antonio area for nearly three centuries. (Courtesy of the Library of Congress.)

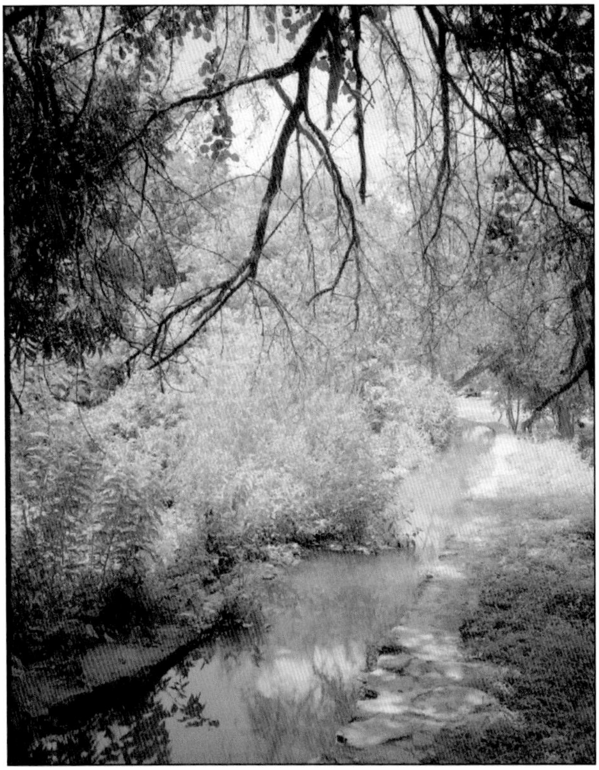

The acequia of Mission Espada has been in existence since the mid-1700s. The acequia is part of the Espada Aqueduct and Dam, and it plays an integral role in the water delivery system. (Courtesy of the Library of Congress.)

Originally founded in 1690 as Mission San Francisco de los Tejas in East Texas, Mission San Francisco de la Espada was established on the San Antonio River in 1731. This pictured sign describes an important feature of the mission: the Espada Dam. Made of stone and measuring 47 varas long, 2 varas wide, and 3 varas high (a vara is a Spanish unit of measurement roughly equivalent to 33 inches), the Espada Dam has been functioning since the mid-1700s and is the oldest Spanish diversion dam in Texas. (Courtesy of Steven Gonzales.)

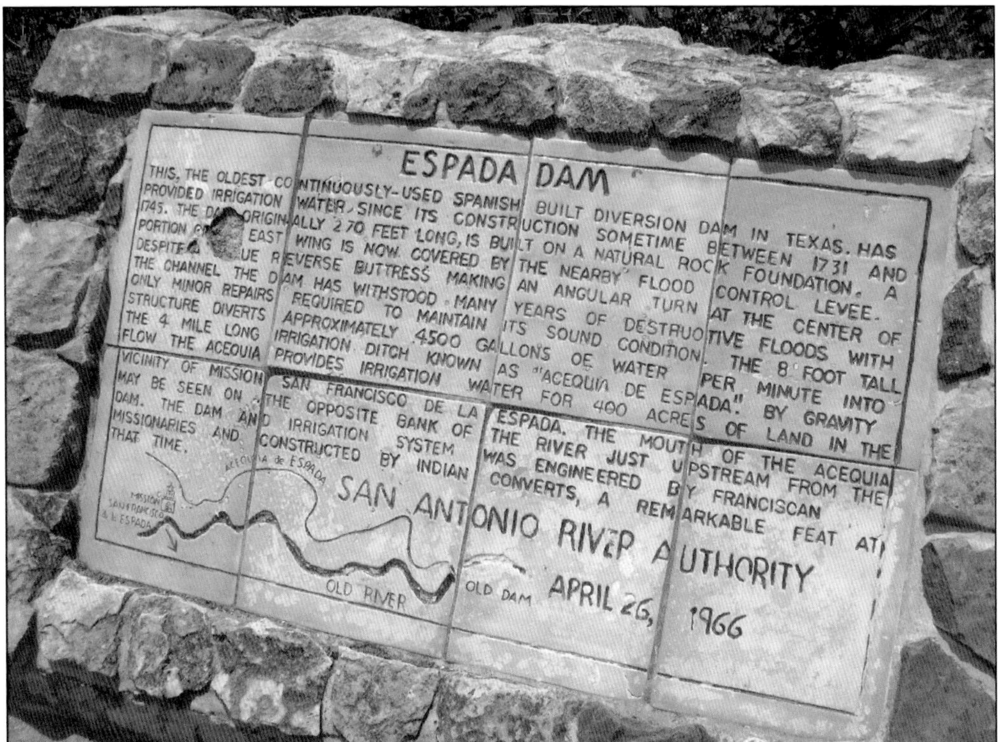

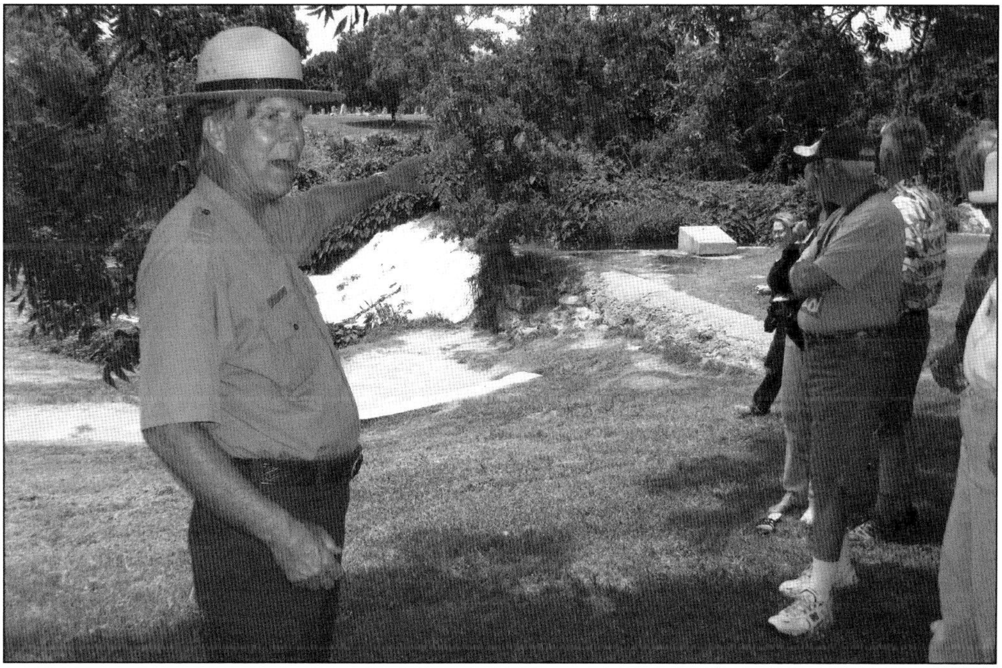

Attendees of the Partnership for the National Trails System's 2010 National Historic Trails workshop are seen here learning about Espada Dam from a Park Service ranger. (Courtesy of Steven Gonzales.)

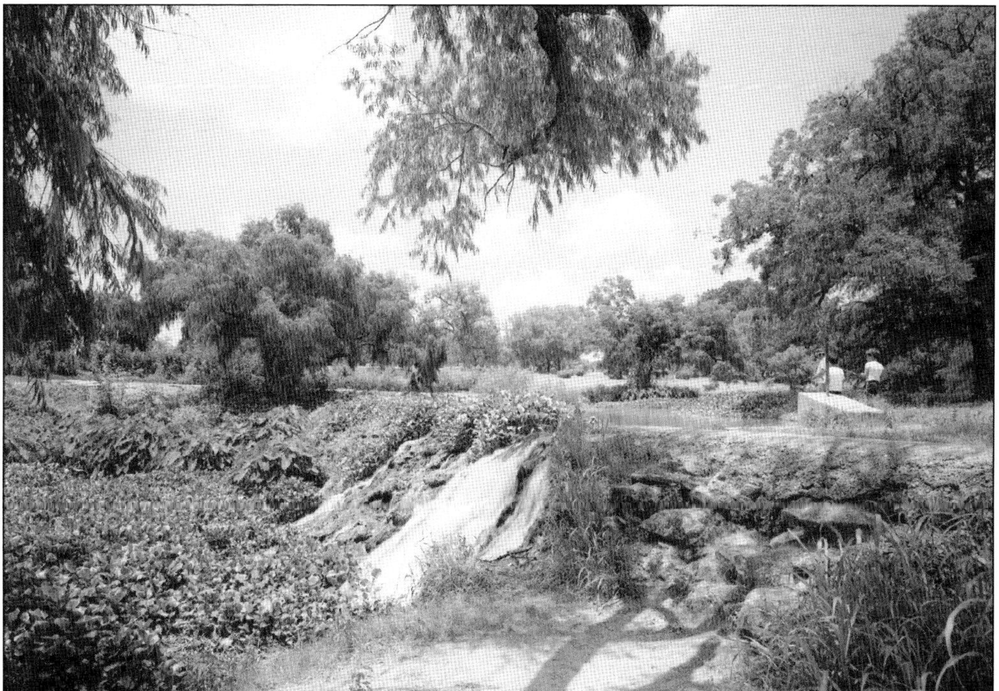

The majestic setting of the Espada Dam is captured beautifully in this photograph. The dam has been functioning for nearly 300 years. (Courtesy of the Library of Congress.)

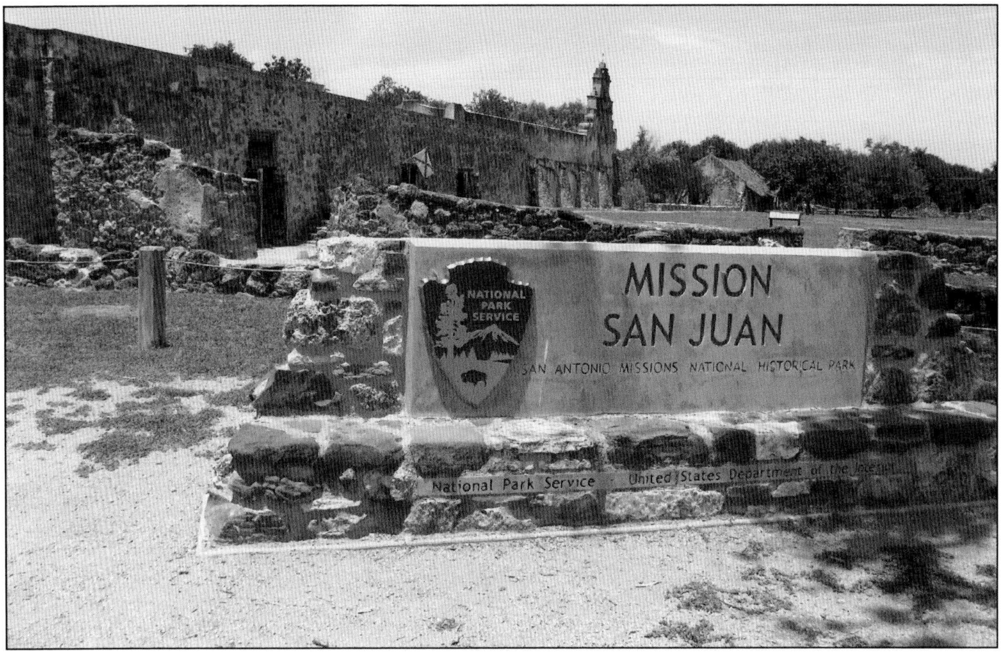


Mission San Juan Capistrano was moved from East Texas and reestablished on the banks of the San Antonio River on March 5, 1731. The church was completed in 1756 and included a granary. Expansion of the church began in 1772; however, due to a lack of indigenous labor, the project came to an end in 1786. (Courtesy of Steven Gonzales.)

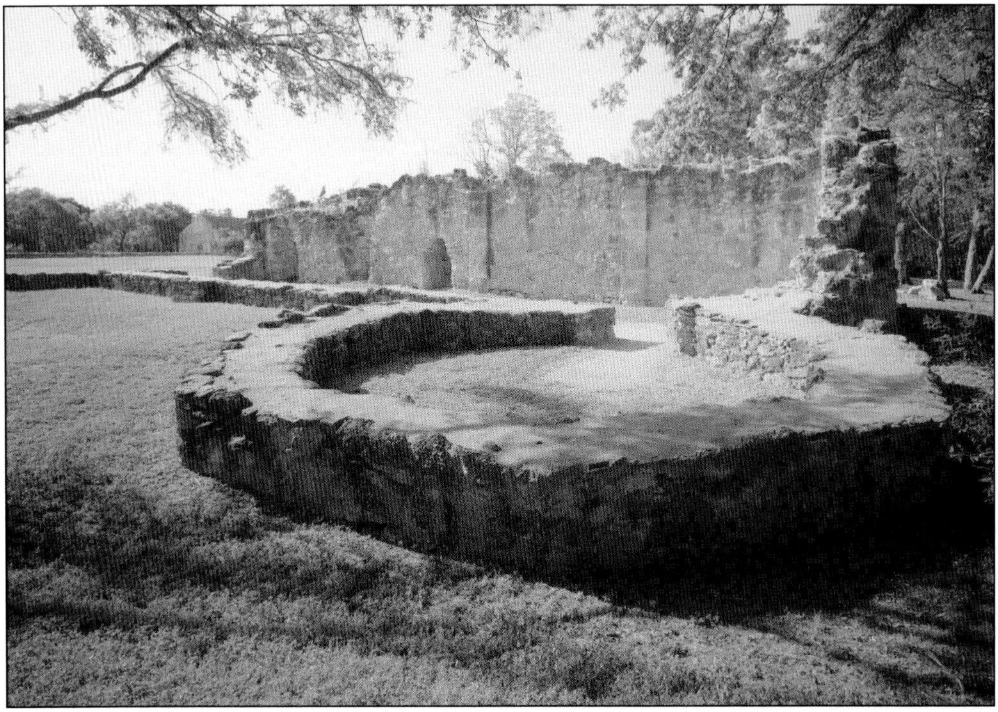

Pictured here are the walls of Mission San Juan Capistrano as they appeared in 1933. (Courtesy of the Library of Congress.)

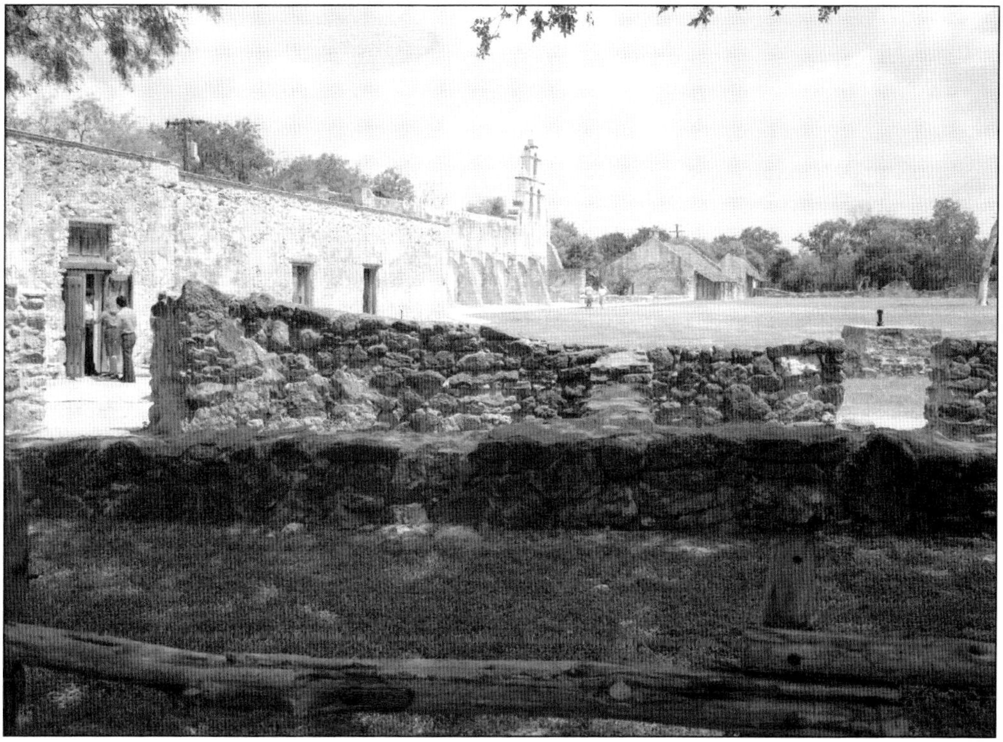

Mission San Juan has been on the banks of the San Antonio River for nearly 300 years. Its beauty and majesty are breathtaking. (Courtesy of the Library of Congress.)

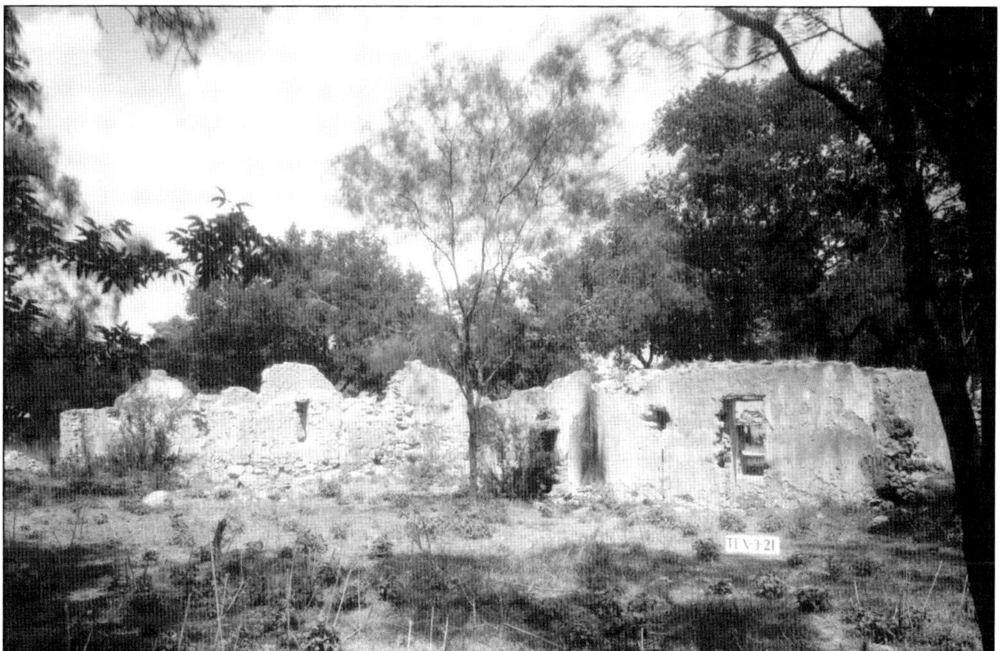

The ruins of the Indian quarters are pictured here as they appeared at Mission San Juan in 1936. (Courtesy of the Library of Congress.)

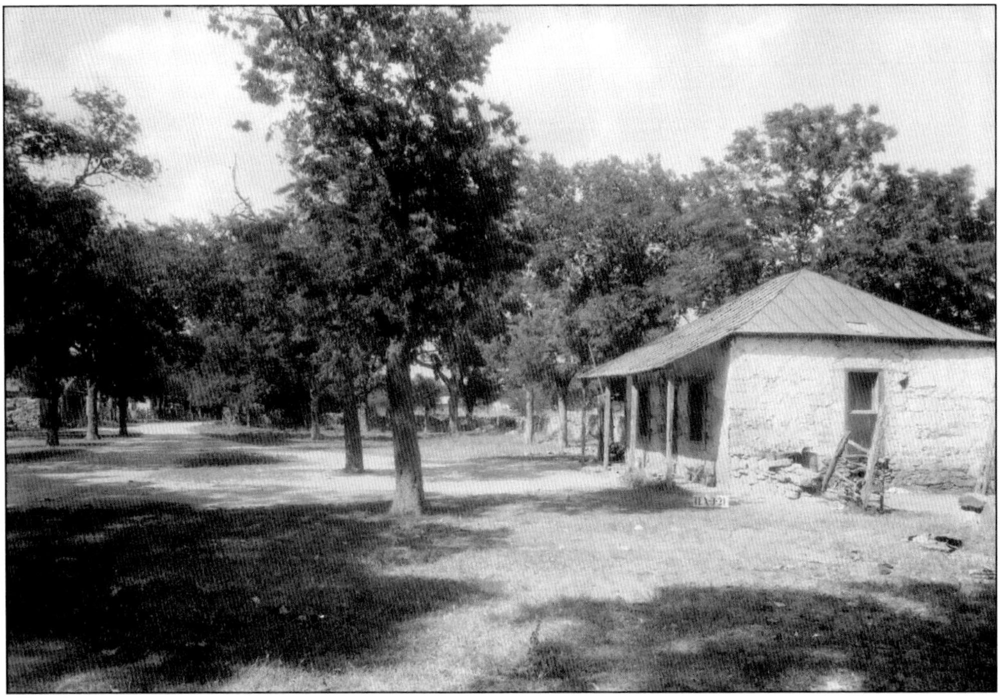

Here is a road passing through Mission San Juan in 1936. (Courtesy of the Library of Congress.)

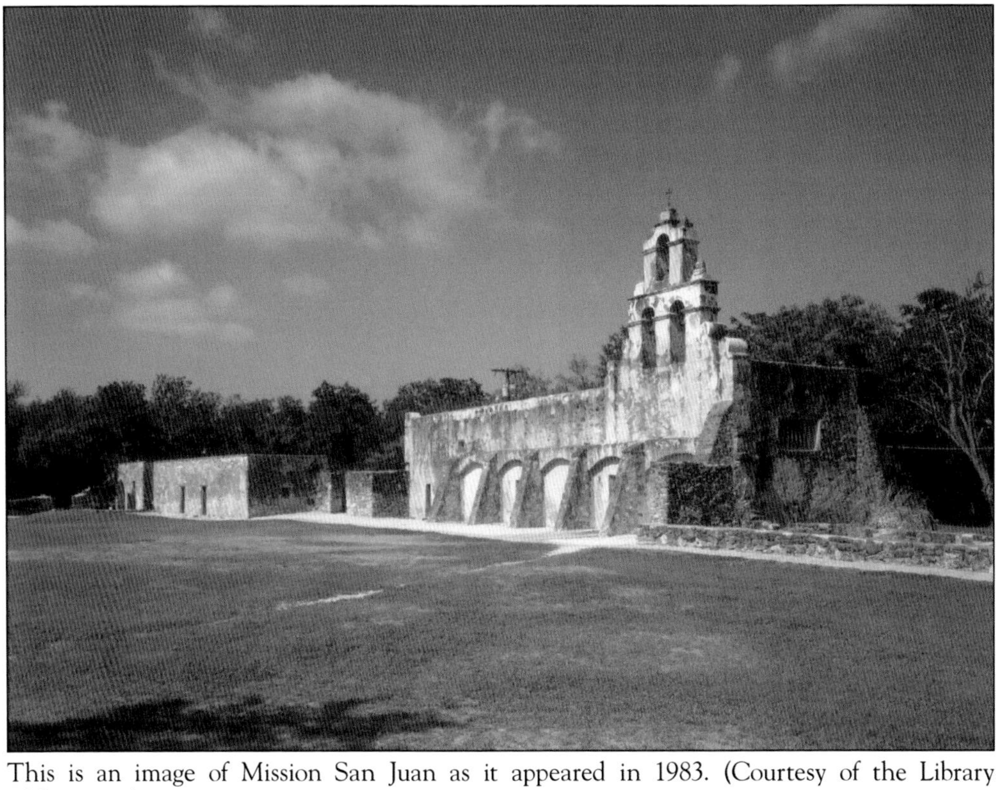

This is an image of Mission San Juan as it appeared in 1983. (Courtesy of the Library of Congress.)

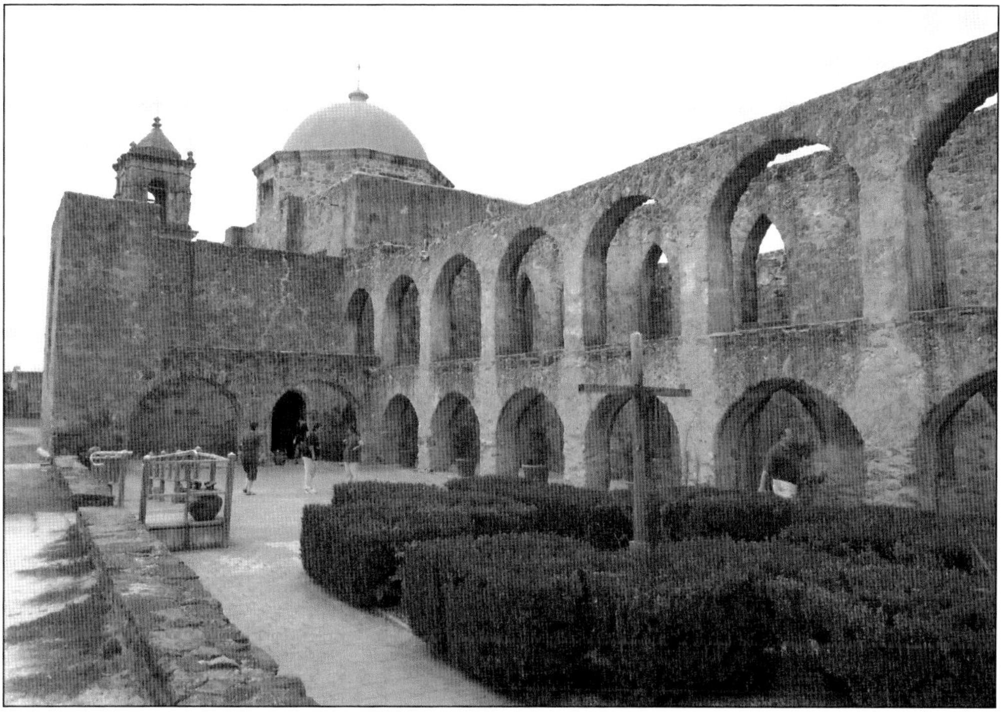

Mission San José y San Miguel de Aguayo is considered to be the "Queen of the Texas Missions." Mission San José, as it is typically referred to, was founded in 1720. The mission was named after San José—also known as Saint Joseph—and the Marqués de Aguayo, who was governor of the province of Coahuila y Tejas at the time. (Courtesy of Steven Gonzales.)

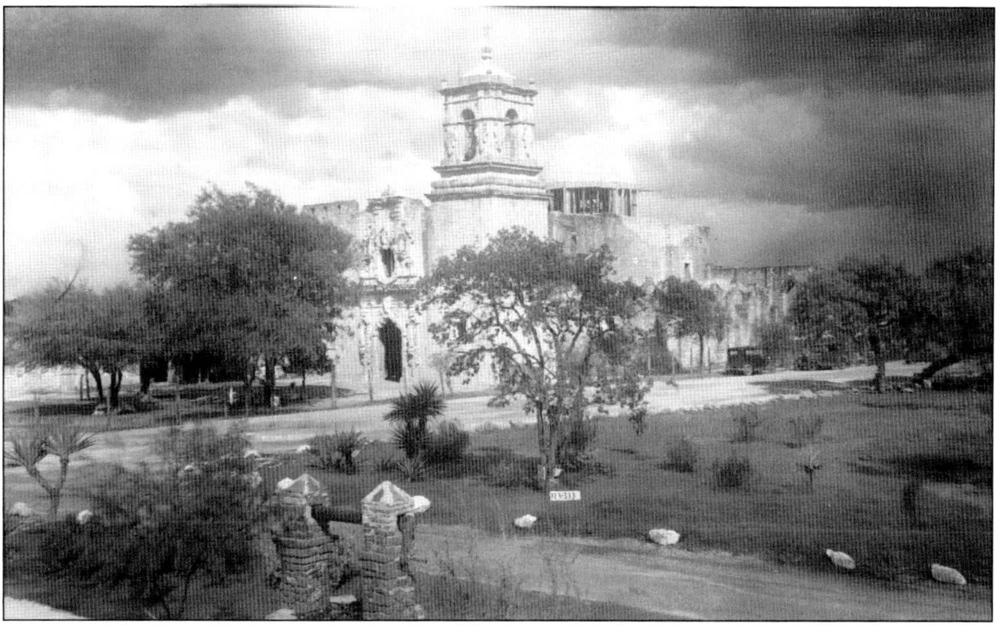

This photograph shows Mission San José as it appeared in the early 1900s. The dome behind the tower has since been rebuilt, and the trees immediately in front of the church are no longer present. (Courtesy of the Library of Congress.)

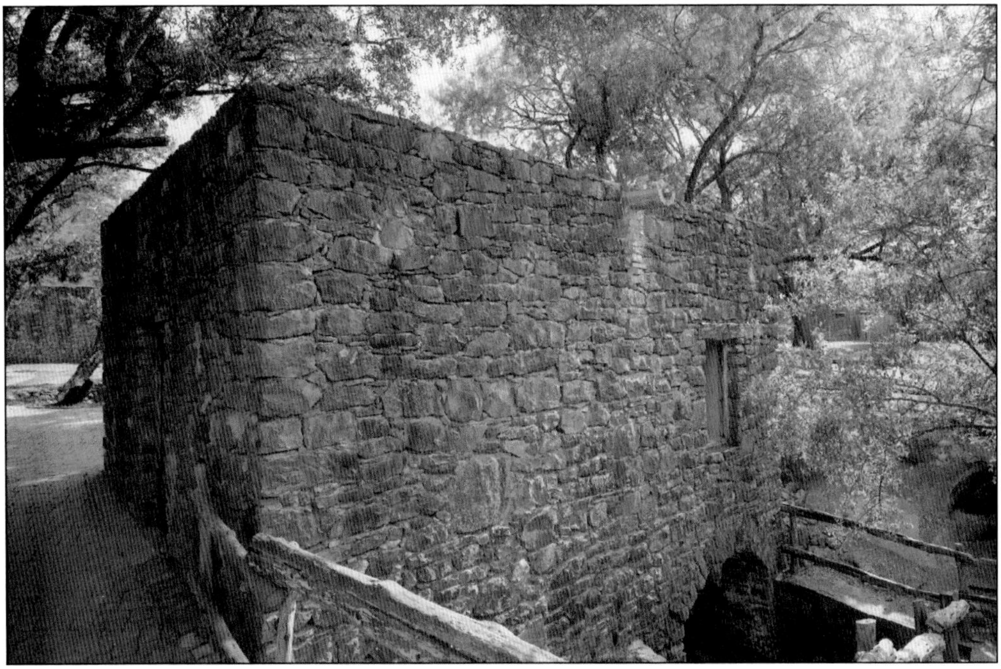

The gristmill at Mission San José is the only Spanish gristmill that still exists in Texas. (Courtesy of the Library of Congress.)

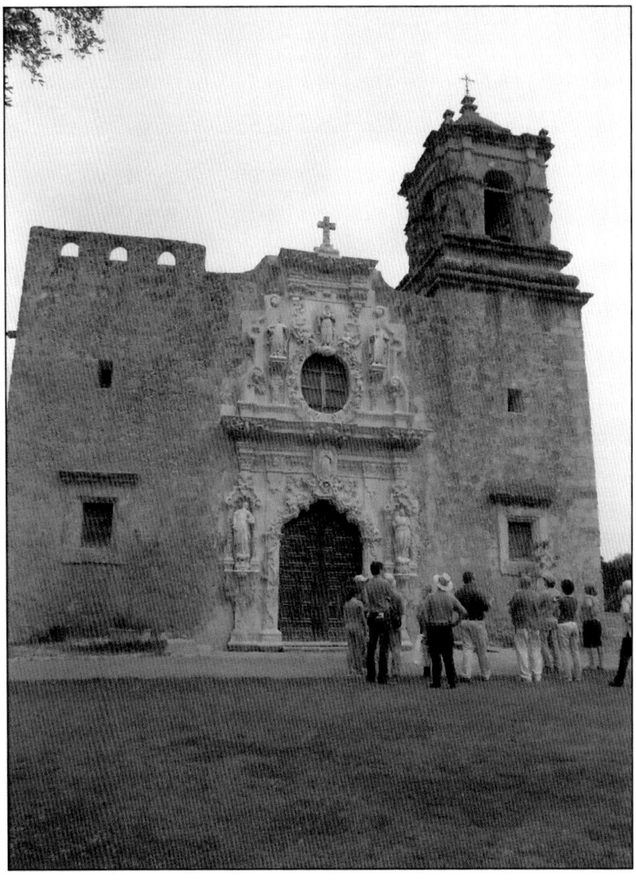

While gathered for a symposium titled El Camino Real and the Southern Route to California: Trails that Shaped the Face of Texas, a group of officials from El Camino Real de los Tejas National Historic Trail Association and the Oregon-California Trails Association took part in a tour of Mission San José. (Courtesy of Steven Gonzales.)

The gristmill at Mission San José was constructed in the late 1700s. Powered by water from the San Antonio River—channeled through acequias—the gristmill produced flour for the various peoples of the mission community. (Courtesy of Steven Gonzales.)

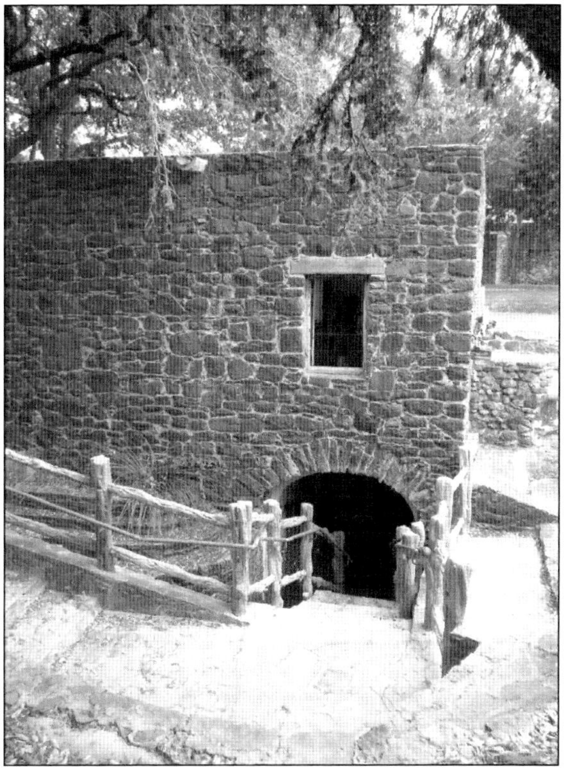

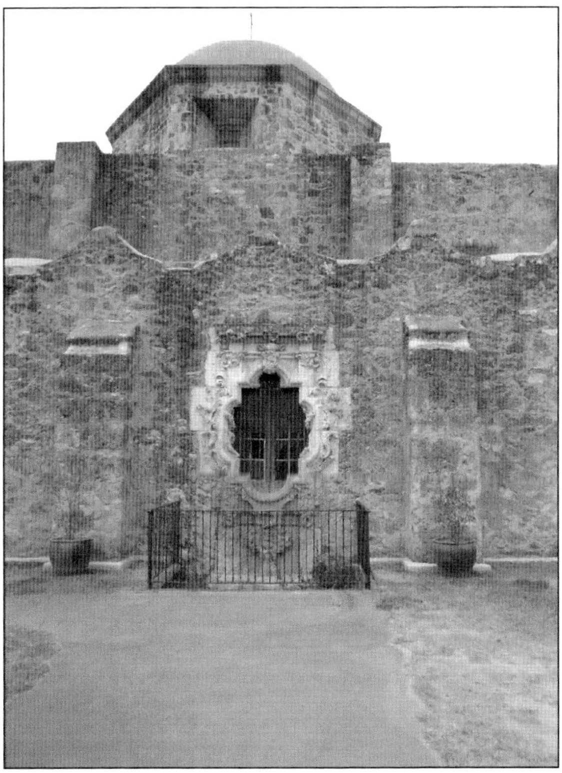

The Rose Window, or la Ventana de Rosa, was sculpted around 1775. The window is believed to have been crafted by Pedro Huízar and named after his lost love, Rosa. The window is one of the most famous aspects of Mission San José. (Courtesy of Steven Gonzales.)

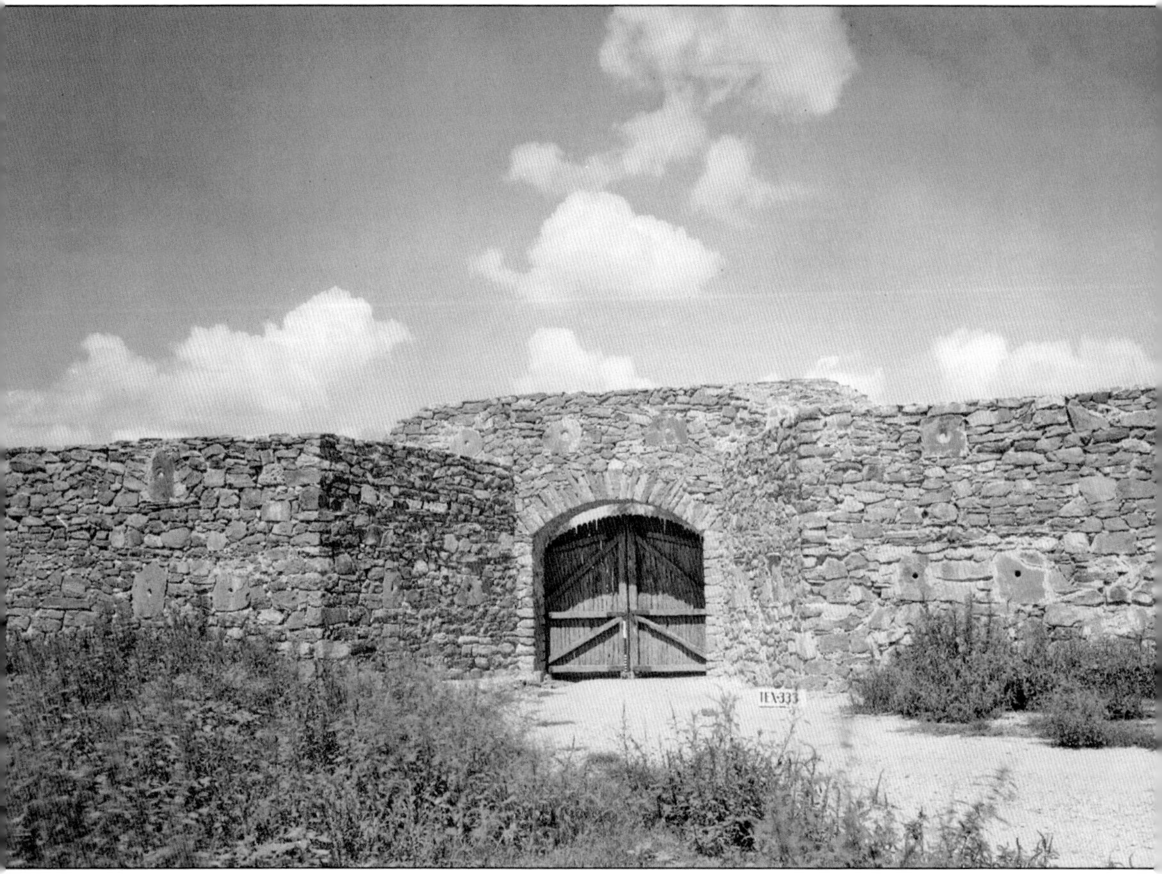

Here are the gates of the courtyard to Mission San José in the early 1900s. (Courtesy of the Library of Congress.)

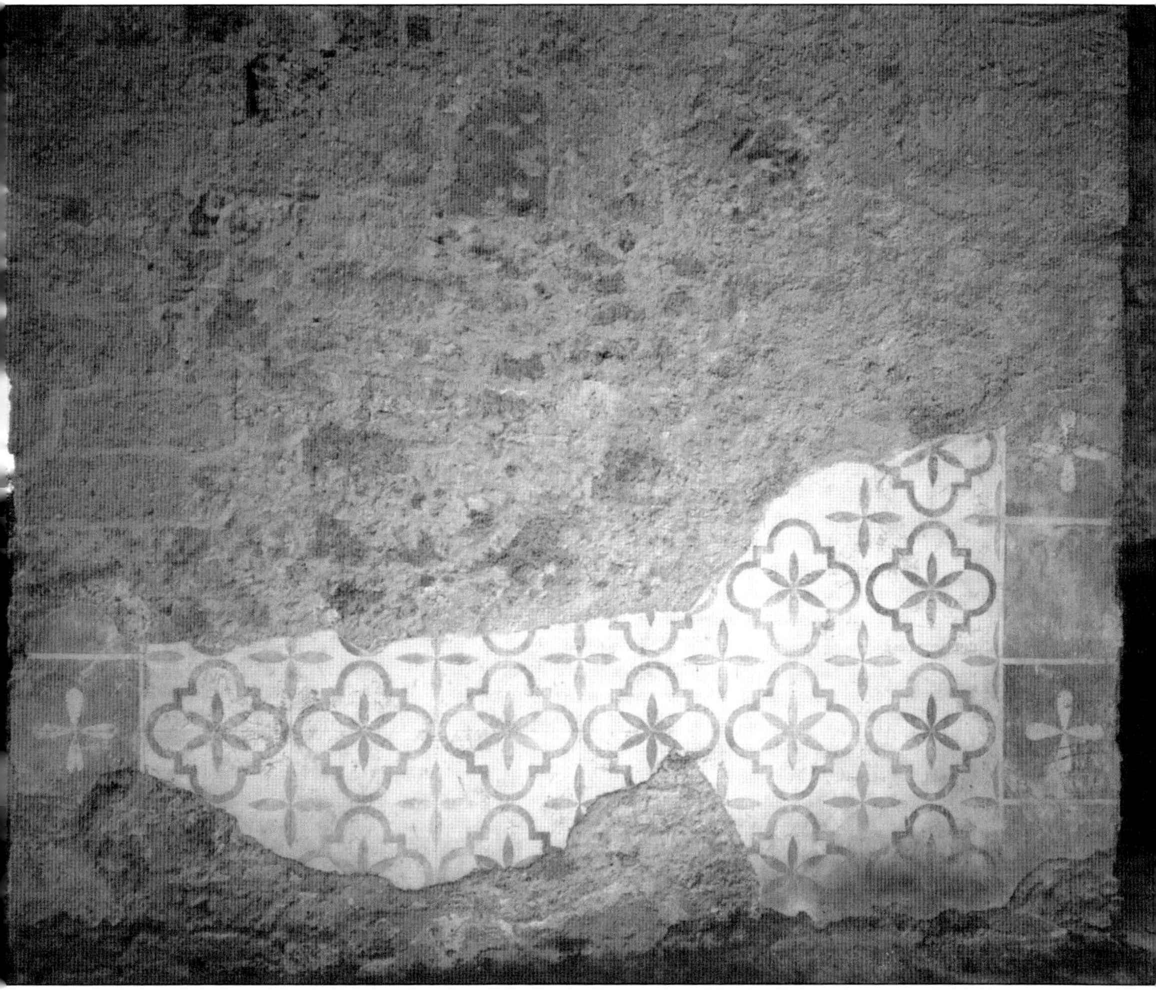

This elaborate stucco remnant at Mission San José illustrates the Mudéjar design influence that was transferred from Spain to the Americas. In the past, Mission San José was covered in this sophisticated design. (Courtesy of the Library of Congress.)

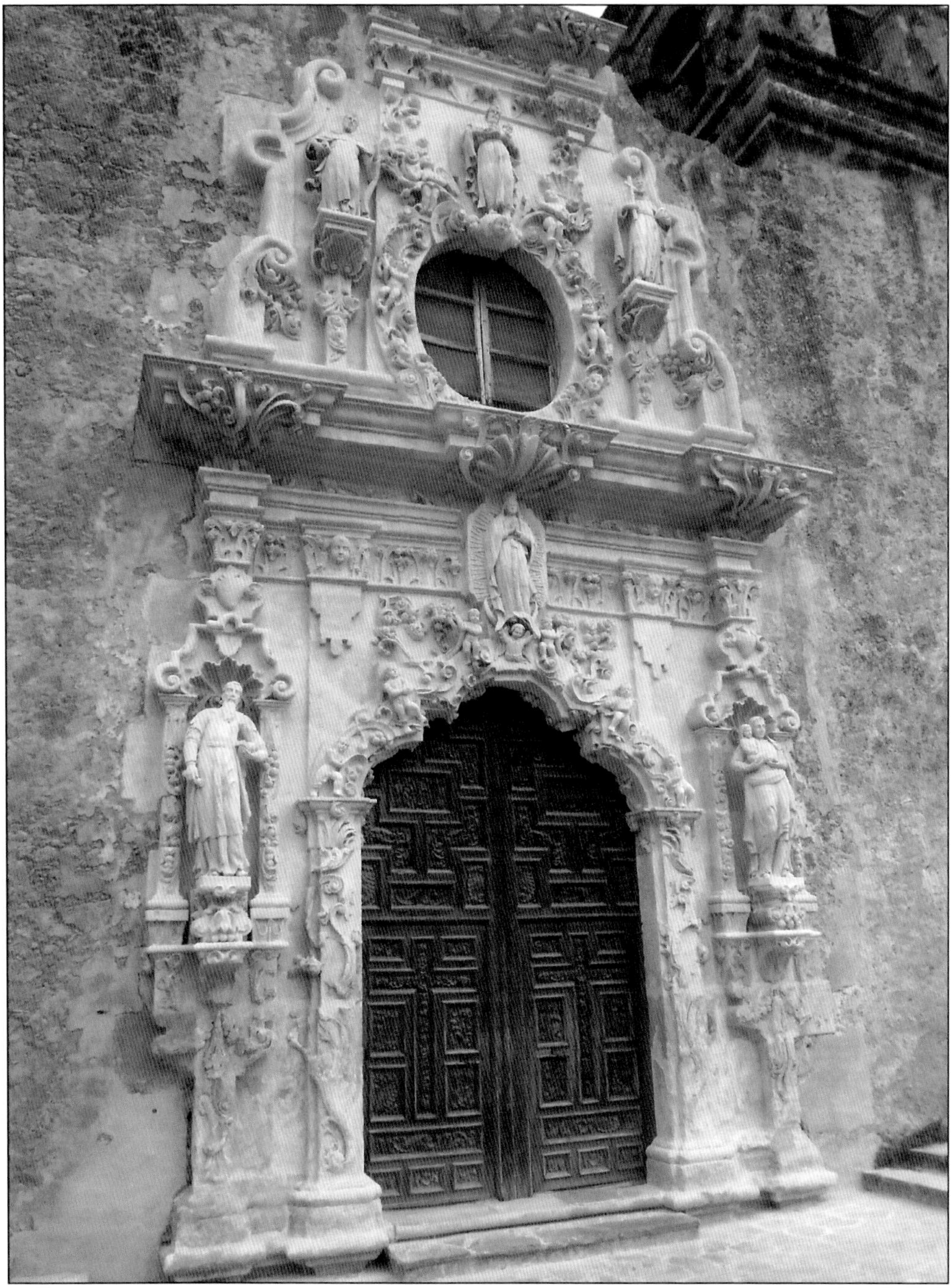

The facade of Mission San José elegantly illustrates the Mudéjar architectural tradition. Mudéjar architecture features a mixture of Muslim, Christian, and Jewish influences, which comingled in Spain before crossing the Atlantic to places such as the missions on the remote northern frontier of New Spain. (Courtesy of Steven Gonzales.)

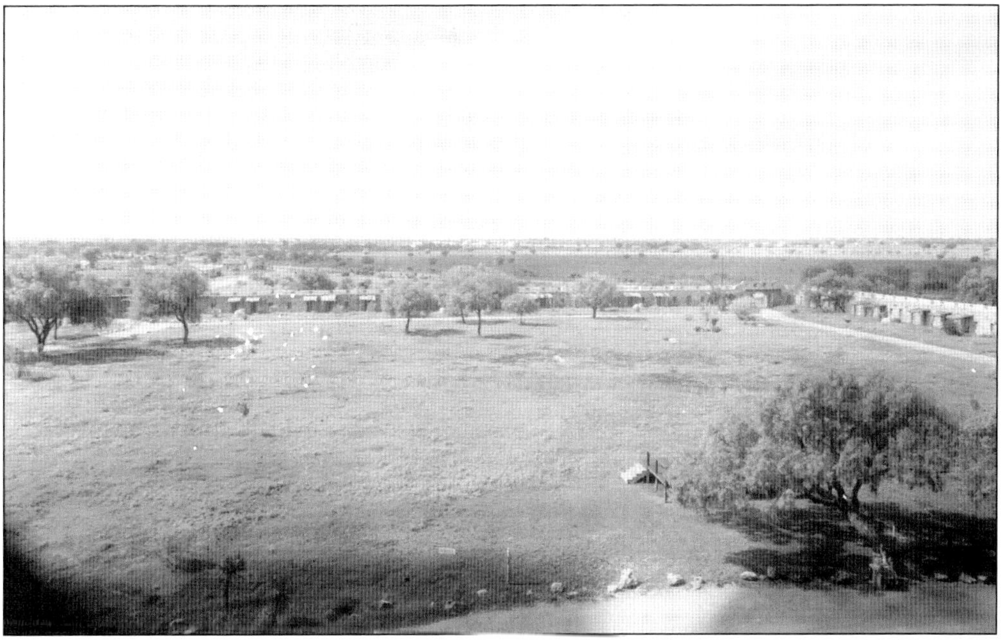

This photograph shows Mission San José and its surroundings as they appeared in 1936. (Courtesy of the Library of Congress.)

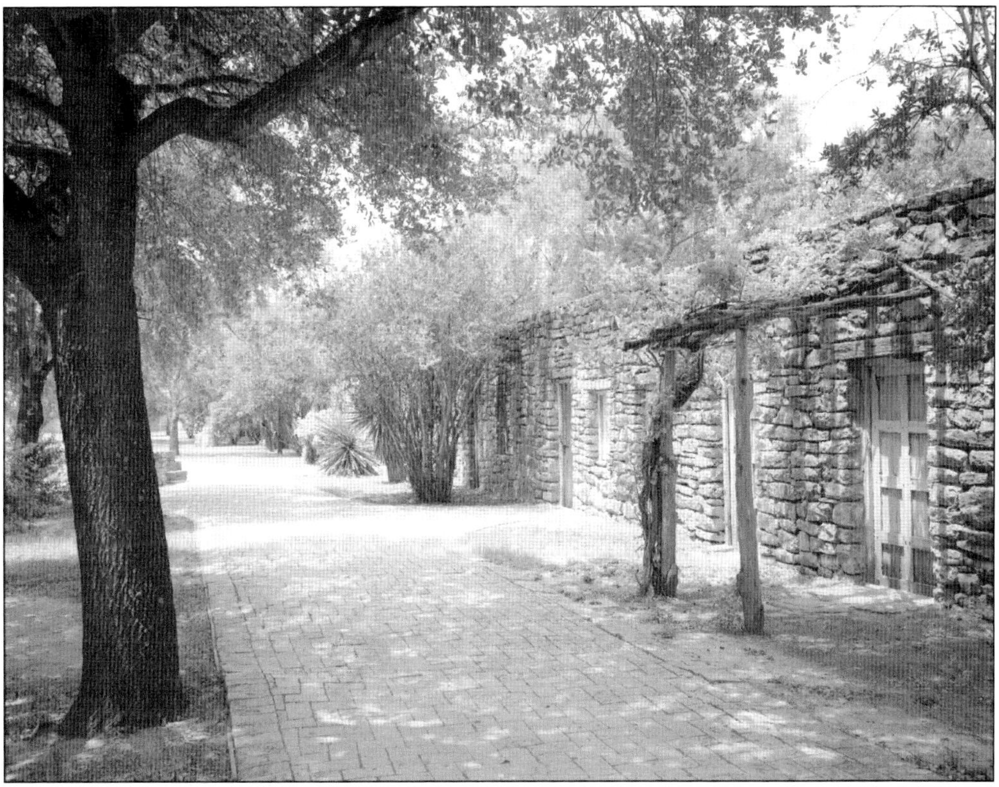

The Indian quarters at Mission San José appear much the same today as they did hundreds of years ago. (Courtesy of the Library of Congress.)

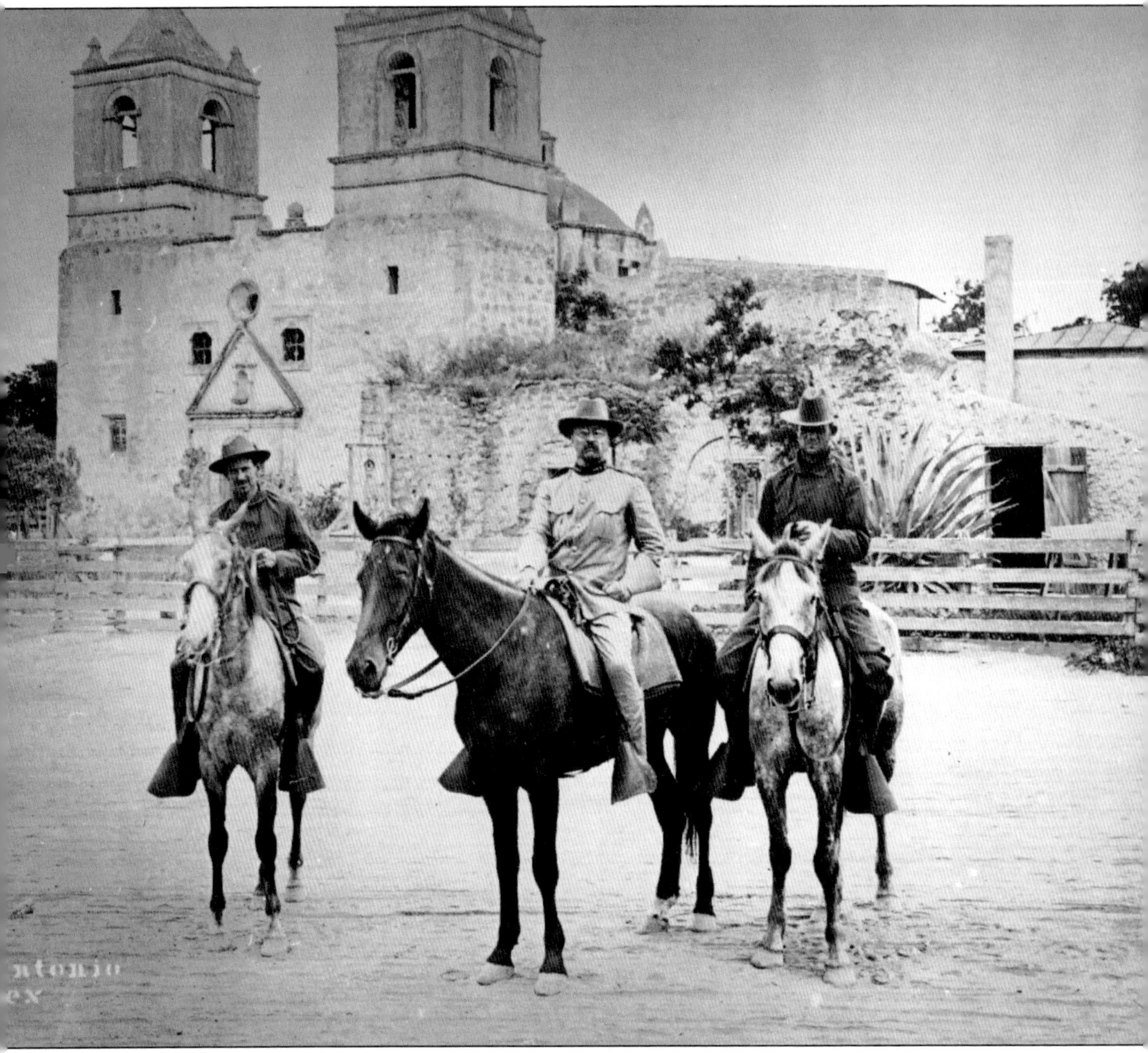

Future president Theodore Roosevelt and members of the Rough Riders are pictured here in front of Mission Concepción in 1898. Roosevelt journeyed to San Antonio under the orders of Pres. William McKinley to form volunteer military regiments from the Southwestern United States for the Spanish-American War. (Courtesy of the Library of Congress.)

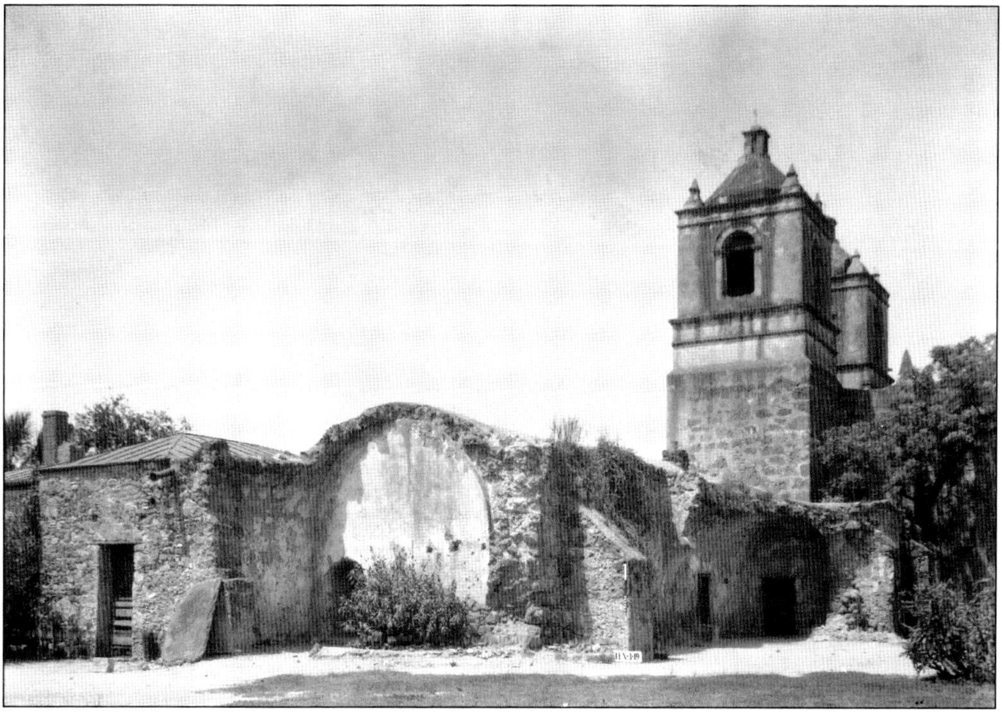

This 1936 photograph shows how Mission Concepción appeared prior to its renovation and before it was part of the National Park System. At the time this photograph was taken, the mission was nearly 200 years old. (Courtesy of the Library of Congress.)

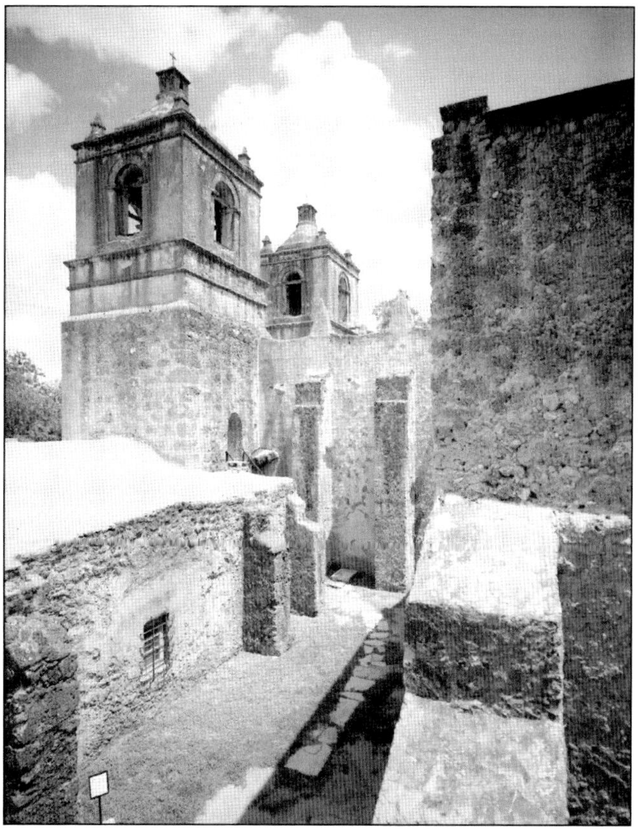

This photograph from 1936 shows a side view of Mission Concepción, with the convent in the background. (Courtesy of the Library of Congress.)

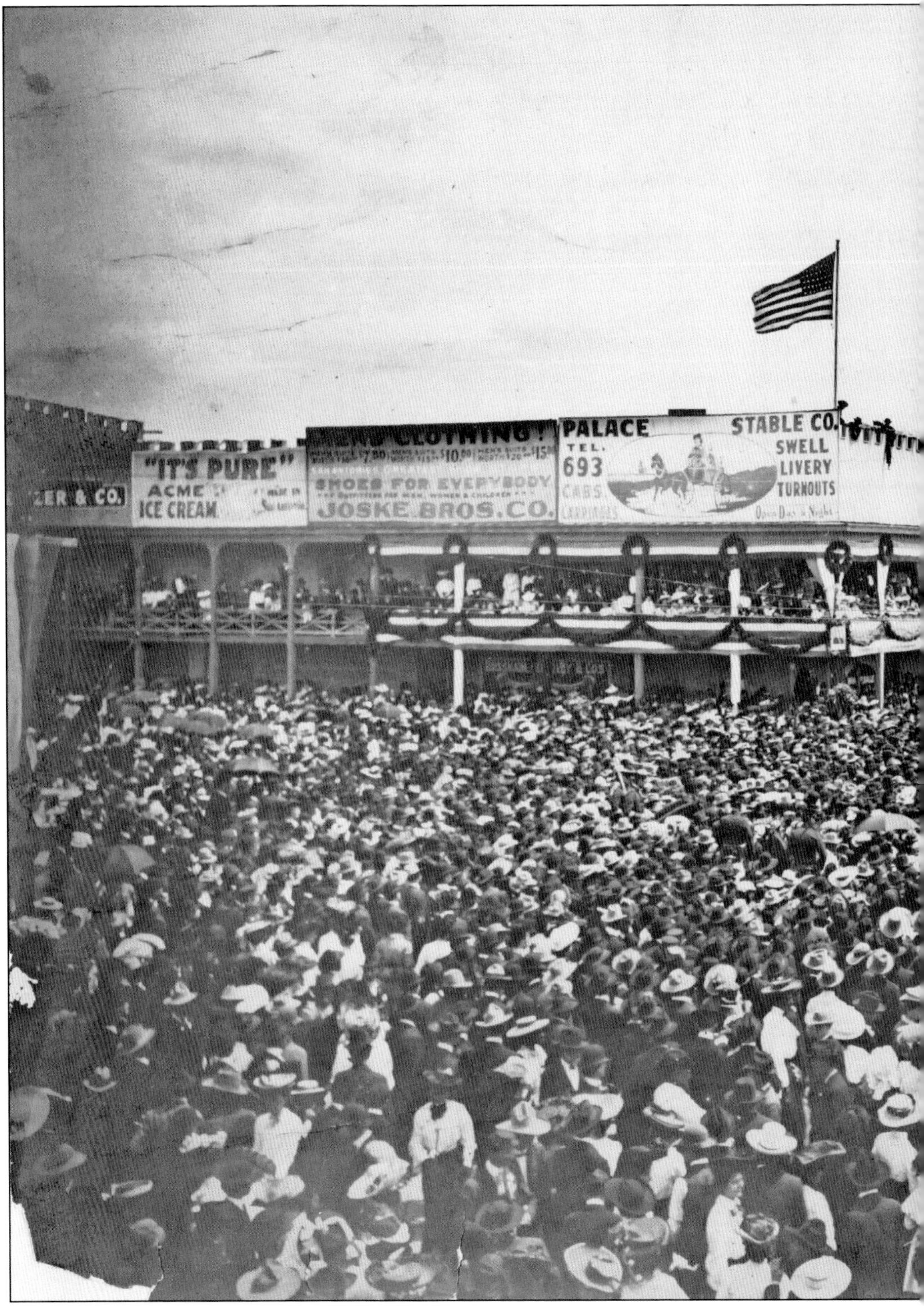


In 1905, Pres. Theodore Roosevelt returned to Texas for a Rough Riders reunion in San Antonio. Speaking in front of the Alamo, his appearance was attended by thousands. (Courtesy of the

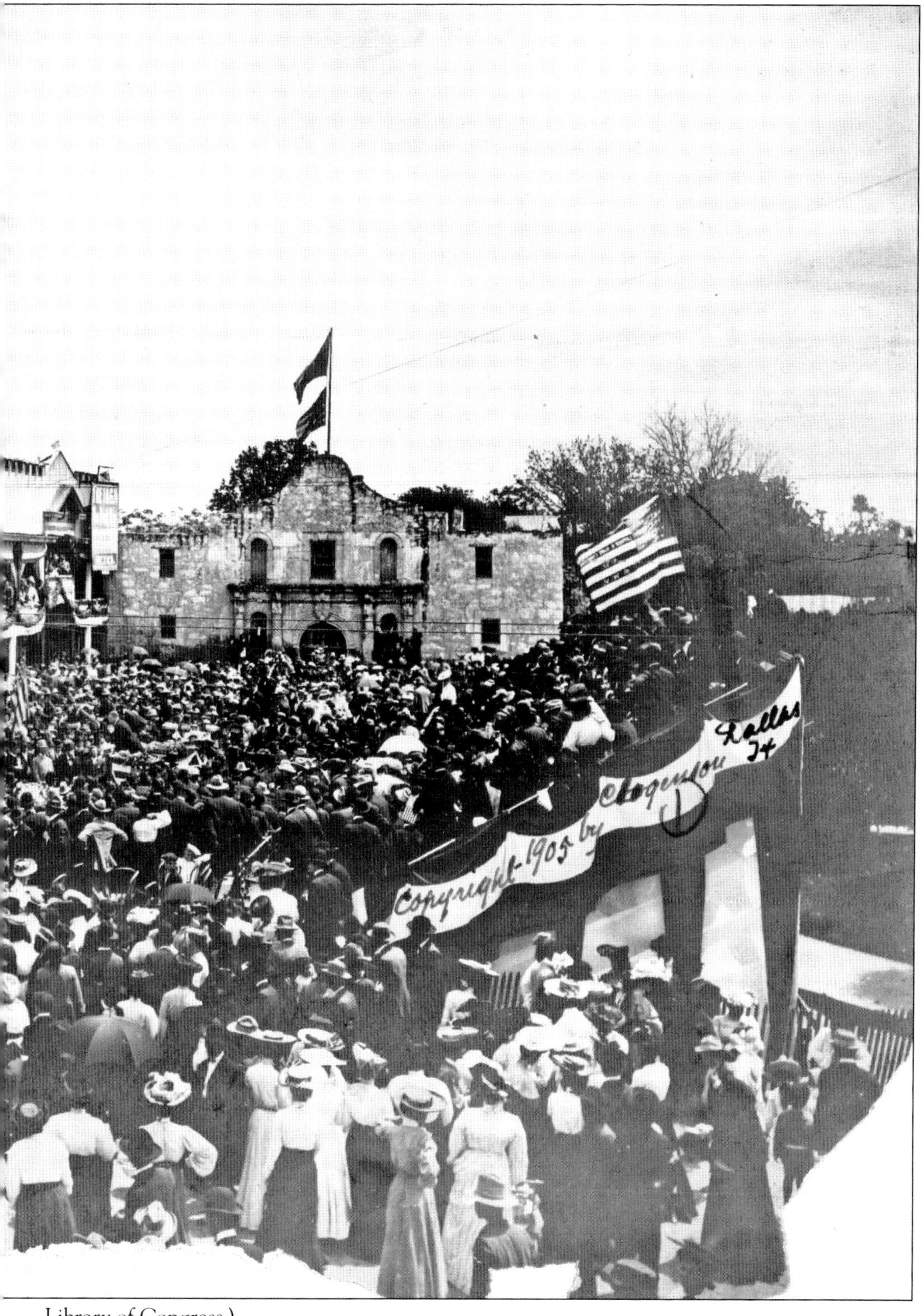


Library of Congress.)

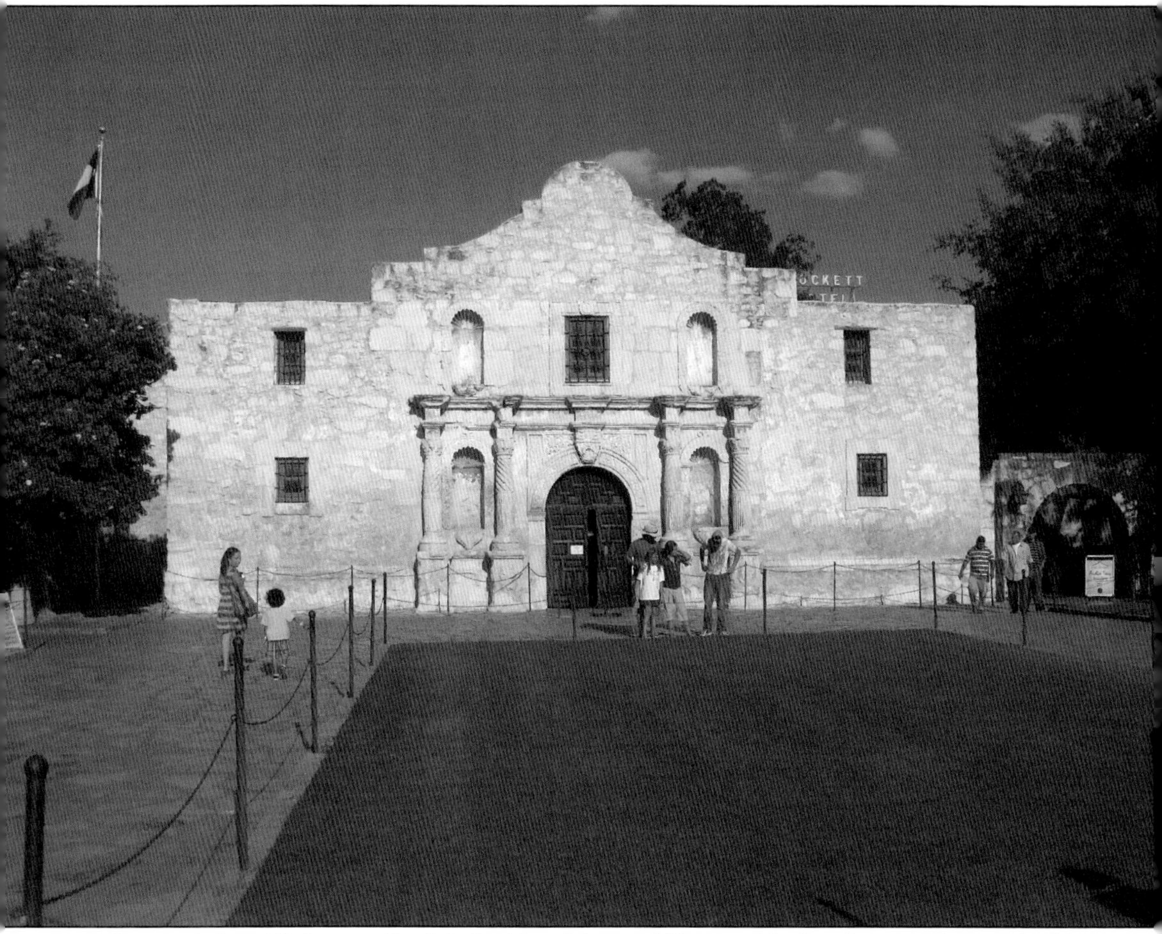

Situated along El Camino Real de los Tejas National Historic Trail is the most famous building in Texas, and possibly one of the most famous buildings in the world: the Alamo. Originally known as Mission San Antonio de Valero, the mission was founded on May 1, 1718, near San Pedro Springs. The mission moved three times and eventually reached its current location on the east bank of the San Antonio River. The name "the Alamo" comes from La Segunda Compañía Volante de San Carlos de Parras (Álamo de Parras), or the Second Flying Company of San Carlos de Parras. La Compañía del Álamo came from the area of Parras, Coahuila, and the men were designated as presidial soldiers of the secularized Mission San Antonio de Valero. (Courtesy of Steven Gonzales.)

A state historic marker illustrates the role of Canary Islander families in the founding of San Fernando de Béxar in the early 1700s. The families of Béxar constituted the first organized civil government in Texas. (Courtesy of Steven Gonzales.)

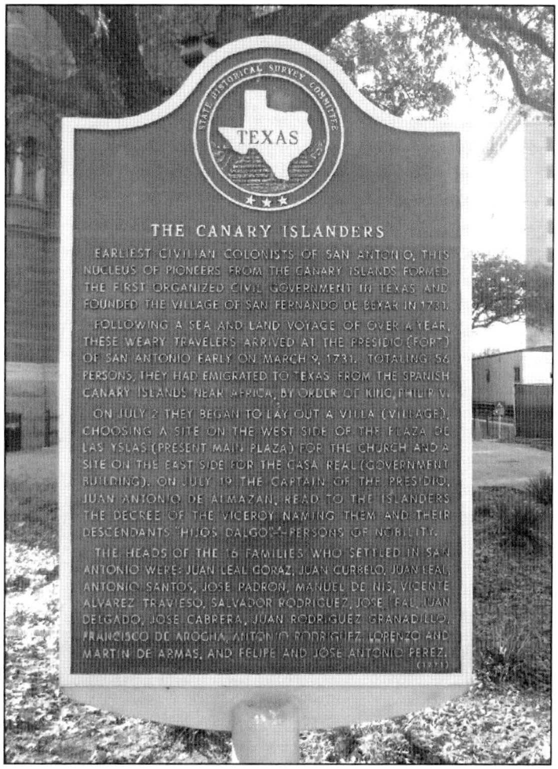


Main Plaza, also known as la Plaza de las Islas because of the Canary Islanders, is still the heart of the city. It is the site of the original settlement of civilian families in San Antonio and home to many festivities to this day. (Courtesy of Steven Gonzales.)

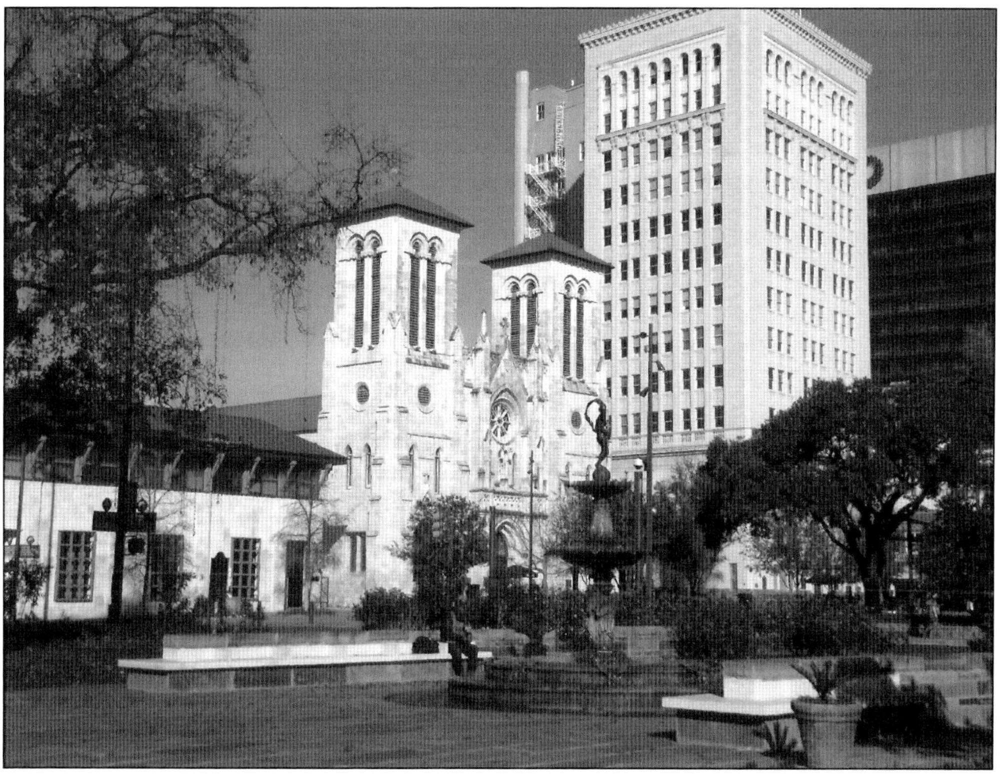

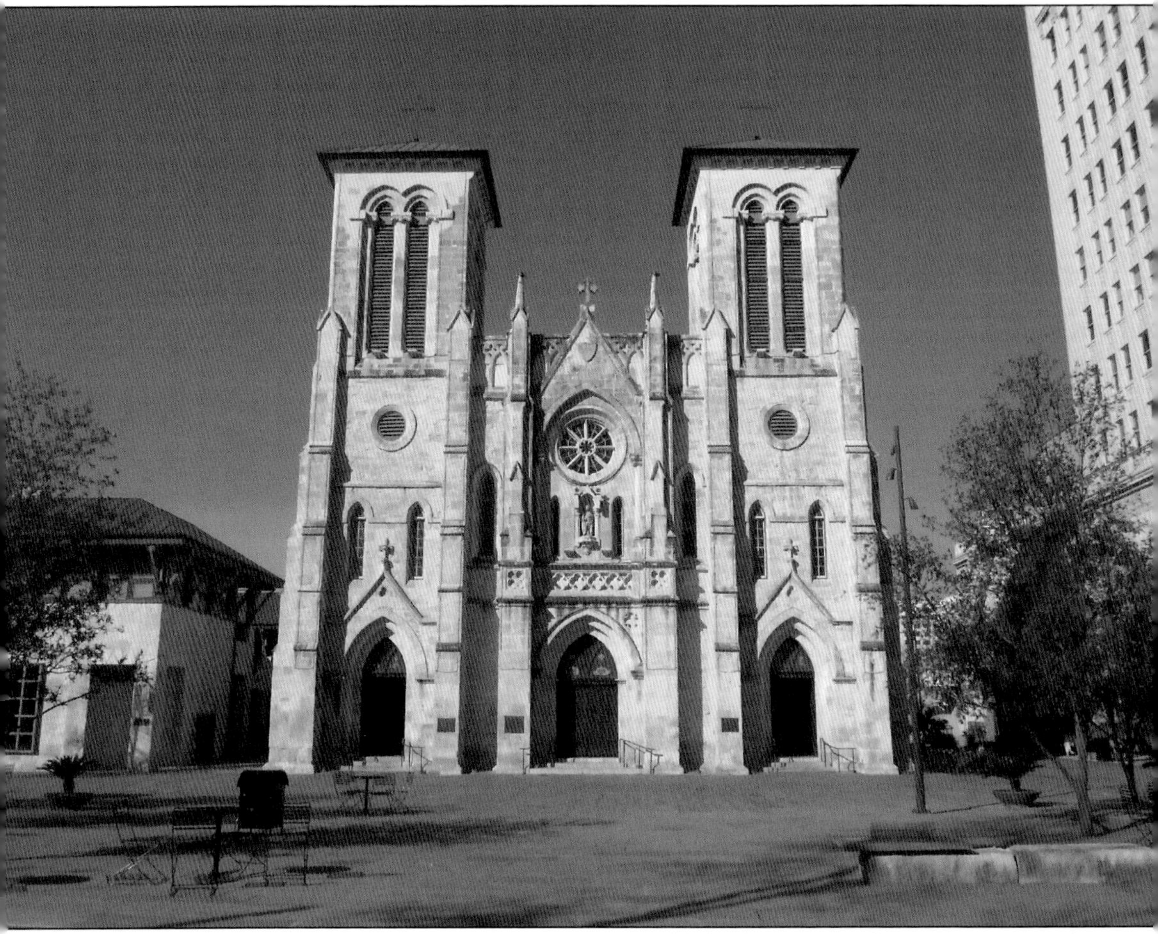

The location of the San Fernando Cathedral was established in 1731, and it was constructed in the years following. Located on la Plaza de las Islas, San Fernando was originally created for the civilian public of Béxar and is still an active cathedral in the center of the community. (Courtesy of Steven Gonzales.)

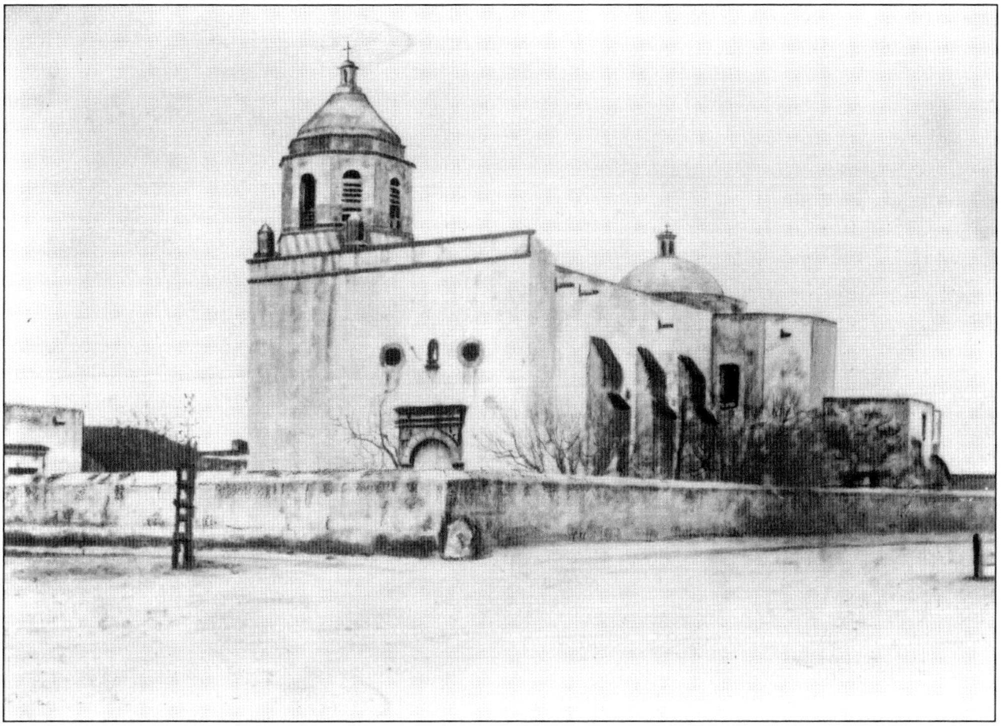

This photograph from the late 1800s illustrates one of the variations in the appearance of the San Fernando Cathedral over the years. Some differences from the cathedral of today are the single tower in the front of the church and the wall surrounding the compound. (Courtesy of the Library of Congress.)

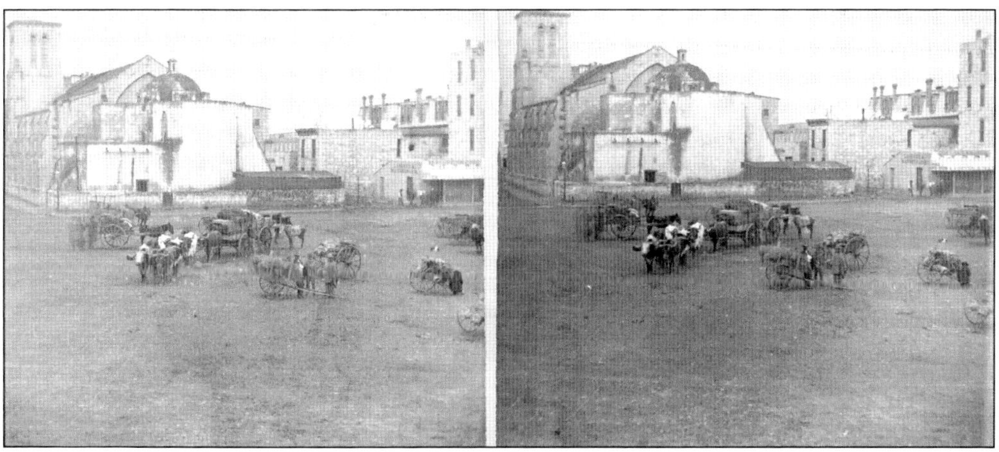

This stereographic photograph was produced between 1860 and 1880. It shows horses and oxen pulling wagons in Military Plaza in San Antonio. The structure to the left is the San Fernando Cathedral, and the image helps to demonstrate the cathedral's consistencies and changes throughout the years. (Courtesy of the Library of Congress.)

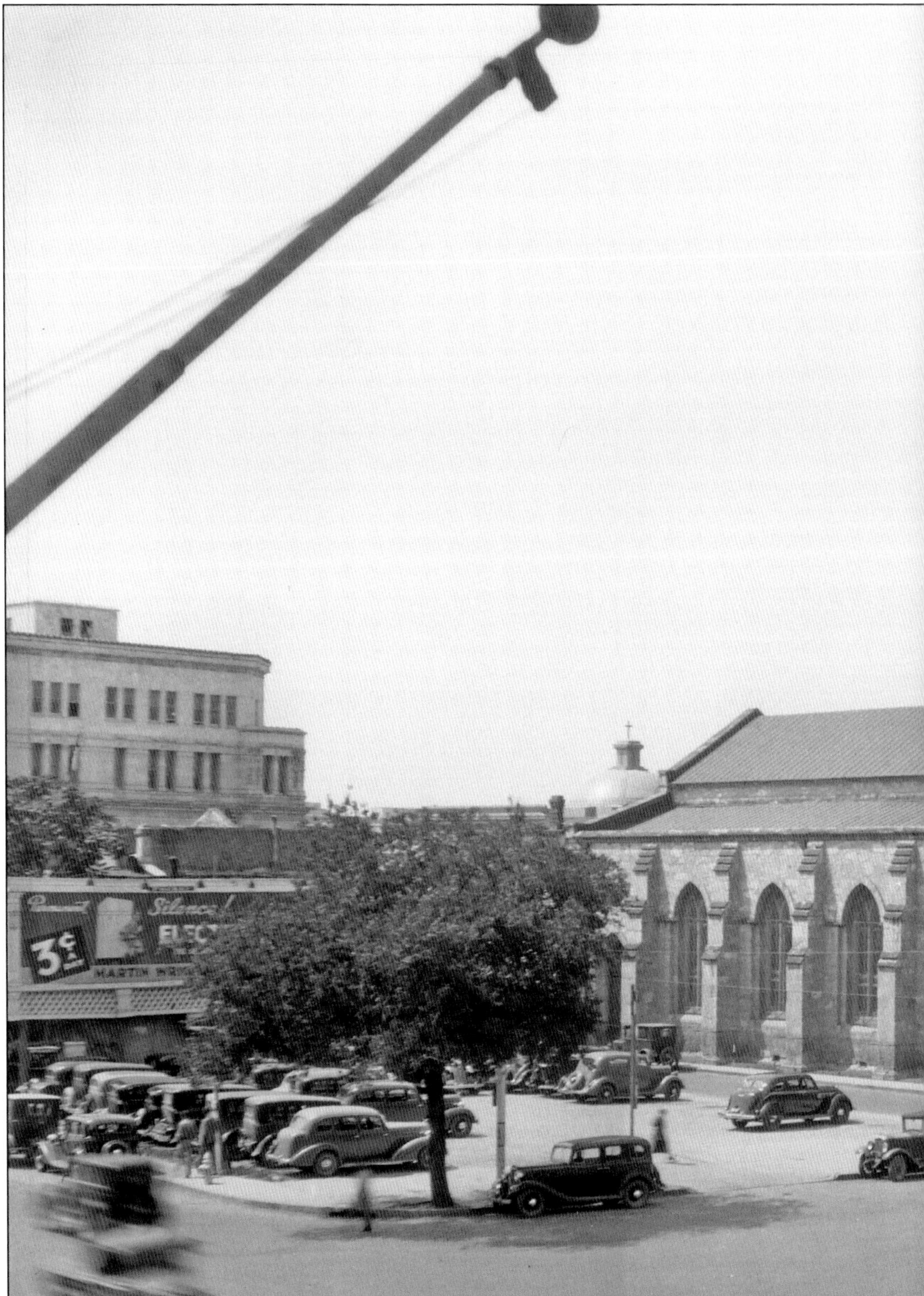


This image of San Fernando in 1936 shows that the cathedral had, by that time, largely taken on its current form. However, the caps on the towers at the front of the cathedral are notably

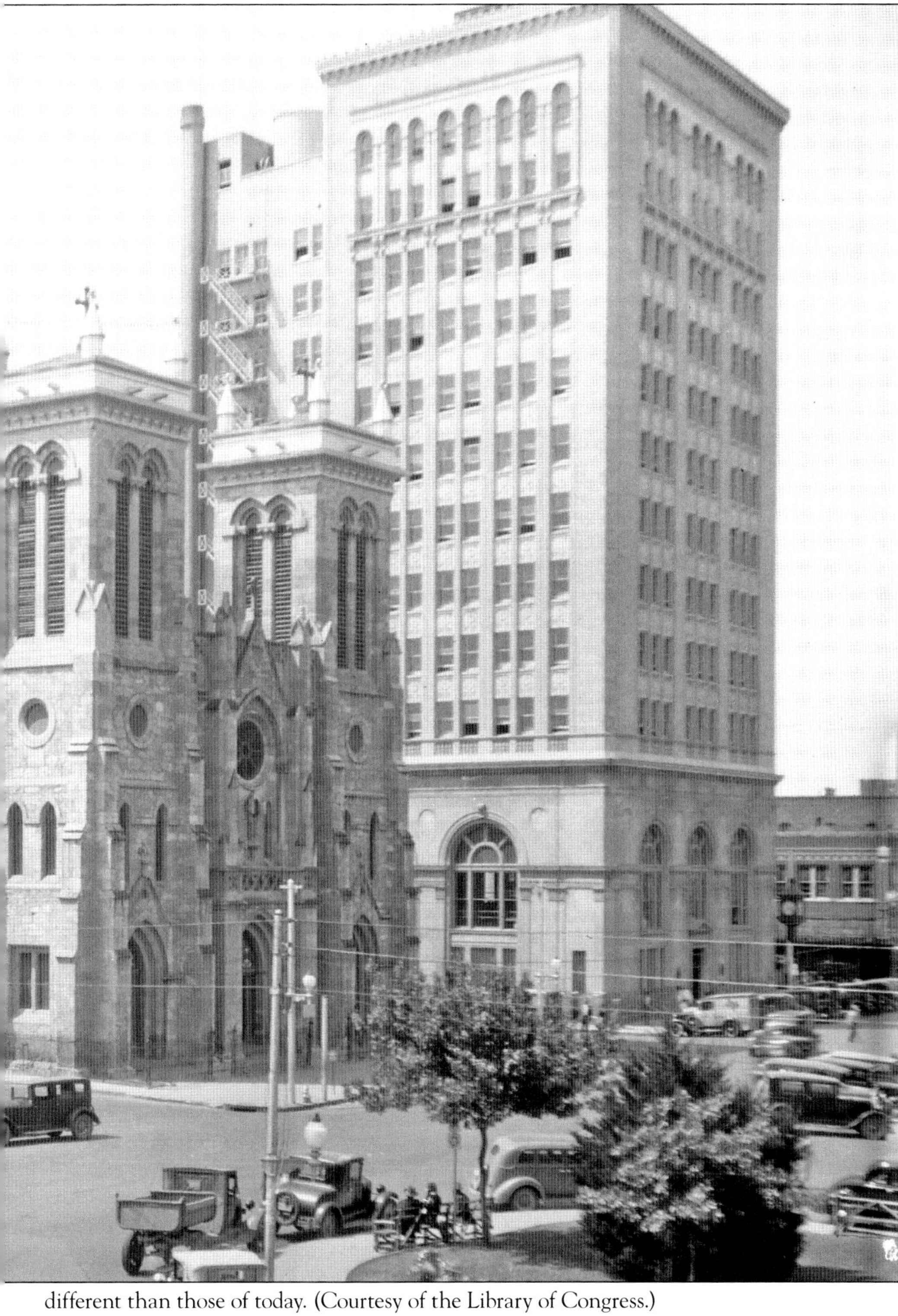

different than those of today. (Courtesy of the Library of Congress.)

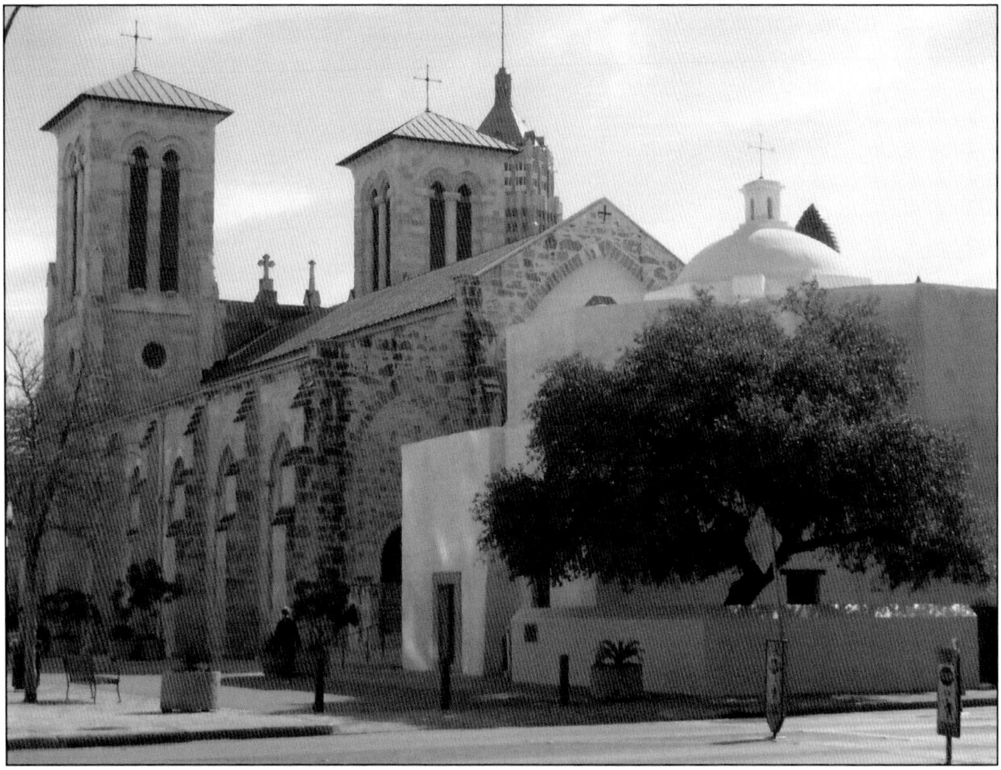

The San Fernando Cathedral is an impressive structure that has undergone multiple renovations and repairs over the years. (Courtesy of Steven Gonzales.)

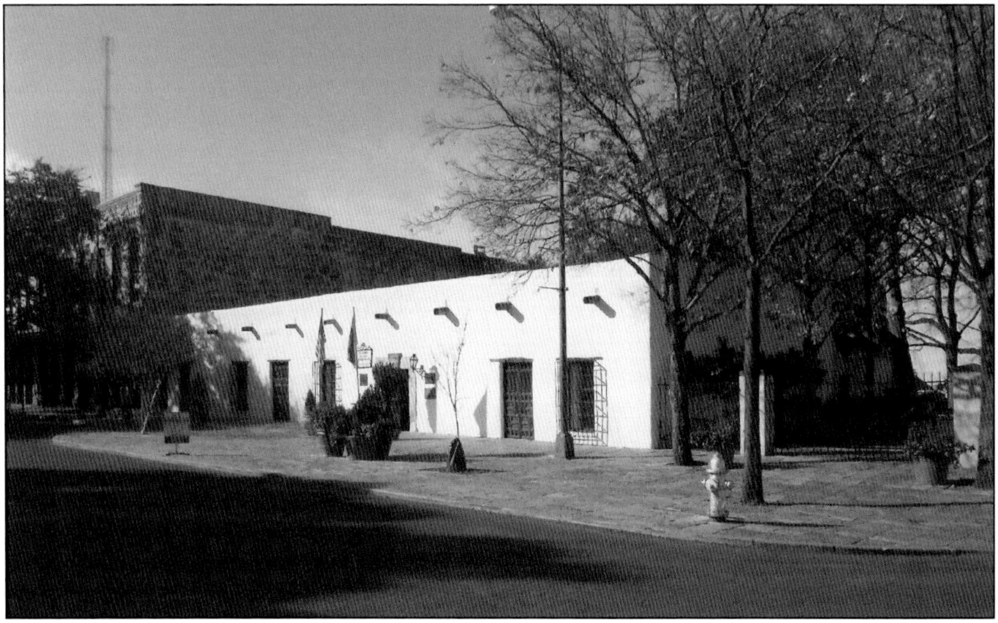

Military Plaza is an official site along El Camino Real de los Tejas National Historic Trail. First established in 1722 as a market for Spanish soldiers, Military Plaza has been a focus of the local community since the 18th century. (Courtesy of Steven Gonzales.)

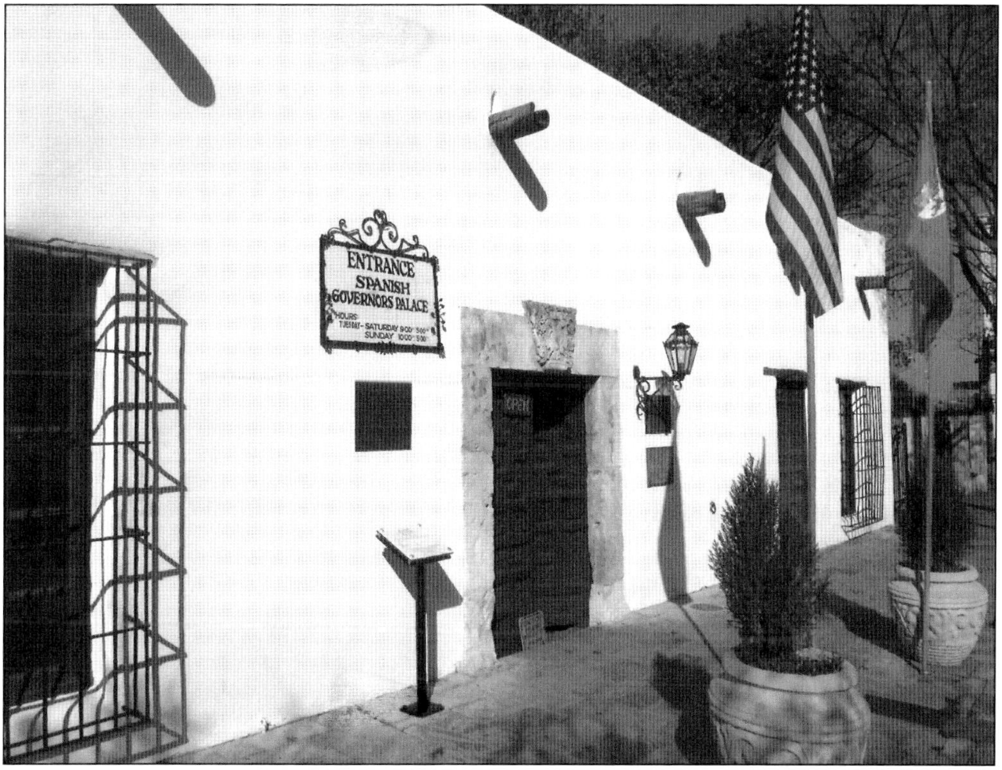


The Spanish Governor's Palace is the site of the original Presidio de San Antonio de Béxar. Plans for the site originated in 1722, under the Marqués de Aguayo, and the date "1749" is carved above the entrance of the facility. Though referred to as the Governor's Palace, the building actually housed the original comandancia, or residence and headquarters for local presidio captains. (Courtesy of Steven Gonzales.)

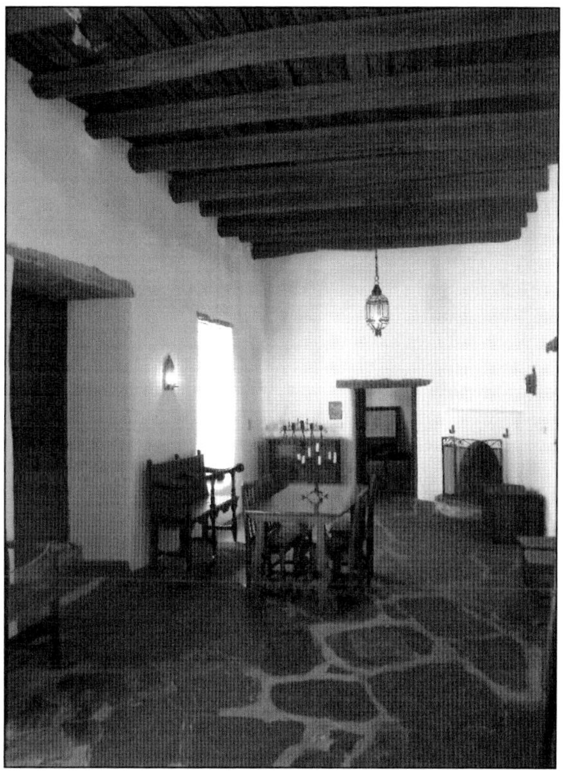

The interior of the Spanish Governor's Palace is a rustic look into what life was like for Spanish officials headquartered along El Camino Real de los Tejas. (Courtesy of Steven Gonzales.)

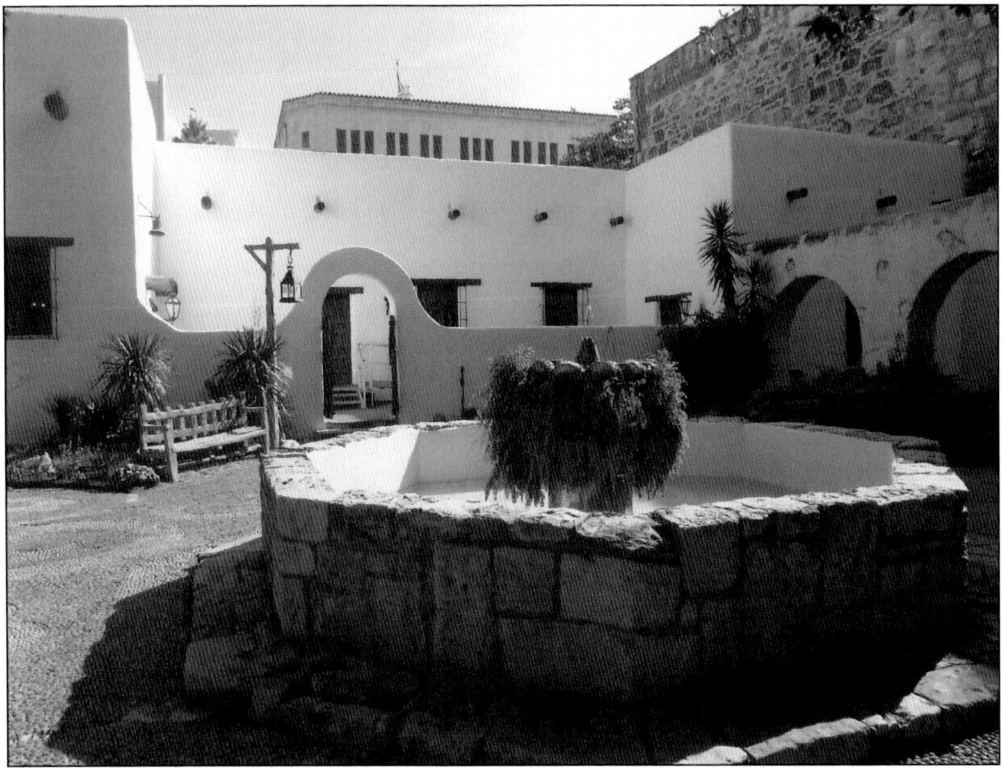

The courtyard of the Spanish Governor's Palace is a tranquil place to spend an afternoon contemplating the history and legends of the trail. (Courtesy of Steven Gonzales.)

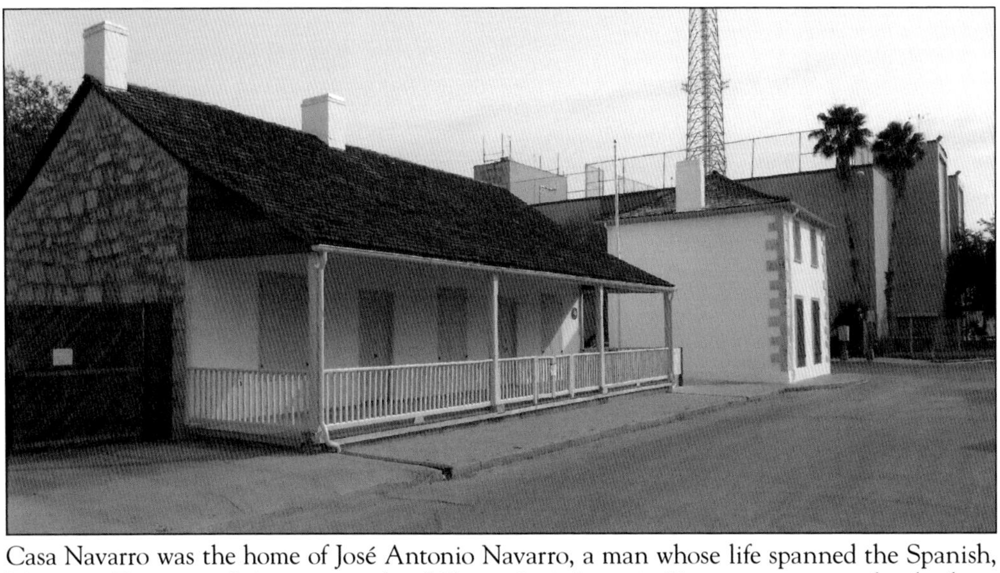

Casa Navarro was the home of José Antonio Navarro, a man whose life spanned the Spanish, Mexican, Texian, and American rule of Texas. José Antonio Navarro was one of only three Native Texans (Tejanos) to sign the Texas Declaration of Independence. Situated on the Laredo Road portion of El Camino Real de los Tejas, the site of Casa Navarro was purchased by José in 1832. The pictured limestone, adobe, and caliche structures were built on the property between 1832 and 1855. (Courtesy of Steven Gonzales.)

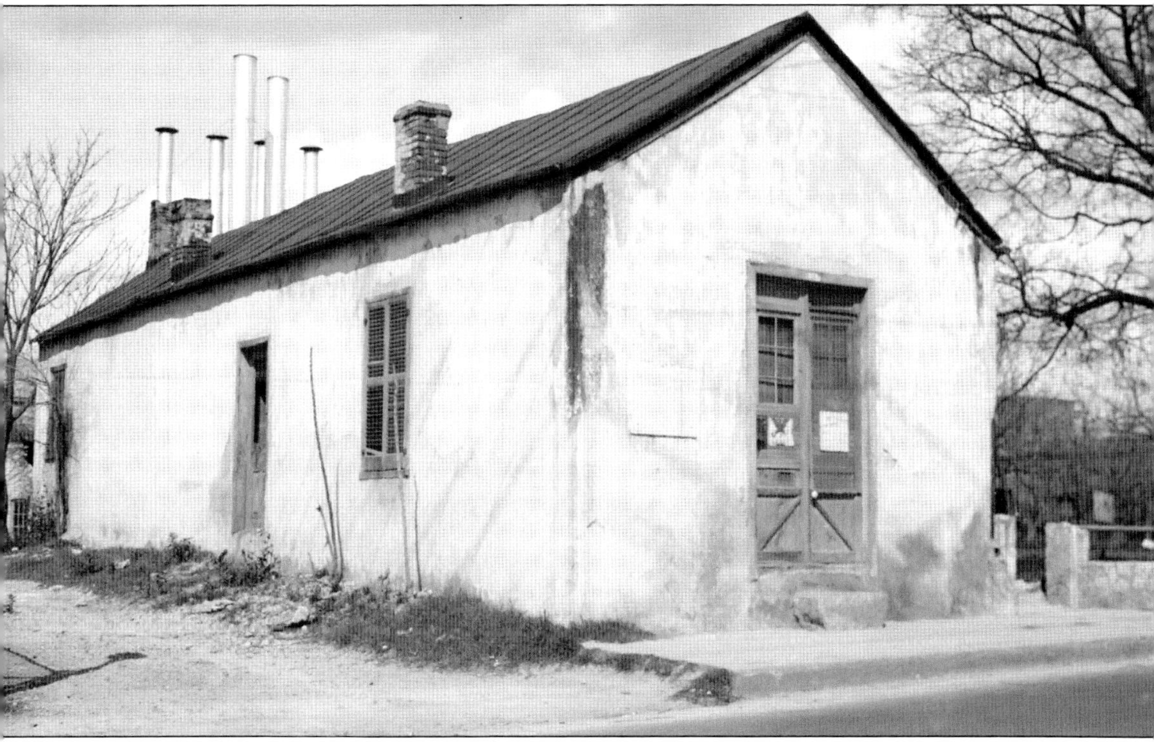

La Villita was a civil settlement that grew up as a barrio around the Presidio de San Antonio de Béxar. Listed in the National Register of Historic Places, this historic district includes 27 contributing buildings, structures, and archaeological remnants dating to the Spanish period or later. (Courtesy of the Library of Congress.)

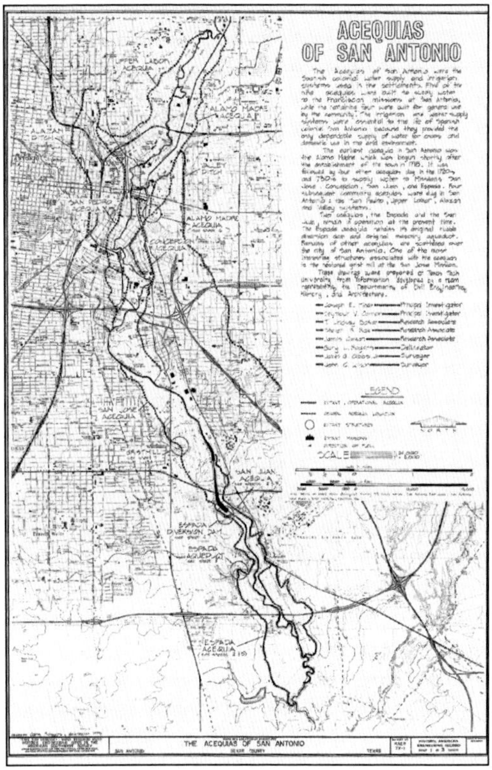


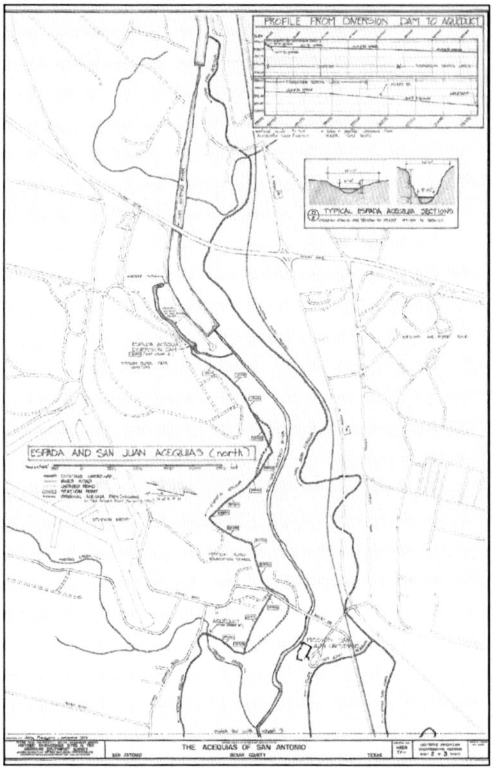


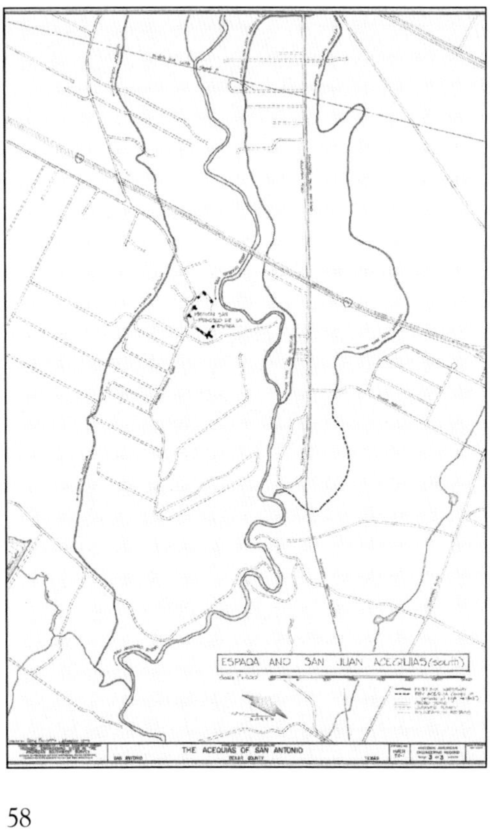


The acequias of San Antonio were the Spanish colonial water supply and the irrigation systems used to support the region's earliest European settlements. Five of the nine acequias were built to supply water to the Franciscan missions at San Antonio, while the remaining four were built for general use by the community. The irrigation and water supply systems were essential lifelines of Spanish colonial San Antonio, because they provided the only dependable supply of water for crops and domestic use in the arid environment. (All courtesy of the Library of Congress.)

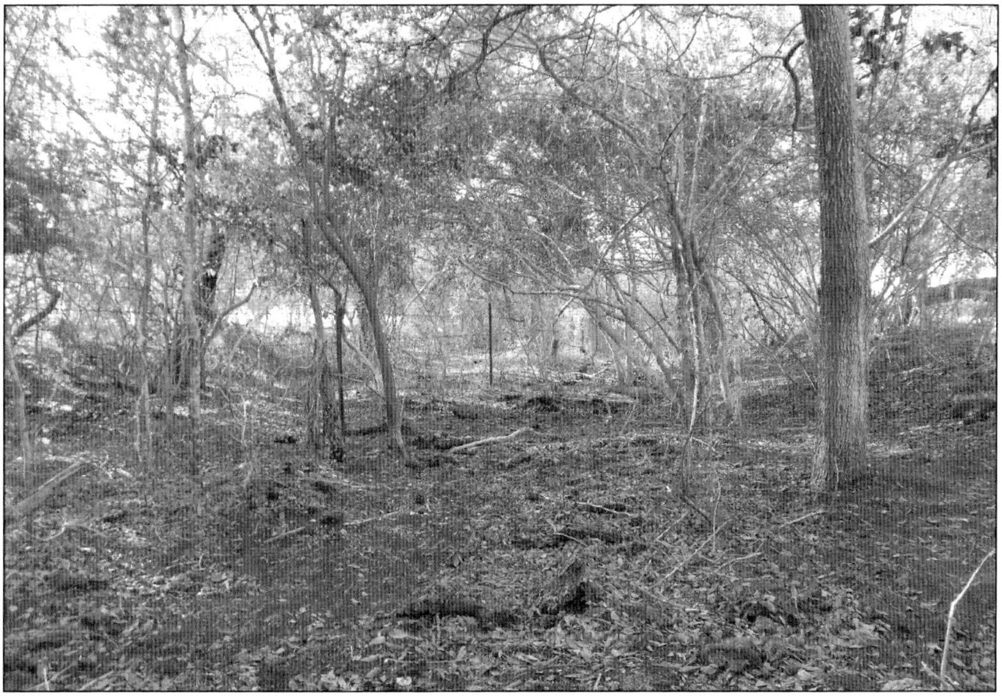

A barbed wire fence and trees can be seen running down the middle of the Salt Creek Swales in this photograph. Alonso de León's expeditions camped at parajes along the creek in 1689 and 1690. Salt Creek is in DeWitt County, just west of the Karnes County line, near Yorktown and Nordheim. The Salt Creek Swales can be found on the la Bahía portion of El Camino Real de los Tejas National Historic Trail. (Courtesy of Steven Gonzales.)

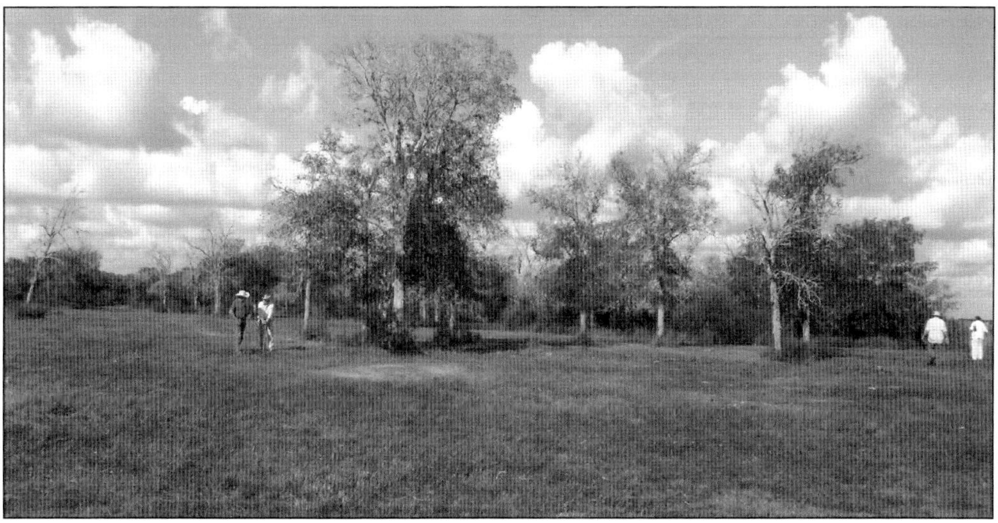

The site of La Salle's French Fort St. Louis is located on Garcitas Creek in Victoria County. Word of the French presence in Spanish territory led Alonso de León to carry out the initial entradas, or expeditions, along El Camino Real in search of La Salle. Upon finding the ruins of the fort, and wanting to deter further French encroachment, the Spanish repurposed the land as the first site of the presidio of Nuestra Señora Santa María de Loreto de la Bahía del Espíritu Santo, better known as Presidio la Bahía. (Courtesy of Steven Gonzales.)

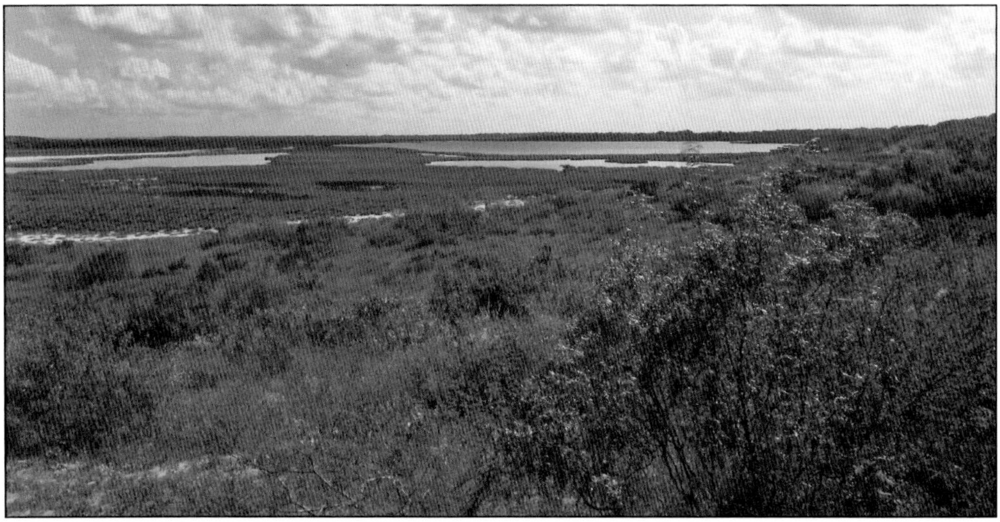

The site of La Bahía del Espíritu Santo in Victoria County still looks much as it did when La Salle and de León first observed it over 325 years ago. (Courtesy of Steven Gonzales.)

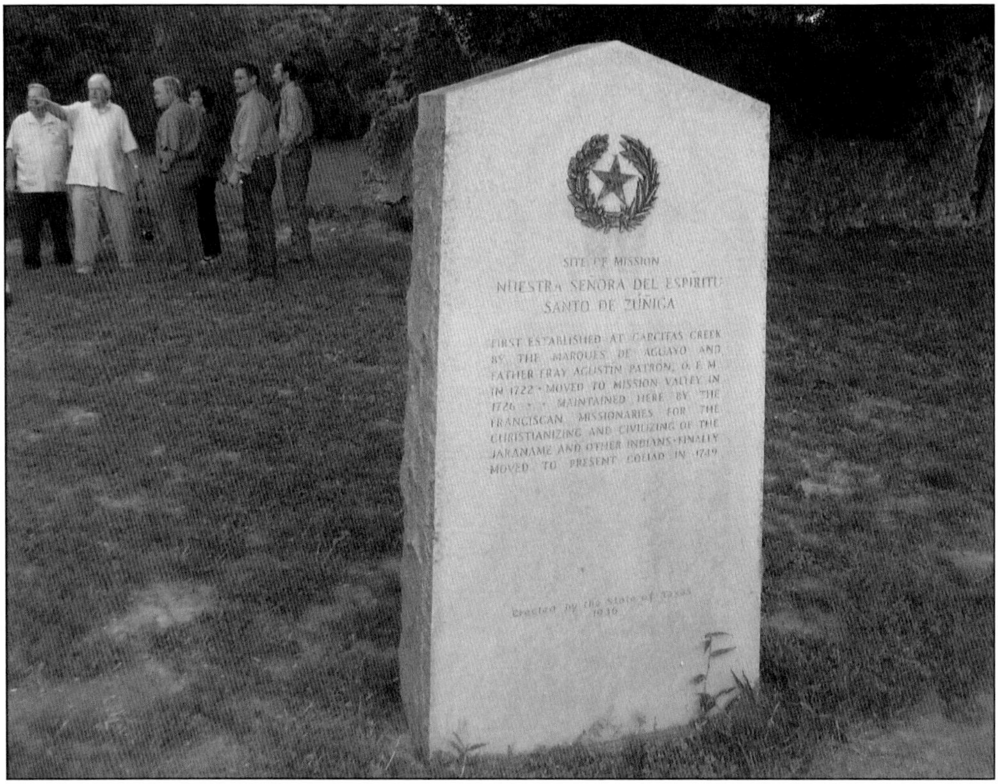


Situated on the banks of the Guadalupe River in Victoria County, this Texas Historic Commission marker notes the location of the third site of Mission Nuestra Señora del Espíritu Santo de Zúñiga, usually referred to as Mission Espíritu Santo, on the banks of the Guadalupe River in Victoria County. El Camino Real de los Tejas National Historic Trail Association board members can be seen touring the site in the background of this photograph. (Courtesy of Steven Gonzales.)

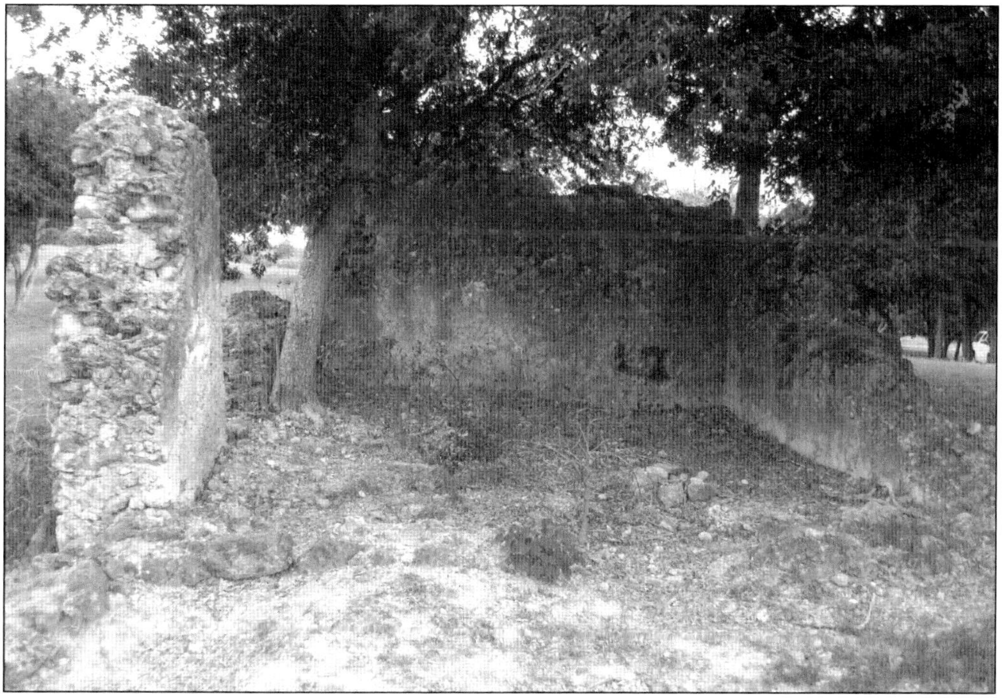

Mission Espíritu Santo was constructed of mortared stone that was quarried 12 miles downriver on a bluff known as Tonkawa Bank. Espíritu Santo's second site was at Tonkawa Bank before being moved upriver to its final location in Victoria County. (Courtesy of Steven Gonzales.)

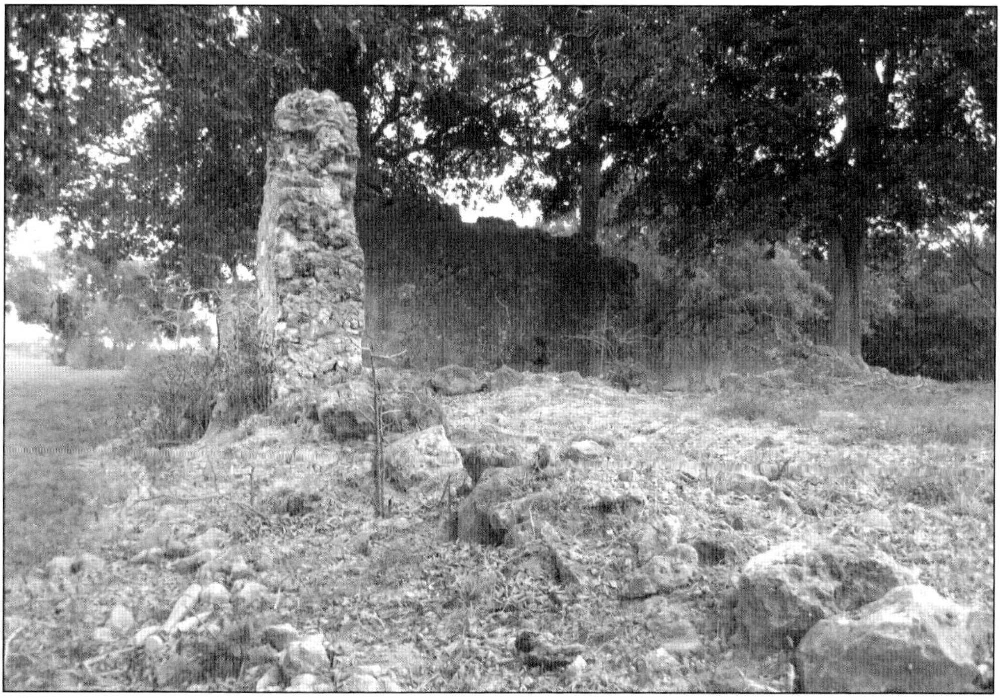

The extensive ruins of Mission Espíritu Santo have not been reconstructed as most missions were during the time of the Works Progress Administration. (Courtesy of Steven Gonzales.)

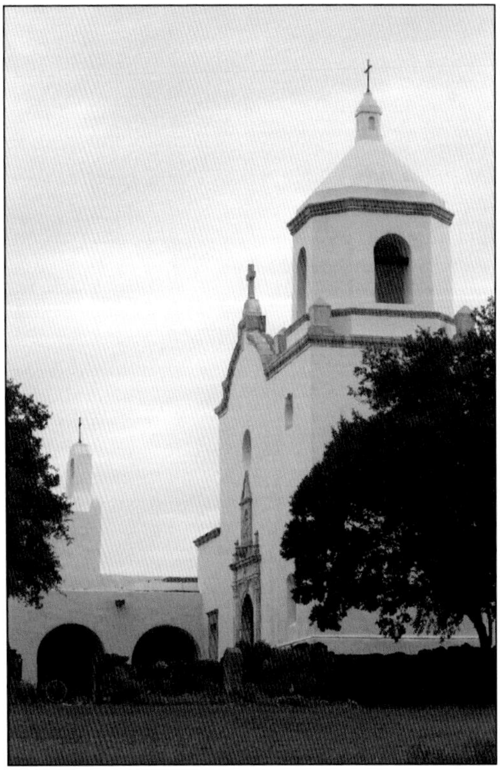

Goliad State Park is the fourth, and final, site of Mission Nuestra Señora del Espíritu Santo de Zúñiga. Mission Espíritu Santo was moved to its present location on the San Antonio River in order to protect the main route of El Camino Real de los Tejas from Mexico to Béxar and East Texas. (Courtesy of the Texas Parks and Wildlife Department.)

Here is a view of the rear of the Presidio la Bahía in 1936. (Courtesy of the Library of Congress.)

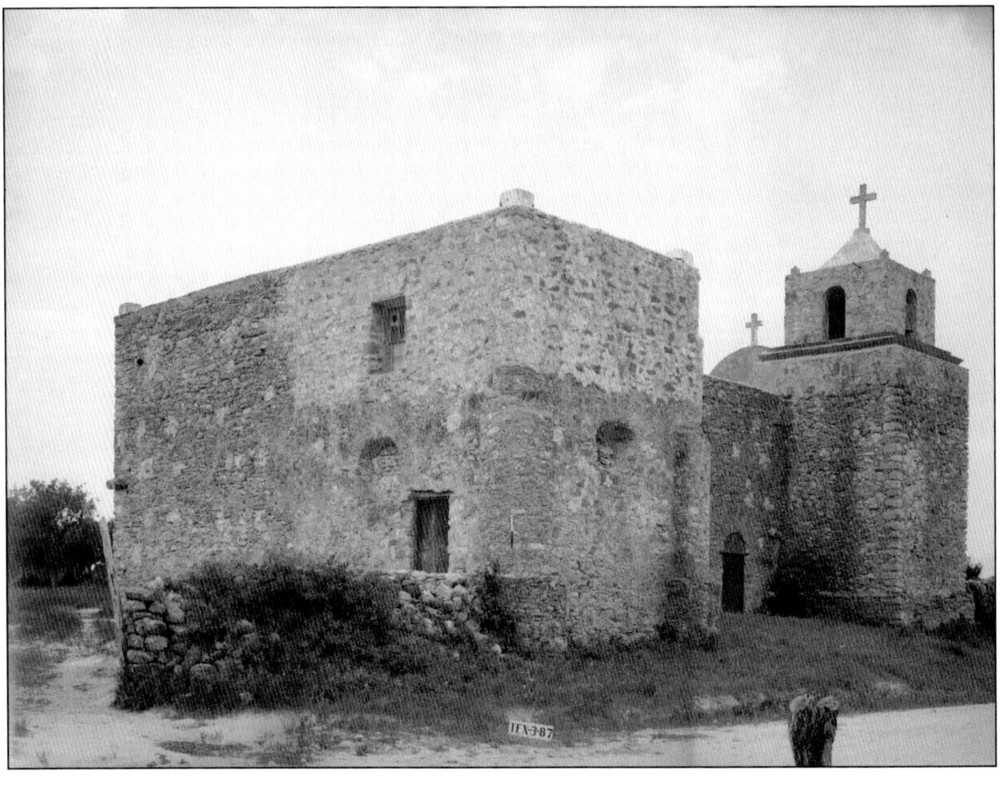

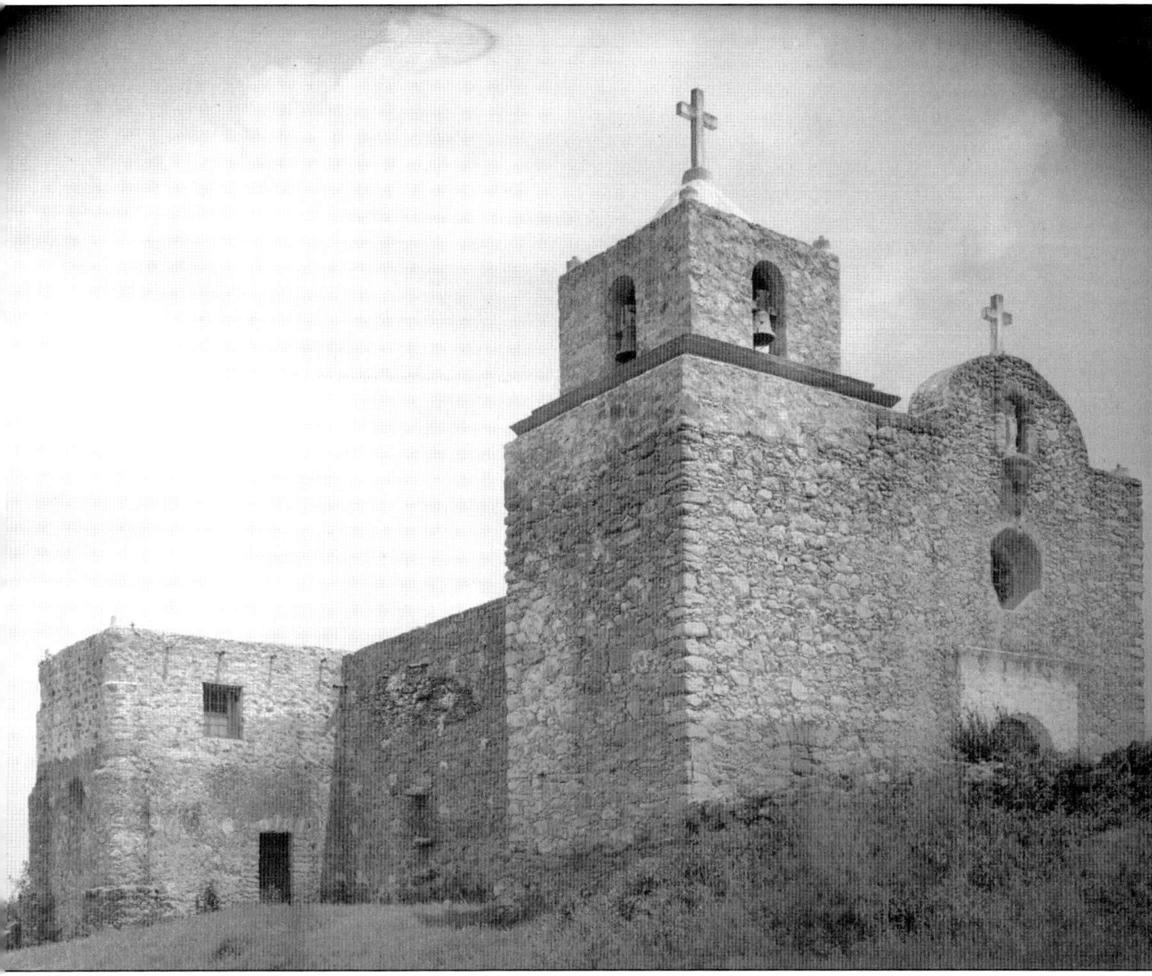

This photograph of Presidio la Bahía was taken in 1936, nearly 30 years before the restoration of the presidio began in 1963. In 1936, the presidio was nearly 200 years old. (Courtesy of the Library of Congress.)

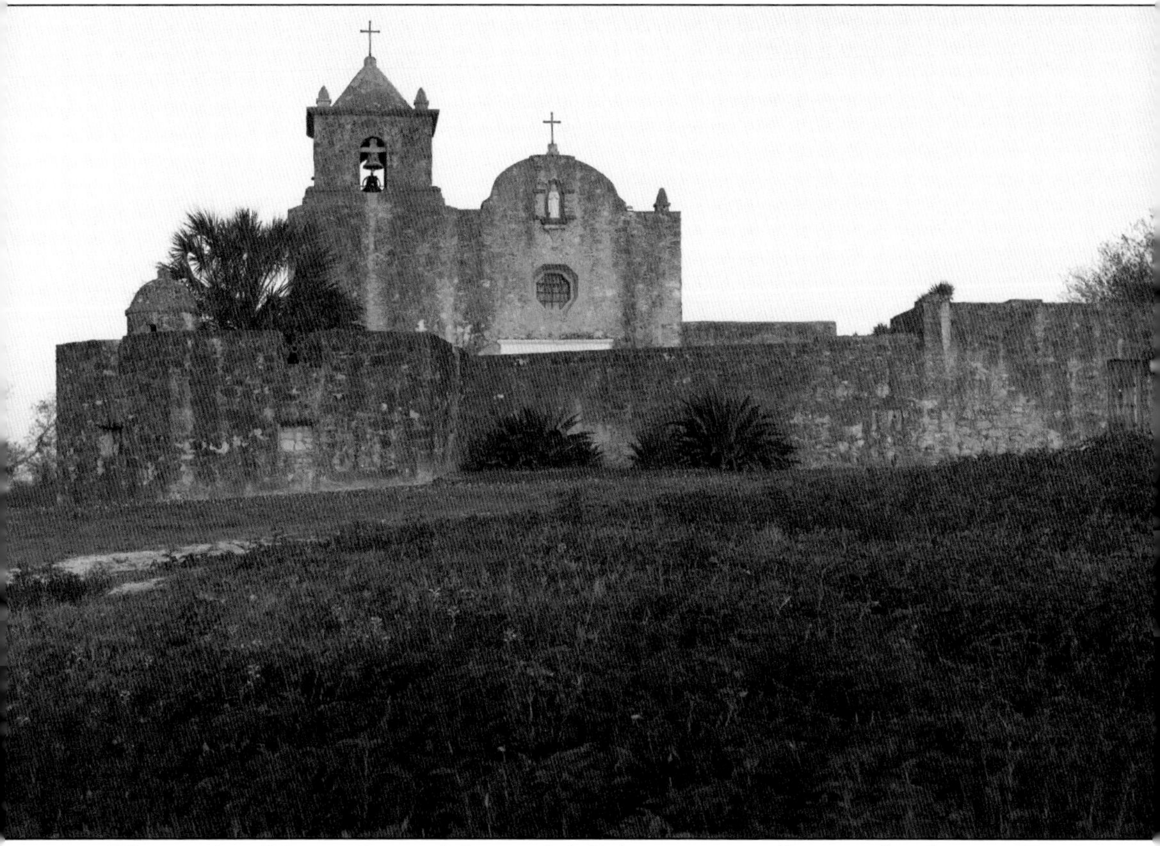

The presidio of Nuestra Señora de Loreto de la Bahía was originally situated at the site of Fort St. Louis on Garcitas Creek in Victoria County. Presidio la Bahía was moved to its third, and final, location on the San Antonio River along with Mission Espíritu Santo in 1749 as part of colonizer José de Escandón's plan to make them the northern anchor of the colony of Nuevo Santander. The plan to bring the presidio under the domain of Nuevo Santander failed. The presidio was rebuilt by the Works Progress Administration in the 1930s and is the best example of a Spanish presidio to be found anywhere in the United States. (Courtesy of Christopher Talbot.)

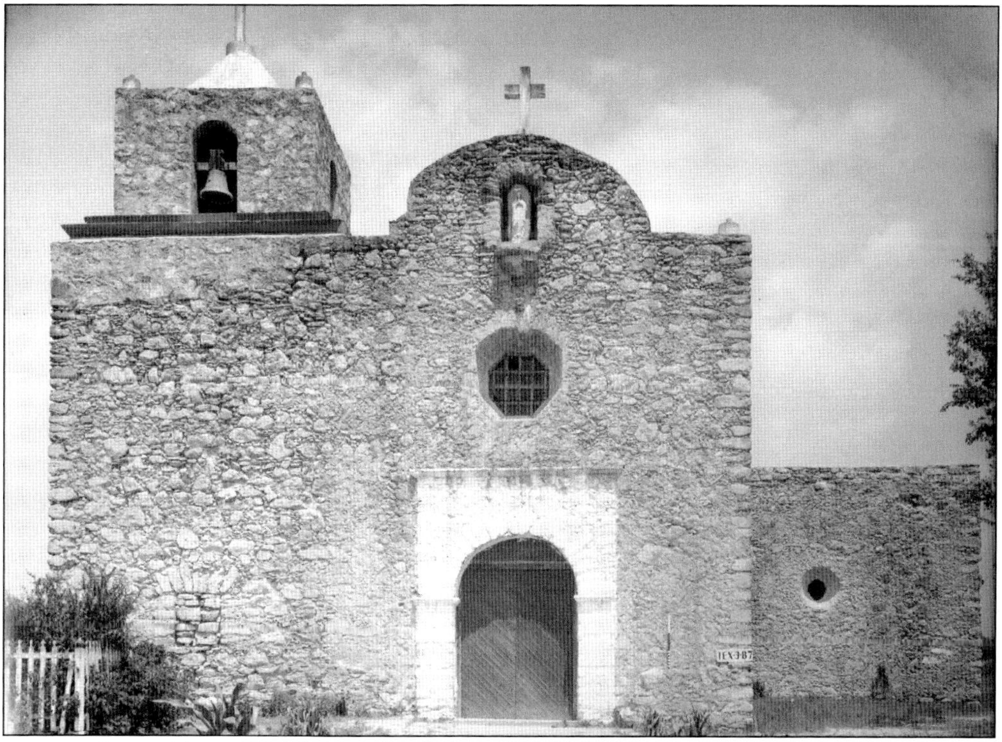

Here is a beautiful image of the facade of the Presidio la Bahía prior to its restoration. (Courtesy of the Library of Congress.)

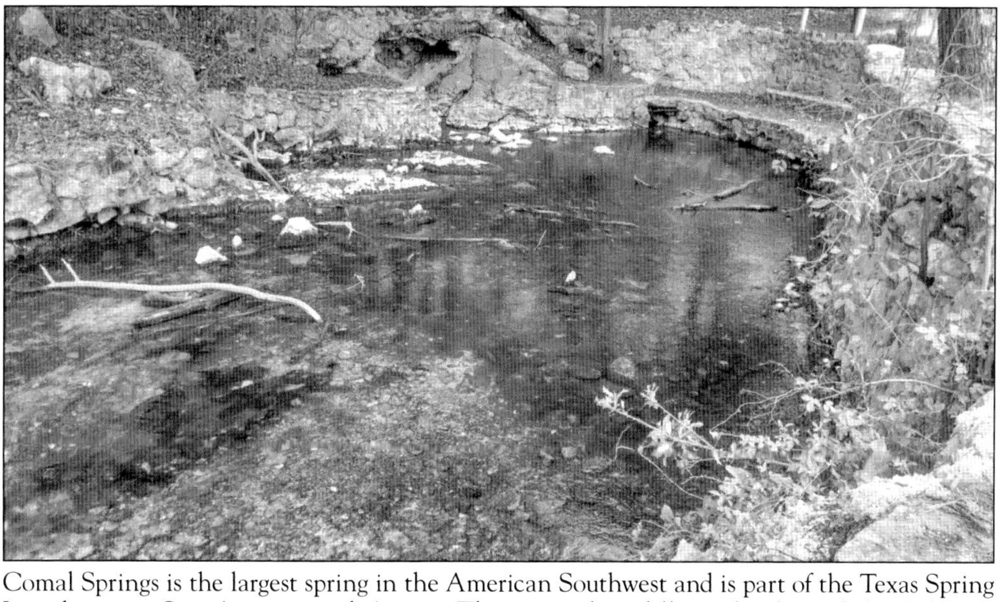

Comal Springs is the largest spring in the American Southwest and is part of the Texas Spring Line between San Antonio and Austin. The spring line follows the foot of the Balcones Escarpment along the southern and eastern edges of the Edwards Plateau. Native peoples and, later, European explorers followed this path due to its abundant water resources and because of the ease of travel in the Blackland Prairie at the edge of the escarpment. Comal Springs can be found at Landa Park in the city of New Braunfels. (Courtesy of Steven Gonzales.)

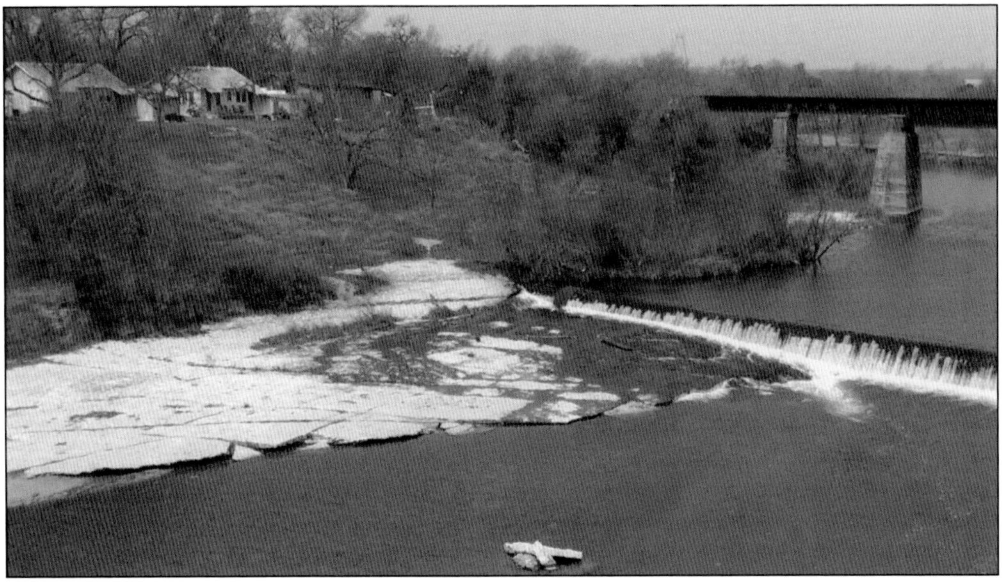

The Faust Street Footbridge in New Braunfels affords this beautiful view of the Guadalupe River crossing of El Camino Real de los Tejas National Historic Trail. One can see the path that travelers took to this low-water crossing on the Guadalupe. A segment of the Camino Real known as the Old Nacogdoches Road descends the riverbank where the railroad bridge meets the homes on the hillside. The path to the crossing is just to the left of the dam and continues down the extensive limestone slab into the river. Shallow crossings with durable surfaces such as this allowed the trail to be funneled down into tight corridors. River crossings are some of the best places to see remnants of the trail. (Courtesy of Steven Gonzales.)

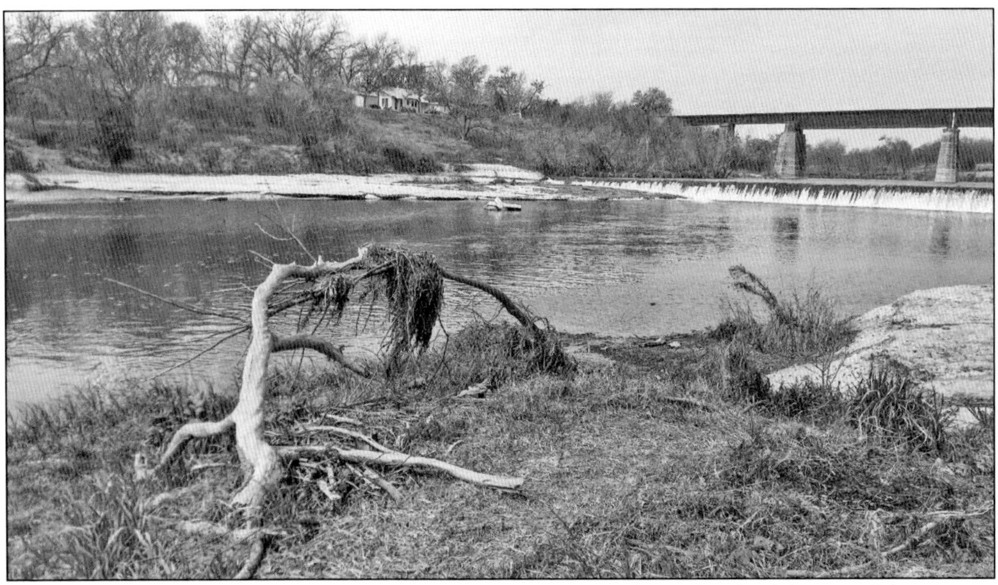

This photograph shows one of two swales coming up the northeast bank of the Guadalupe River in New Braunfels. The swale is just to the right of the tree, next to the limestone slab in the immediate foreground. (Courtesy of Steven Gonzales.)

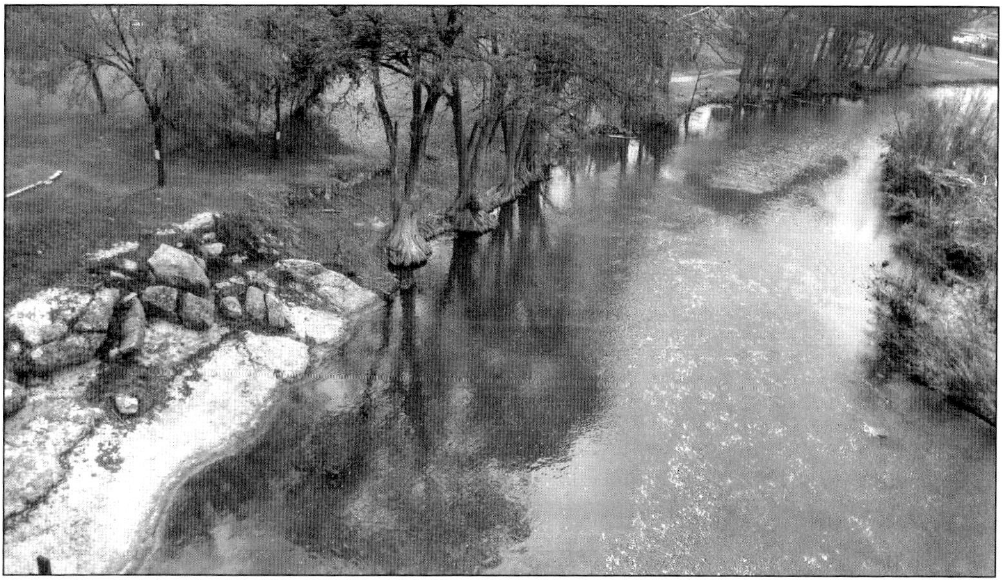

A second swale can be seen coming up the northeast bank of the river. It is between the limestone slab on the left and the line of bald cypress trees on the right The exposed dirt ridge behind the tree line indicates where the path of travel was. (Courtesy of Steven Gonzales.)

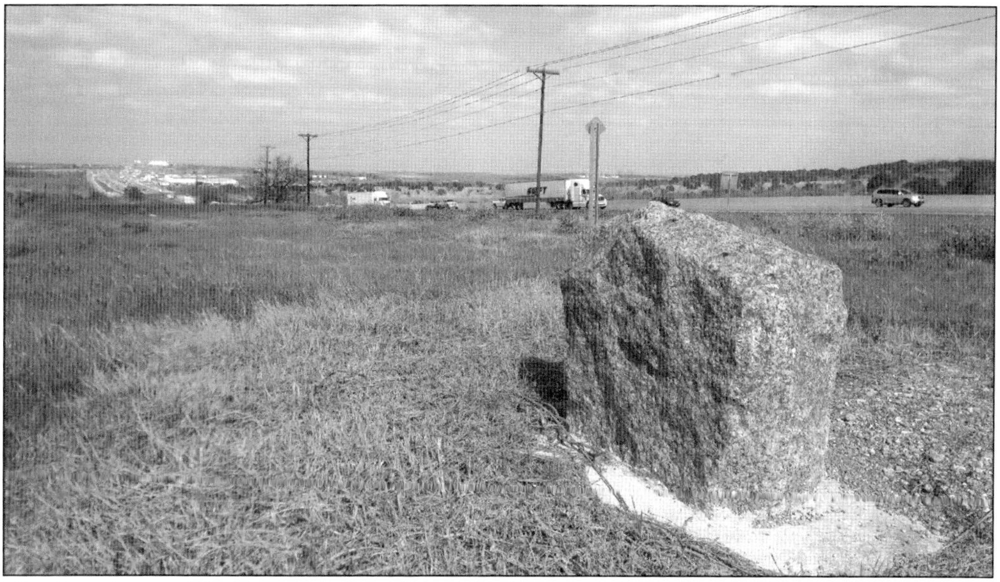

This Daughters of the American Revolution marker was placed along a segment of the Camino Real in 1918. In total, about 125 markers were placed between the Río Grande and the Sabine River. This particular marker is on Interstate 35 in Comal County, just south of its intersection with the Old Bastrop Road. When the markers were placed in 1918, the Camino was still a caliche road traveled by horses and very few automobiles. As is evident in this photograph, this portion of the road became so highly traveled that it was eventually made into an interstate highway. (Courtesy of Steven Gonzales.)

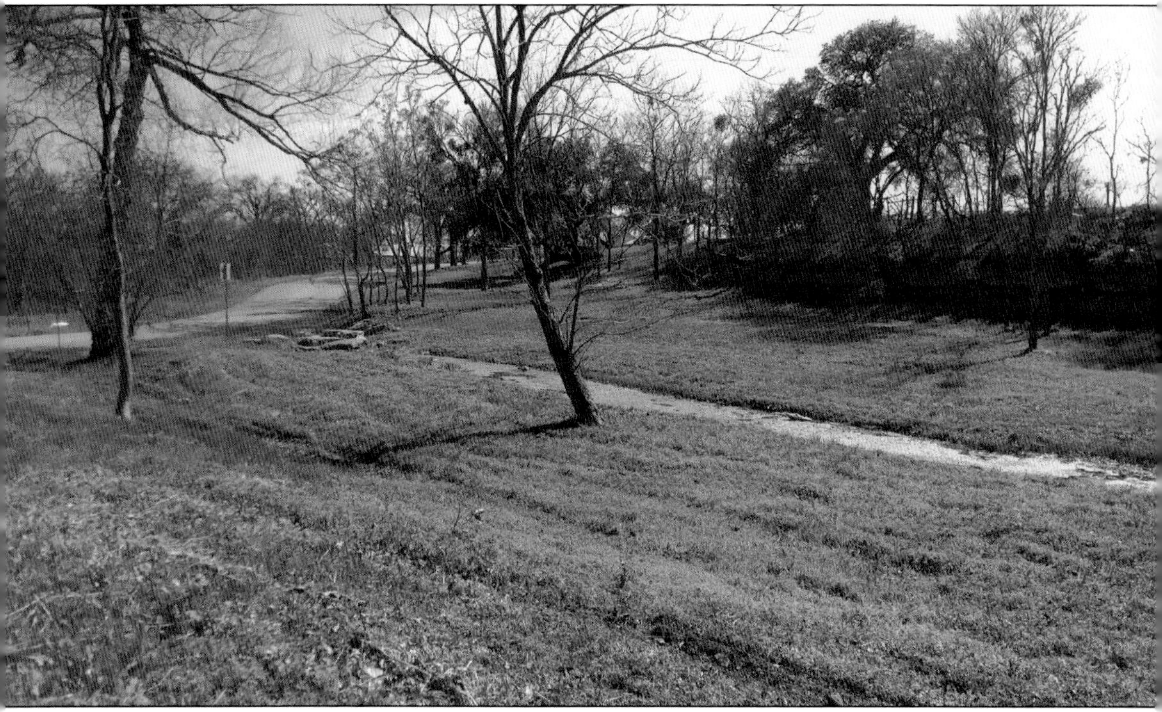

This Camino segment, known as the Old Bastrop Road, is another great example of how water crossings forced the trail to be funneled into certain places. The Camino crossing of York Creek is in Comal County, just south of the Hays County line. The modern roadway was built right on top of the trail in this location. As one can see, the trail was forced to cross the waterway to the left of the sheer limestone bank of the creek. The precipitous nature of creek and river crossings ensured that certain paths of travel had to be followed across the trail. (Courtesy of Steven Gonzales.)

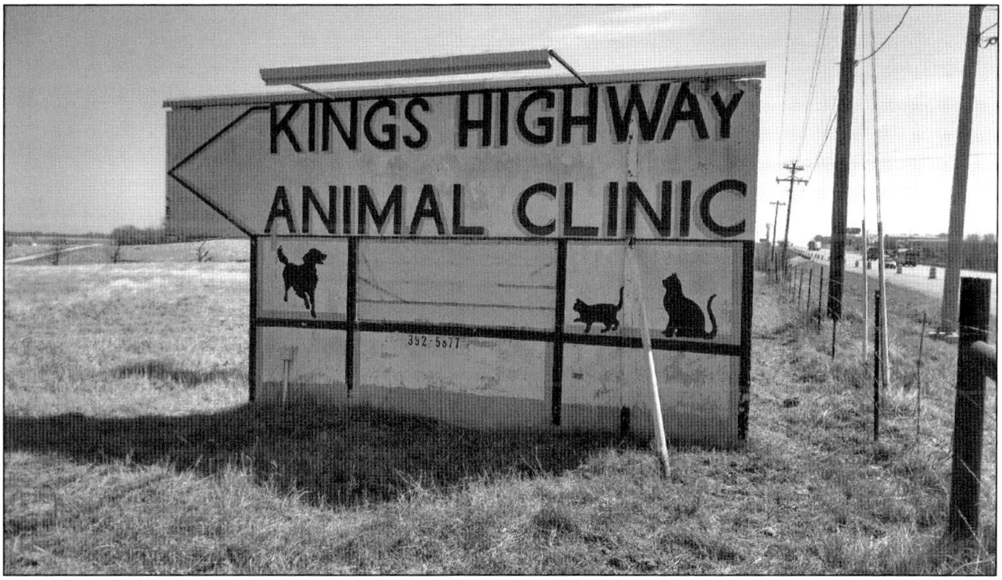

Signs of the trail can be found on the cultural landscape as well. This sign is located in Hays County at the intersection of the Old Bastrop Highway (known as the Old Bastrop Road in Comal County) and Highway 123. El Camino Real is sometimes translated as "The King's Highway" but is more appropriately translated as "The Royal Road." Either way, cultural clues such as these are a sign that one is traveling the trail. (Courtesy of Steven Gonzales.)

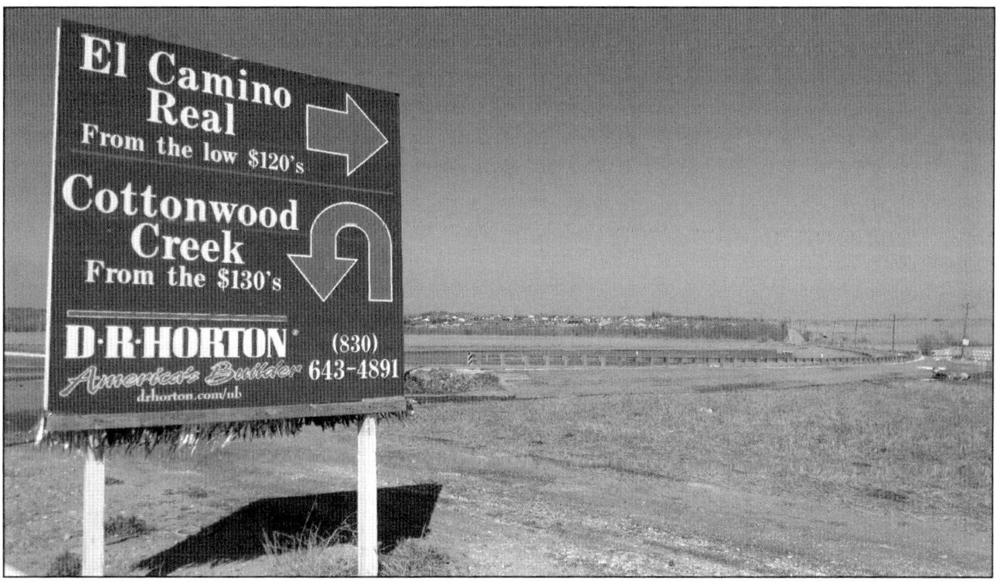

Another example of El Camino Real being recognized on the cultural landscape is seen in this photograph. This sign is also in Hays County, at the intersection of the Old Bastrop Highway and Highway 123. The road is currently being reengineered at this location, and the Old Bastrop Highway is visible in the background. There are swales visible on both sides of the road just beyond here as the trail approaches McGehee Crossing on the San Marcos River. (Courtesy of Steven Gonzales.)

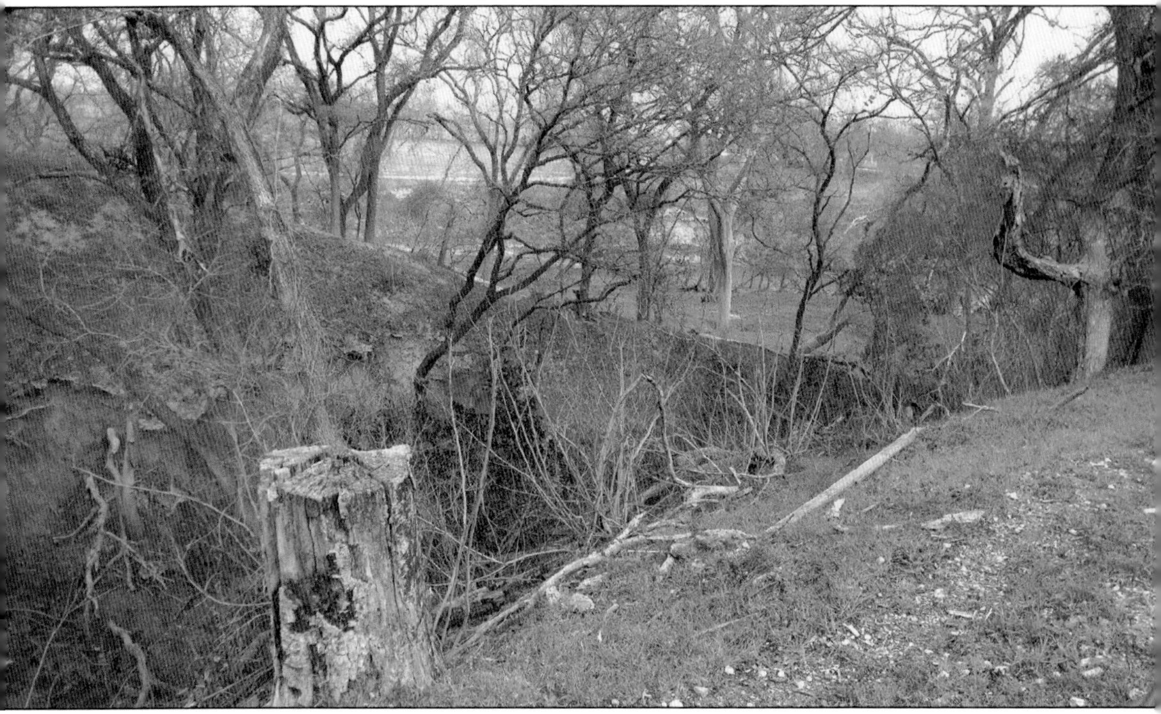

This huge swale can be seen just south and west of McGehee Crossing on the San Marcos River, at the original townsite of San Marcos de Neve. Taken on the Old Bastrop Highway in Hays County, this photograph illustrates the sheer force of the oxcarts and wagons that carved their way into the landscape. The swale is nearly 20 feet deep and 15 feet wide. There are also excellent interpretive markers at the site. The markers highlight the first townsite of San Marcos; the life of Don Felipe Roque de la Portilla, who founded San Marcos; and the story of Lt. Zebulon M. Pike, who was escorted by Spanish officials along El Camino Real all the way to Natchitoches to ensure he left their territory. (Courtesy of Steven Gonzales.)

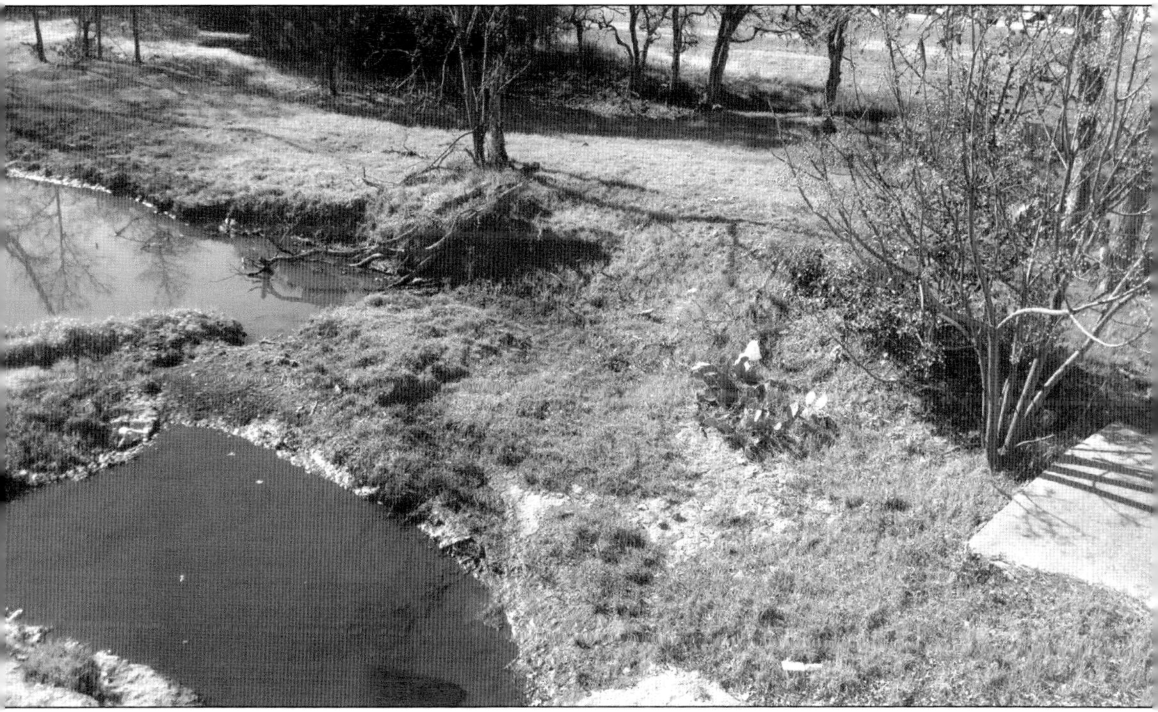

The Willow Springs Creek Crossing is located on Hunter Road in San Marcos. Hunter Road and the crossing follow an upper route of the Camino that approached San Marcos Springs on the Texas Spring Line. This route was north and west of the lower route in Hays County, which crossed the river at McGehee Crossing. The swale remnant is seen between the two trees in the foreground. (Courtesy of Steven Gonzales.)

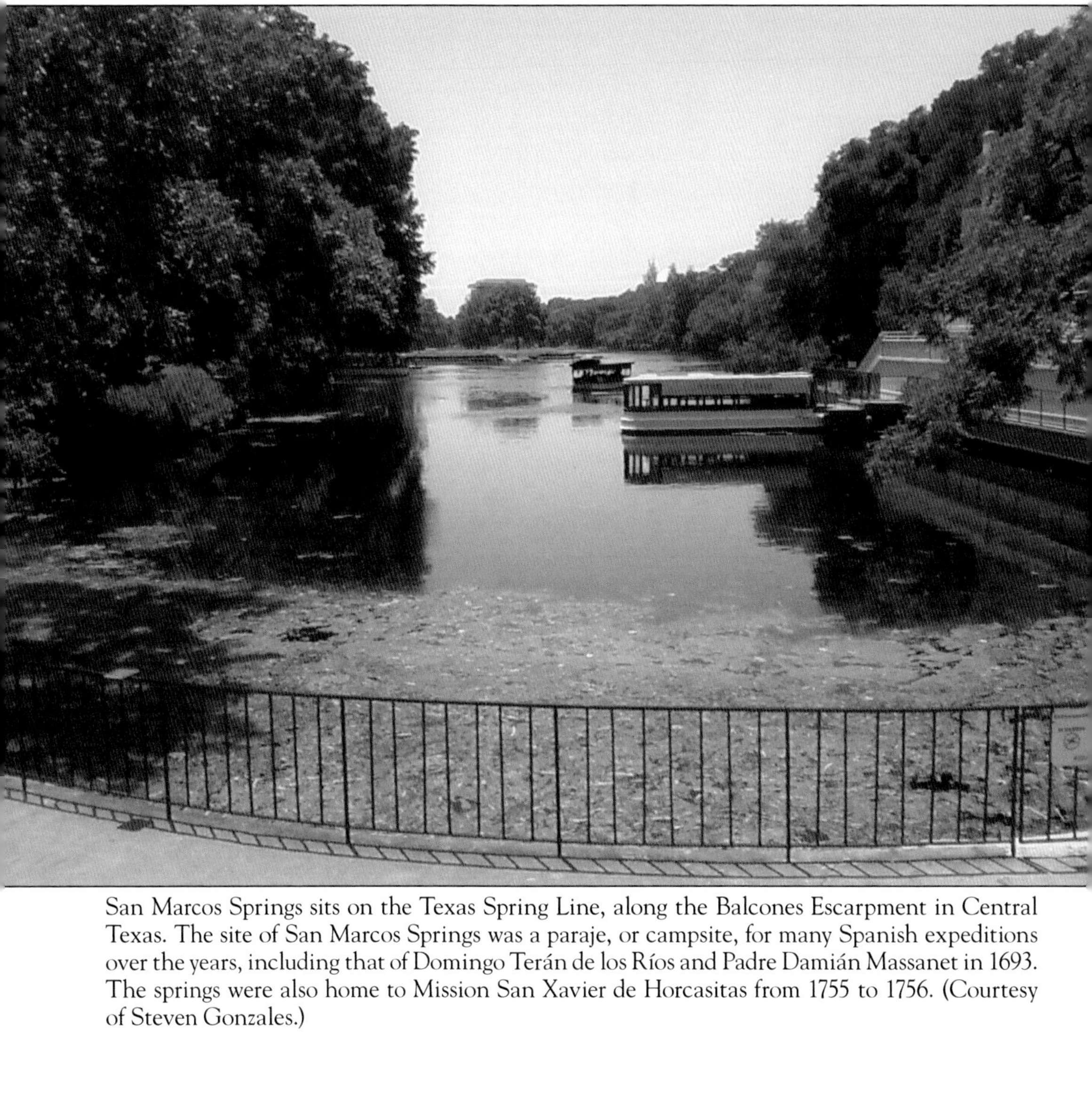

San Marcos Springs sits on the Texas Spring Line, along the Balcones Escarpment in Central Texas. The site of San Marcos Springs was a paraje, or campsite, for many Spanish expeditions over the years, including that of Domingo Terán de los Ríos and Padre Damián Massanet in 1693. The springs were also home to Mission San Xavier de Horcasitas from 1755 to 1756. (Courtesy of Steven Gonzales.)

# *Three*

# Brazos Region

The Brazos Region is in the central area of Texas and is made up of 12 counties: Travis, Williamson, Bastrop, Lee, Milam, Robertson, Burleson, Brazos, Fayette, Washington, Leon, and Madison. The Brazos Region joins the San Antonio–Goliad Region to the west and the East Texas–Caddo Region to the east. The trail splits into four routes from the east of Travis County to the west side of Leon and Madison Counties.

The Upper Route (El Camino Real de los Tejas) includes Travis, Williamson, Milam, Robertson, and Leon Counties, while the Lower Route includes Fayette, Washington, and Burleson Counties and joins the Old San Antonio Road (OSR) in Brazos east to Madison County. The OSR route includes Bastrop, Lee, Burleson, Brazos, and Madison Counties. Burleson, Brazos, and Madison Counties are on both the OSR and the Lower Route.

Dr. Kathleen Gilmore researched the San Xavier Mission Complex along Apache Pass River Crossing in the 1960s and also worked with a Texas Historical Commission (THC) archeologist to confirm the location of Presidio San Francisco Xavier de Gigedo in Milam County. The THC also published Dr. Gilmore's master's thesis in 1969. After the US Congress designated the Camino Real a National Historic Trail in October 2004, Dr. Gilmore and the THC worked from 2005 to 2010 validating the locations of Mission Candelaria, Mission Ildefonso, and the presidio. In 2010, the Texas Historical Commission and Milam County offered a republication of her work.

Some historic sites and points of interest in the Brazos Region are McKinney Falls State Park in Travis County; the Rye Loop Swales and the Old Bastrop Road/County Line Road Trail Segment in Bastrop County; Apache Pass, Missions Nuestra Señora de la Candelaria, San Ildefonso, and San Francisco Xavier de Horcasitas, Presidio San Francisco Xavier de Gigedo, and Sugarloaf Mountain in Milam County; and Kickapoo Rapids in Leon County.

National Historic Trail signs were dedicated in Milam County on October 8, 2012. Fourth- and seventh-grade students of seven schools; officials from the county, the state, and the National Park Service; and a thousand additional people attended the dedication ceremony held on the trail at Apache Pass in Rockdale, Texas.

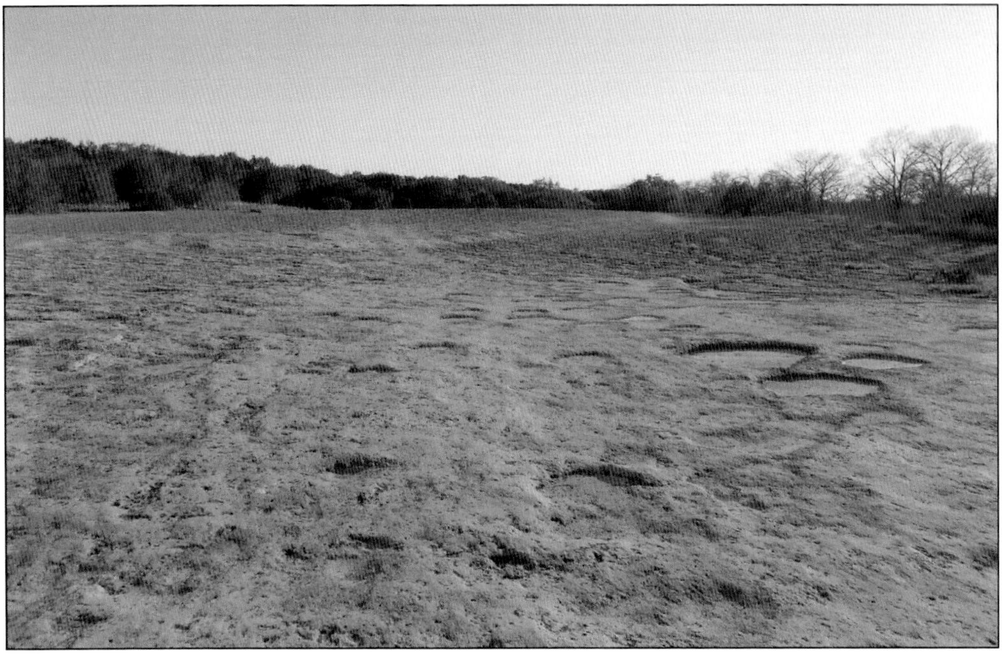

In 1716, Spanish military commander Domingo Ramón followed the left bank of Onion Creek, on the western edge of McKinney Falls State Park, to McKinney Falls at Williamson Creek. These indentions in the rock resulted from extensive use of the area. (Courtesy of Steven Gonzales.)

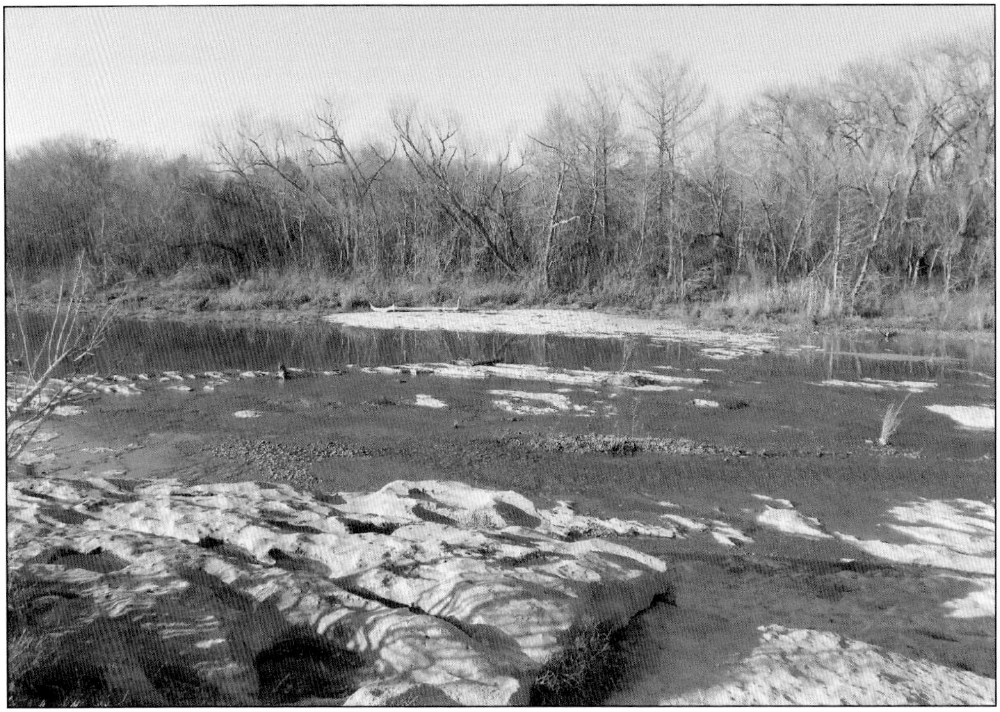

McKinney Falls State Park includes the falls at Onion Creek and the remains of the McKinney Homestead. The land was donated for use as a state park by the Smith family in 1970. (Courtesy of Steven Gonzales.)

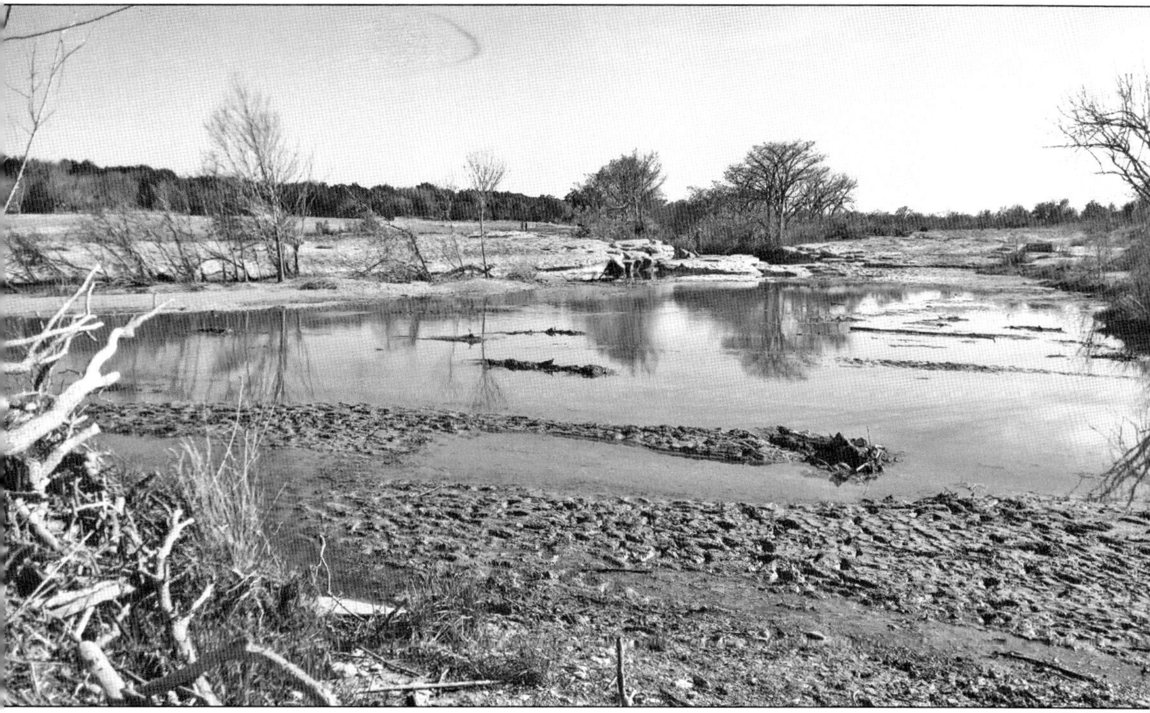

The immense limestone slab at the lower falls area of McKinney Falls State Park served as a perfect shallow-water crossing of El Camino Real on Onion Creek. In this image, parallel routes of the Camino can be seen. Notice the canyon of Onion Creek lined with leafless trees on either side of it toward the rear center of the picture. To the left of this chasm is one route of the trail that approaches the creek just above McKinney Falls. To the right is another route that crossed Onion Creek at the upper falls area within the park. Both routes converged here at the junction of Onion and Williamson Creeks and made their way along the creek and up the hillside toward the McKinney Homestead. (Courtesy of Steven Gonzales.)

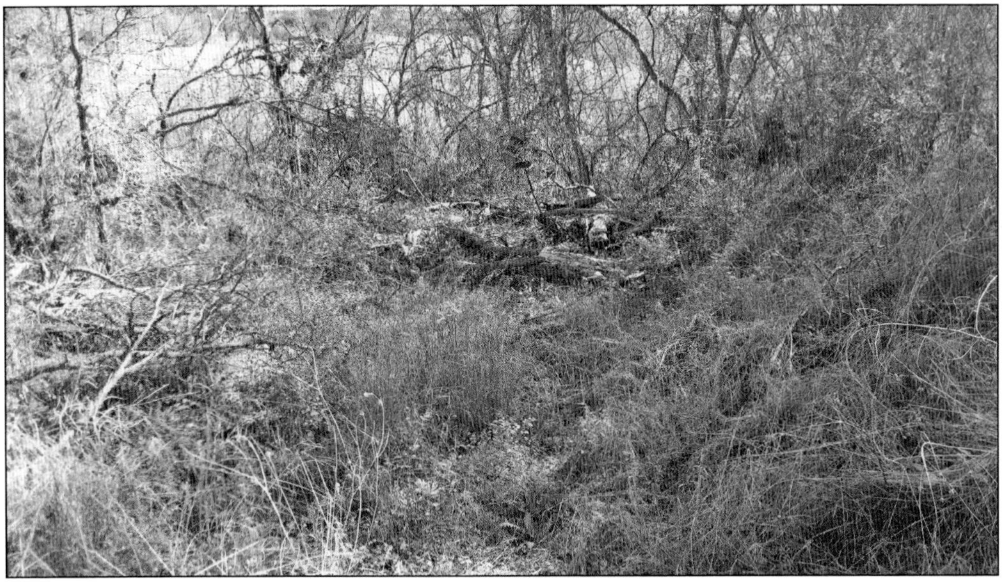

This huge swale can be seen coming up the bank of Onion Creek towards the McKinney Homestead in McKinney State Park. (Courtesy of Steven Gonzales.)

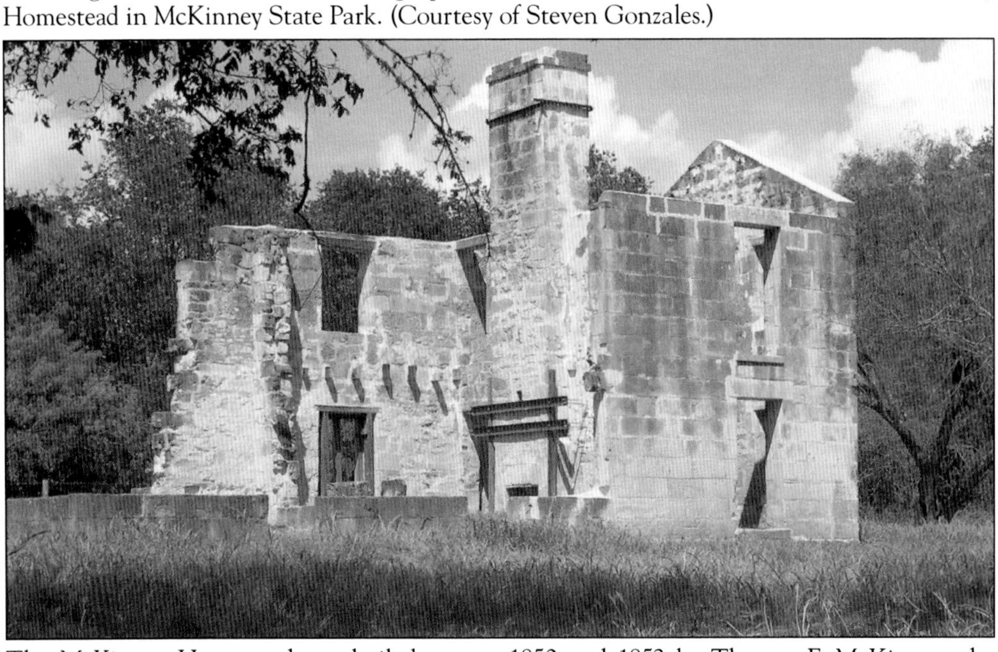

The McKinney Homestead was built between 1850 and 1852 by Thomas F. McKinney, the owner of the surrounding land. The two-story homestead was continuously occupied until it burned in the 1940s. Archaeological investigations in 1974 determined that the house was built with limestone quarried from Onion Creek. The house and most of McKinney's land were sold to James W. Smith in 1885, and Smith's grandchildren granted 638 acres to the State of Texas in 1970. It opened as McKinney Falls State Park in 1976. The homestead was added to the National Register of Historic Places in 1974, and it has since been stabilized to prevent further deterioration of the stone structure. The ruins can be accessed via the park's designated Homestead Trail. Several swale remnants of El Camino Real can be seen adjacent to the homestead. (Courtesy of Steven Gonzales.)

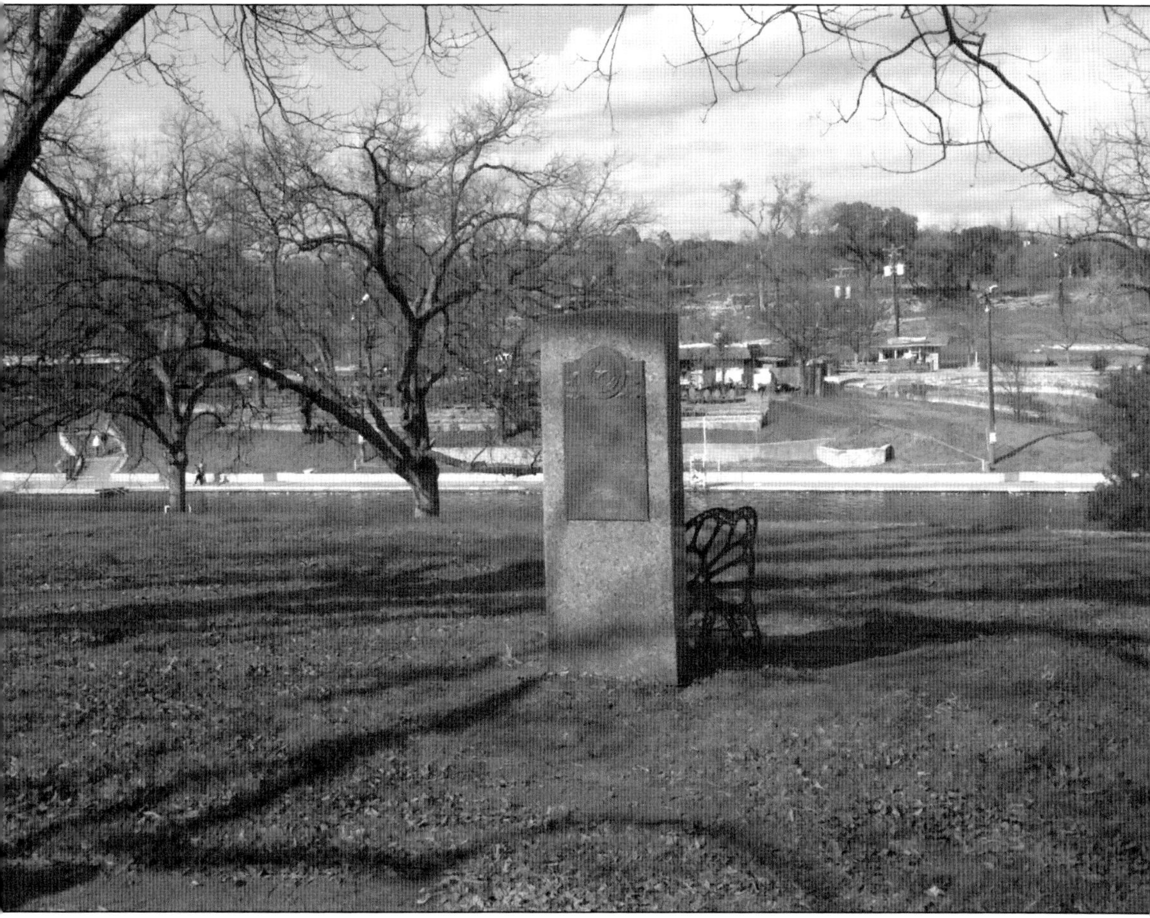

Missions San Francisco de los Neches, Nuestra Señora de la Purísima Concepción, and San José de los Nazonis were removed from East Texas to Barton Springs in 1730. The ephemeral missions did not remain long at this site, as they were soon moved to San Antonio. Pictured here is a Texas Centennial Marker. (Courtesy of the Texas Historical Commission.)

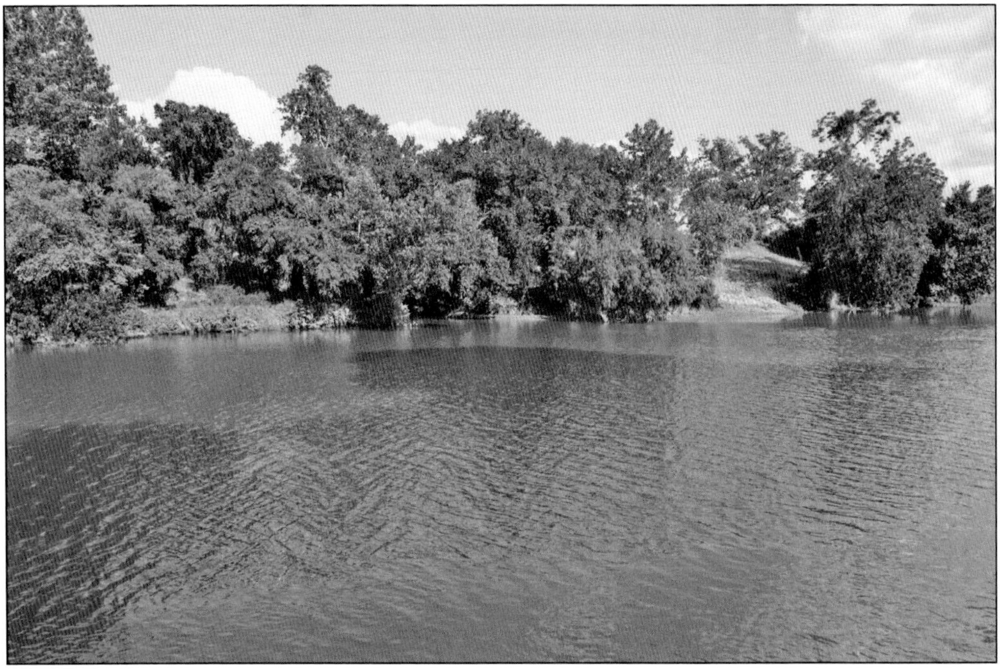

The Camino crossing of the Colorado River in Bastrop, Texas, is a beautiful sight to see. (Courtesy of Joy Graham.)

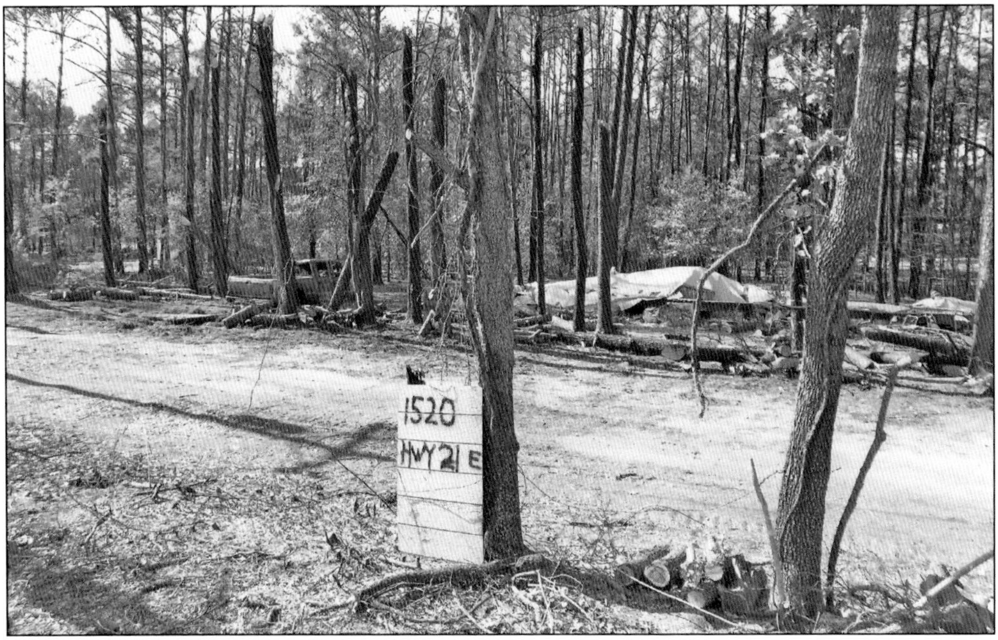


On Labor Day Weekend in 2011, the enormous Bastrop Fire engulfed much of Bastrop County and ravaged Highway 21, which is the Old San Antonio Road portion of the Camino Real. This portion of the Camino is in the Lost Pines region of the state, so named because the stand of pines in Bastrop is situated over 100 miles away from the nearest pine forests of East Texas. As can be seen in this image, much of the Lost Pines was destroyed, and the Camino was forever altered in the process. (Courtesy of Steven Gonzales.)

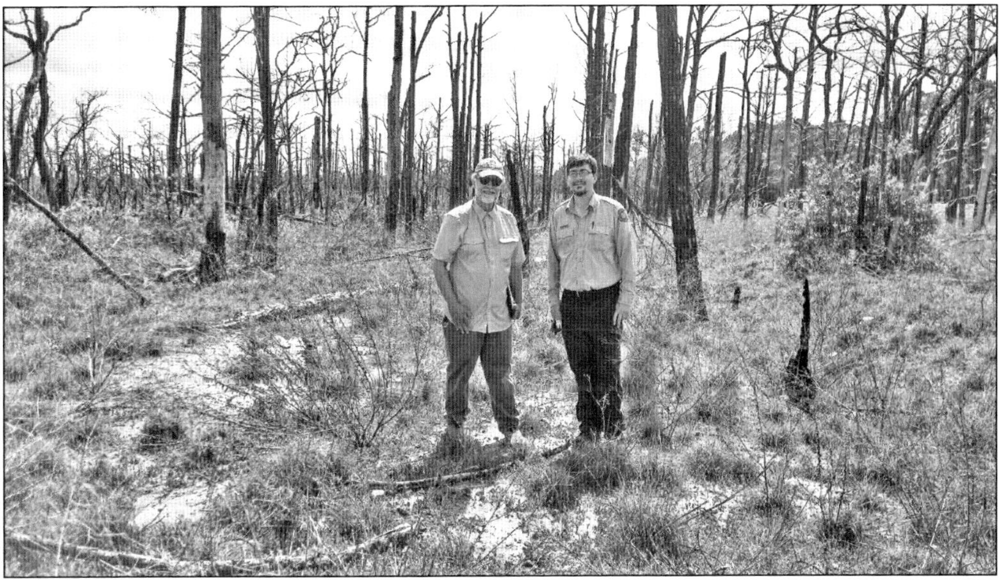

If there is anything positive that can be said about the Bastrop Fire, perhaps it is that it exposed trail resources that had been hidden by underbrush for many years. In this image, Mike Elliott of the National Park Service (left) and Mick Haven of the Texas Parks and Wildlife Department (right) explore trail swales in Bastrop State Park. (Courtesy of Steven Gonzales.)

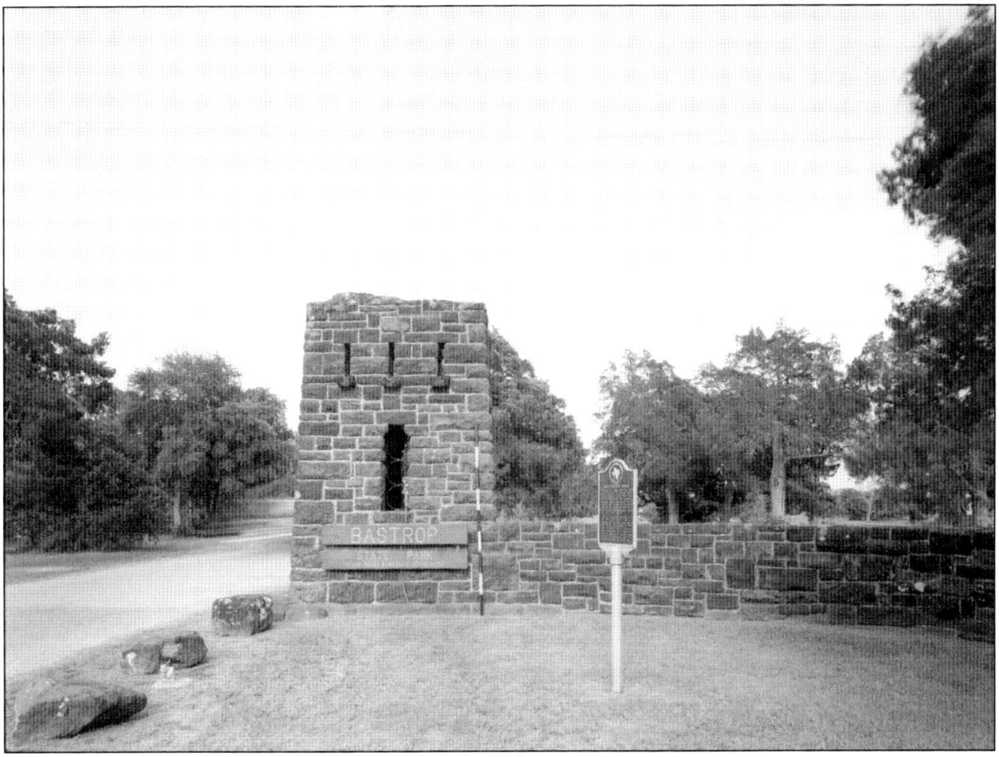


Bastrop State Park has recently been identified by the National Park Service as an official site on the trail. Due to the Bastrop Fire of 2011, trail resources long thought to be in the park were confirmed. (Courtesy of Joy Graham.)

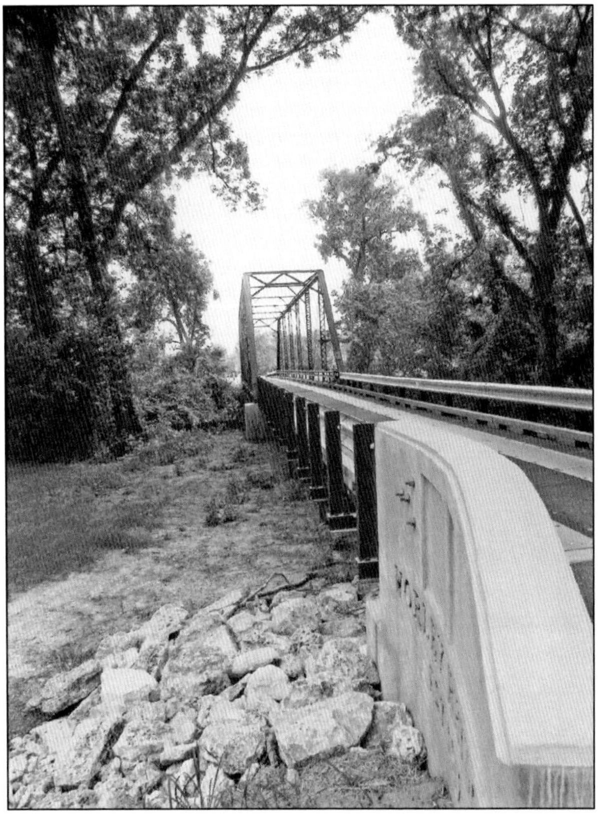

The historic Worley Bridge was built in 1911 and opened for use in 1913. It is located near Camino Real resources on County Road 428, which crosses the San Gabriel River just east of Apache Pass. The Texas Department of Transportation and Milam County restored the bridge beginning in 2012 and completed the restoration in May 2014. The bridge was rededicated on June 22, 2014, to limited traffic. (Courtesy of Candace Velvin.)

The DAR Marker Series has a total of 20 maps that depict DAR markers from the Río Grande to the Sabine River. This map highlights the location of markers in Burleson County. (Courtesy of El Camino Real de los Tejas National Historic Trail Association; map by Nathan Garza.)

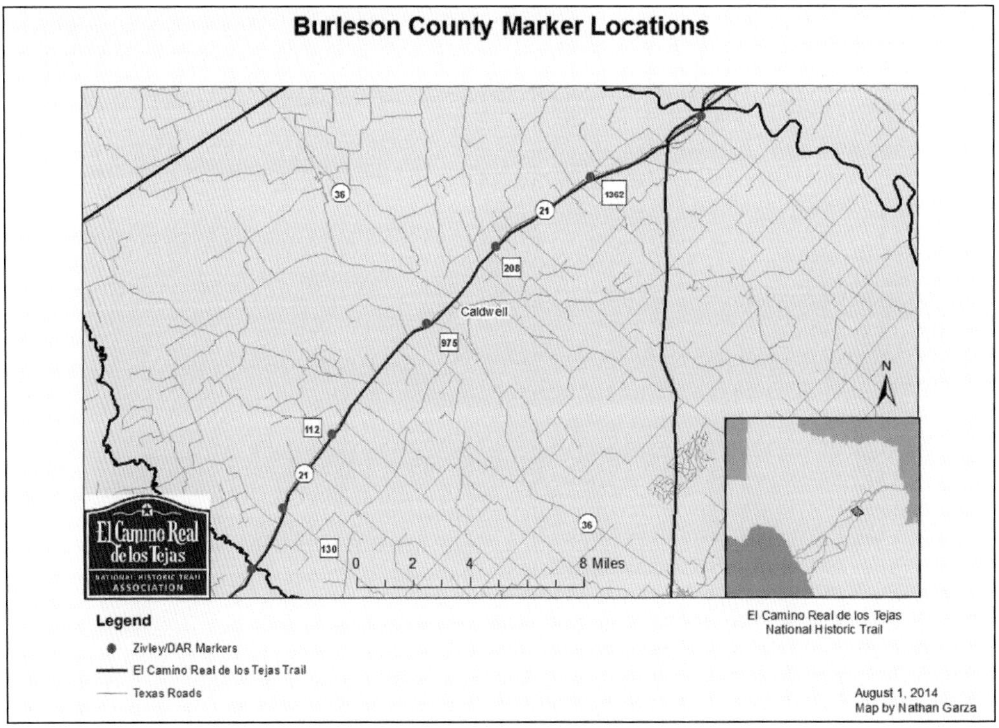

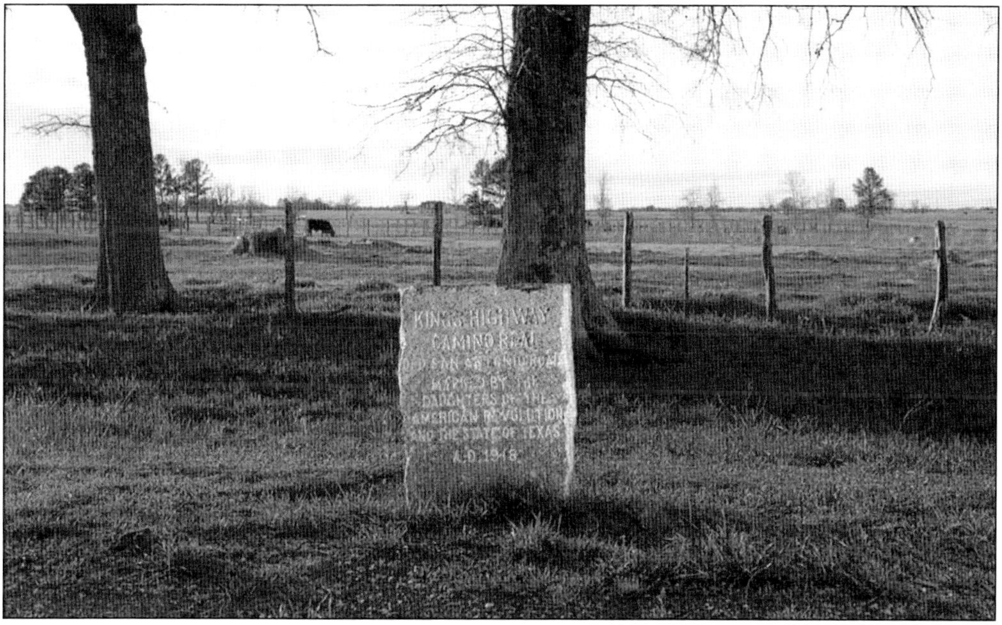


This marker was placed on Highway 21, otherwise known as the Old San Antonio Road, in Bastrop. The Texas Society Daughters of the American Revolution placed these markers across Texas in memory of El Camino Real de los Tejas. (Courtesy of Kay Wesson.)

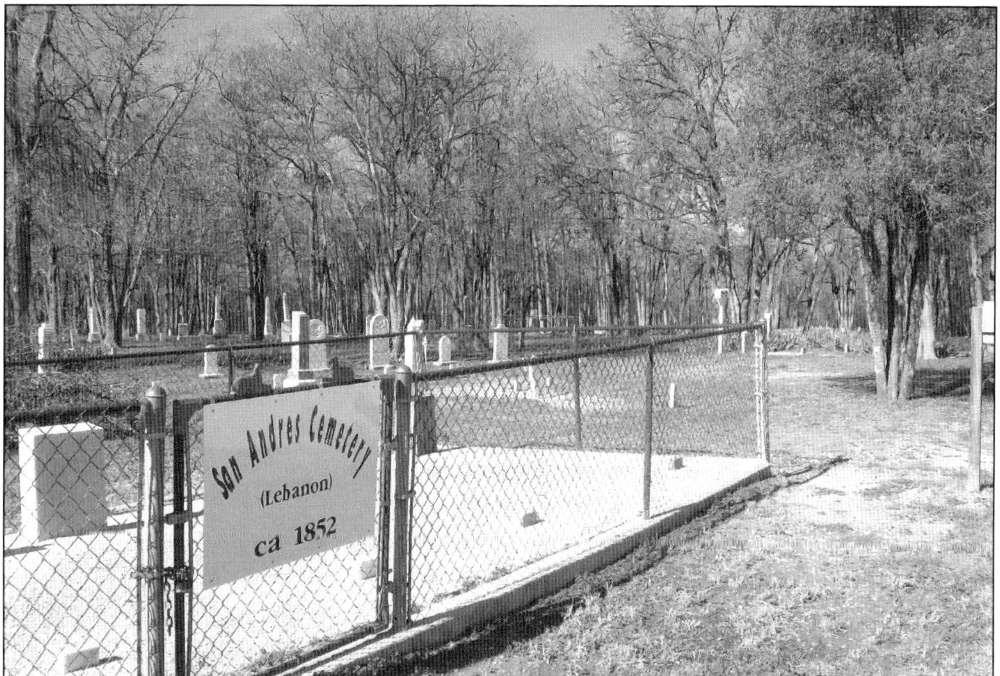


San Andres Cemetery is directly across from Mission Candelaria. The cemetery occupies about five acres, and even though there are unmarked graves in the cemetery, the first burial here was performed in 1852. Jack and Beth Brooks organized and oversaw the restoration of San Andres Cemetery in 2013. (Courtesy of Jack Brooks.)

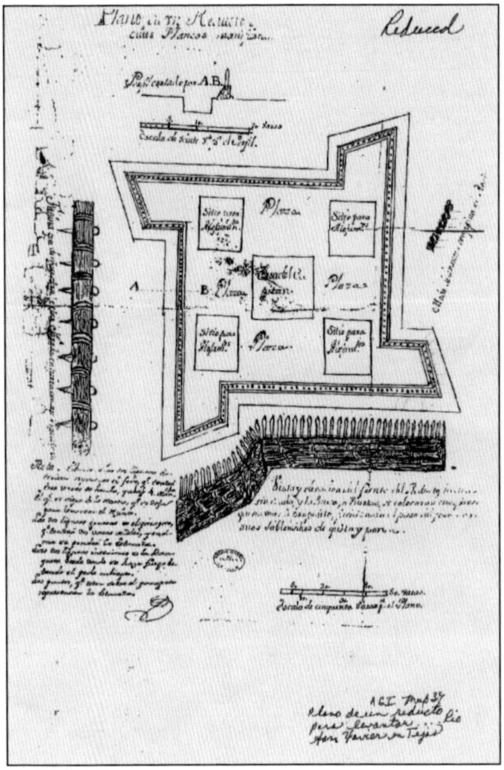

Commander Felipe de Rabago y Teran, along with Spanish missionaries and soldiers from the presidio, explored the river for a place to locate the proposed Presidio San Francisco Xavier de Gigedo. Teran traveled up the San Gabriel River to a crossing called Apache Pass, where he crossed. The presidio is recorded as being established and it functioned for several years, though remnants of its physical structure have yet to be found. (Courtesy of Joy Graham.)

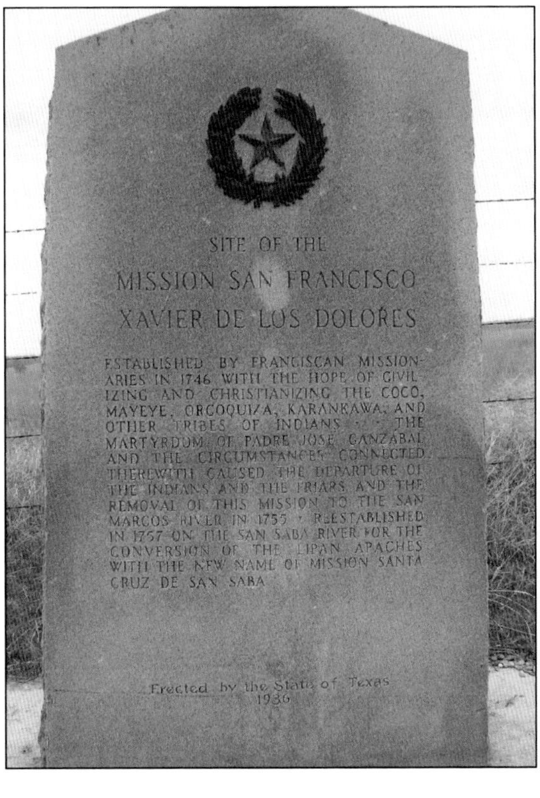


Mission San Francisco Xavier de Horcasitas (1746–1755), also known Nuestra Señora de los Dolores del Río de San Xavier, is now in the National Register of Historic Places. In June 1745, a group of Indians went to San Antonio to ask for a mission. They were granted their request, and the first mission on the banks of the San Gabriel River was built to the east of the Apache Pass crossing. Dr. Kathleen Gilmore began her archeological studies of this area in 1969, and they lasted until 2010. The result of her dedication is the San Xavier Missions Complex in Milam County. (Courtesy of Joy Graham.)

Mission Ildefonso (1749–1755) was located east of Mission San Francisco Xavier. Indians who were housed at this mission were of the Procquisac, Bidai, and Deadose tribes. These groups spoke similar dialects and soon intermarried. These tribes also had contact with the French, with whom they traded. The Franciscan missionary assigned to Ildefonso, Padre Juan José de Ganzabal, was killed at Mission Candelaria. (Courtesy of Joy Graham.)

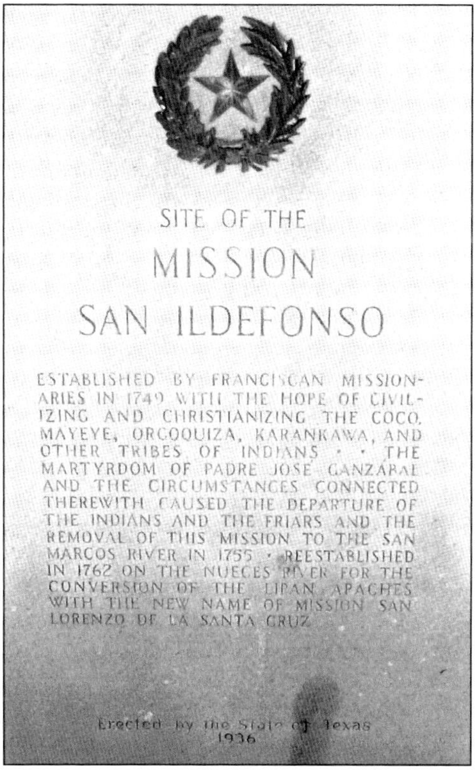


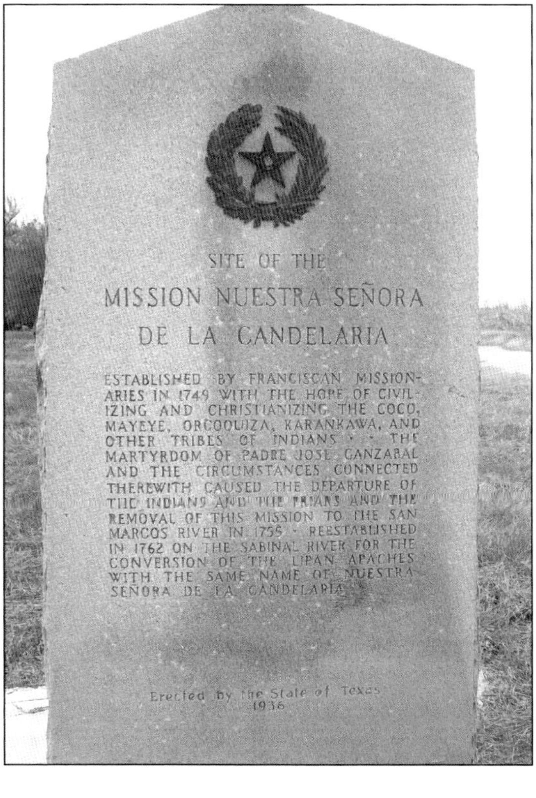


Mission Nuestra Señora de la Candelaria (1749–1755) was occupied by Bidai, Orcoquiza, and Coco Indians. This mission was southeast of the garrison near Apache Pass. Padre Juan José de Ganzabal and a soldier named Ceballos were murdered here in a series of events concerning the garrison. Following these deaths, the Indians in the area became distraught, disease set in, and a drought plagued the land. The decision was eventually made to close the three missions and move them to the San Marcos River. (Courtesy of Joy Graham.)

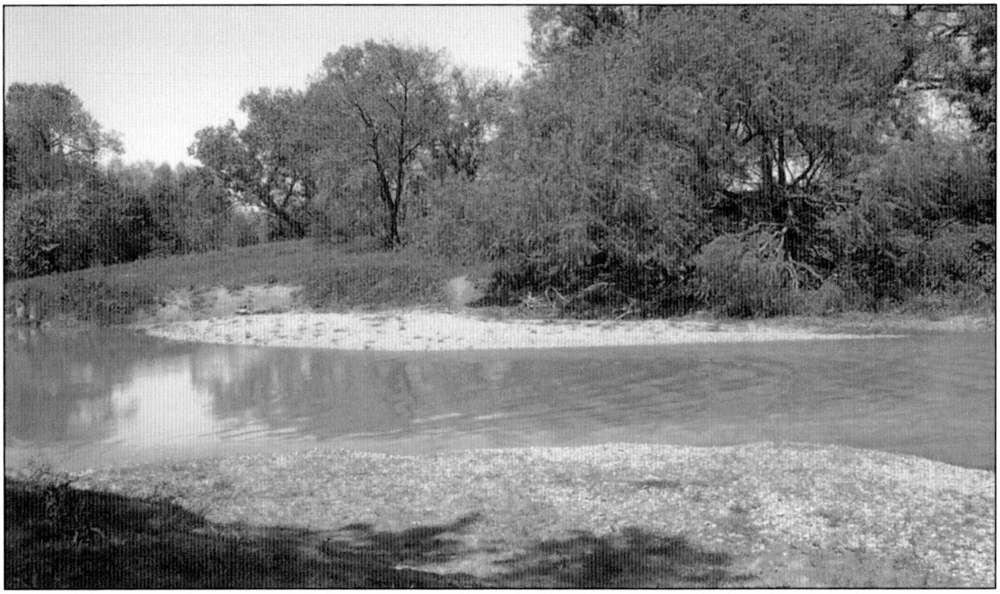

Apache Pass Park is the location of the San Gabriel River crossing named "the Apaches" by Fray Domingo de Arricivita. He made measurements of the bank heights and the width of the riverbed. These measurements were made from the north and west to the three proposed missions to be located east and south of the river. (Courtesy of Lucile Estell.)

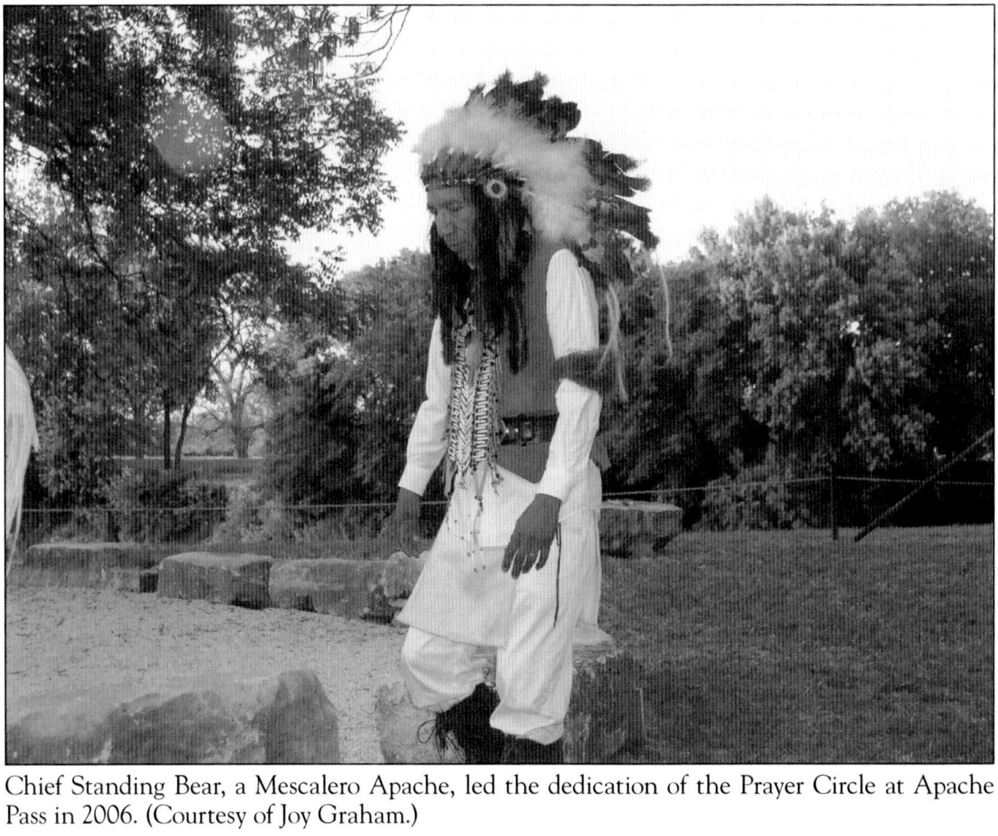

Chief Standing Bear, a Mescalero Apache, led the dedication of the Prayer Circle at Apache Pass in 2006. (Courtesy of Joy Graham.)

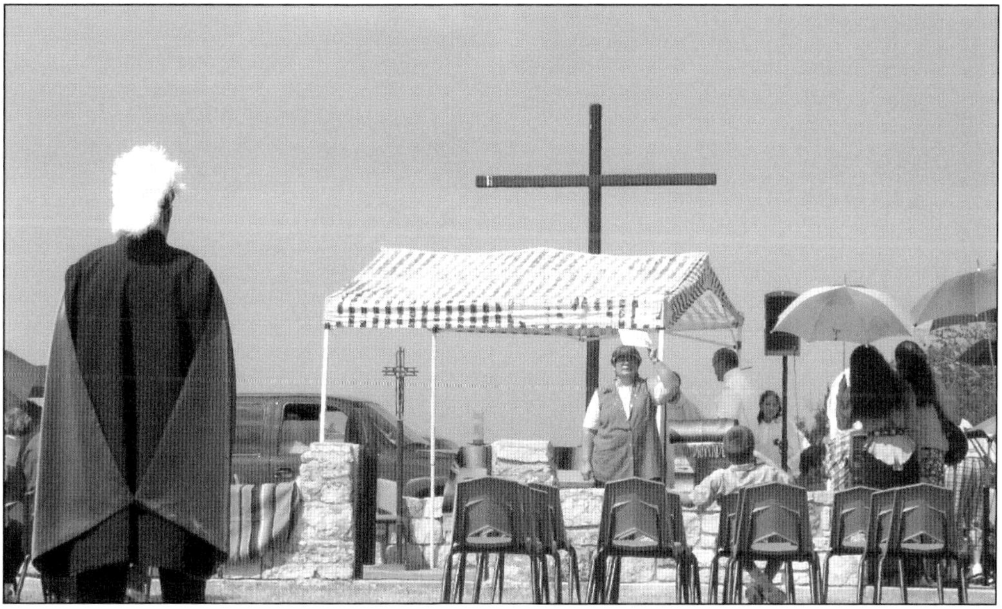

The Austin Catholic Diocese and the St. Joseph Catholic Church held a mass honoring the Native Americans of Mission San Francisco Xavier de Horcasitas in October 2005. The mission site is located on private property. (Courtesy of Lucile Estell.)

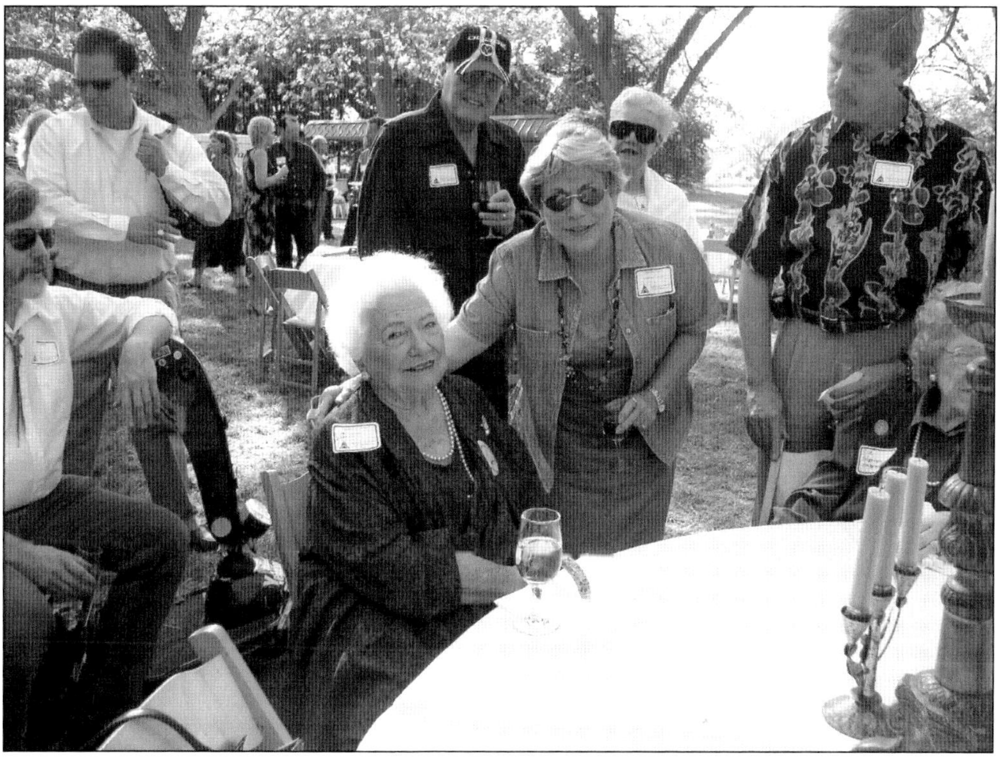

Liz Carpenter (seated at center), former secretary to Pres. Lyndon Baines Johnson, spoke at the El Camino Real de los Tejas symposium in Milam County in 2005. A reception was held at Apache Pass to honor all those who spoke at the symposium. (Courtesy of Joy Graham.)

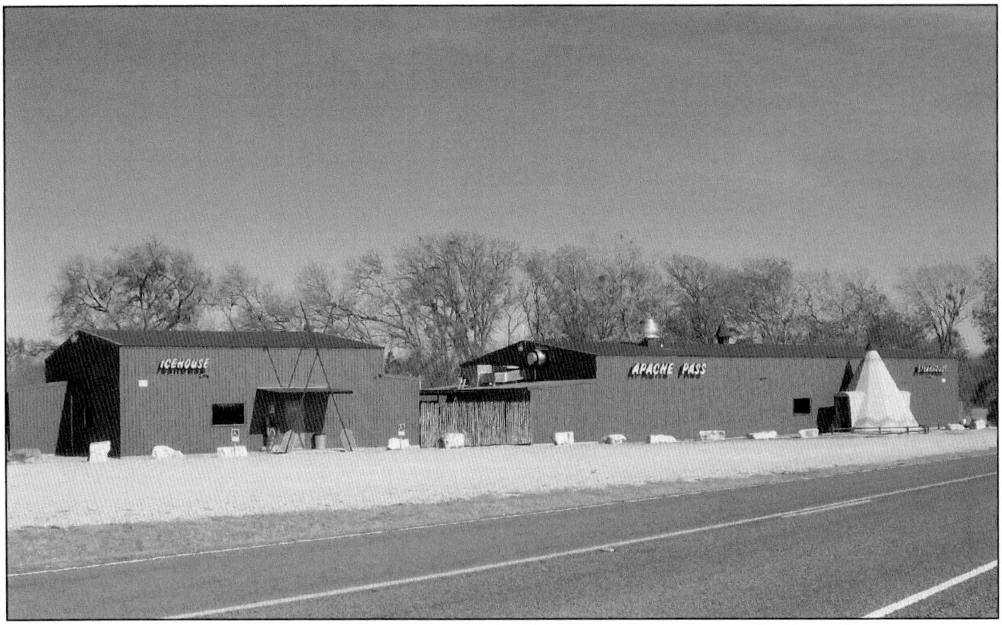


The Apache Pass Ice House & Restaurant was built to serve visitors to the San Xavier Missions Complex and provides both an indoor and outdoor venue for recreation and entertainment. It is located eight miles northwest of Rockdale, Texas, along FM 908. (Courtesy of Joy Graham.)

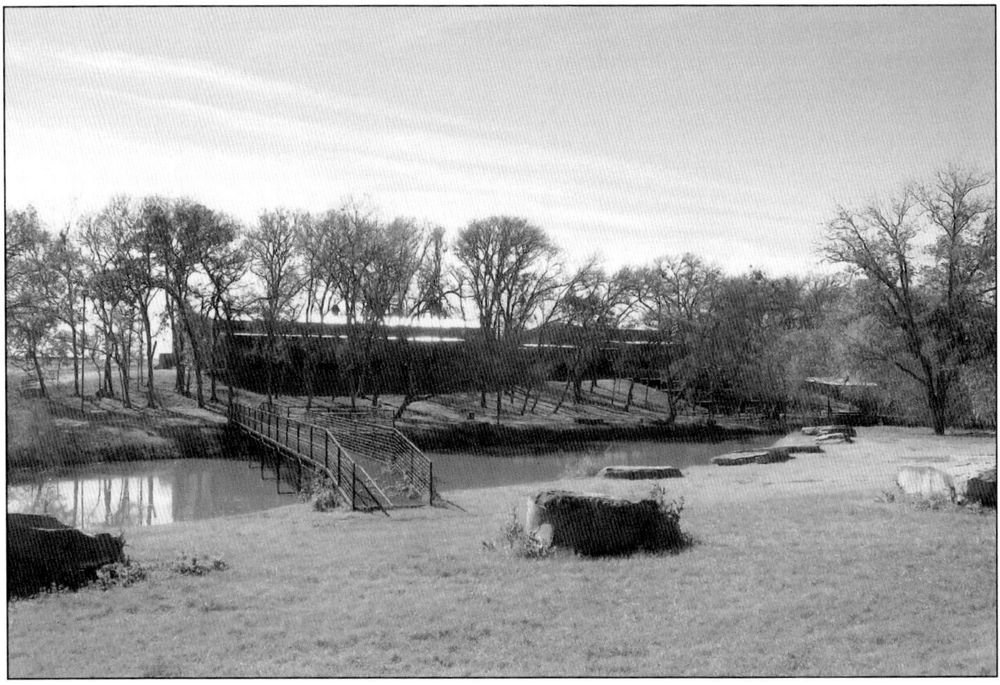

The view of Dream Catcher Lake from the Apache Pass Ice House & Restaurant captivates those who visit this area. These two venues also provide a stage for outdoor music and dancing. Dream Catcher Lake is just south of this area and features a path for those who want to walk to the river crossing. (Courtesy of Joy Graham.)

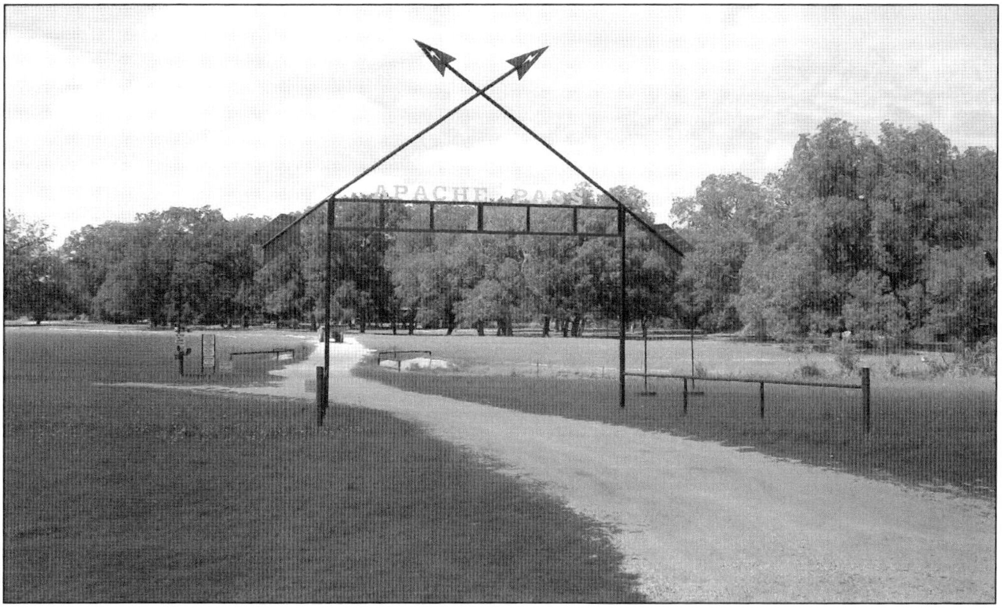


Here is the entrance to Apache Pass Park. (Courtesy of Joy Graham.)

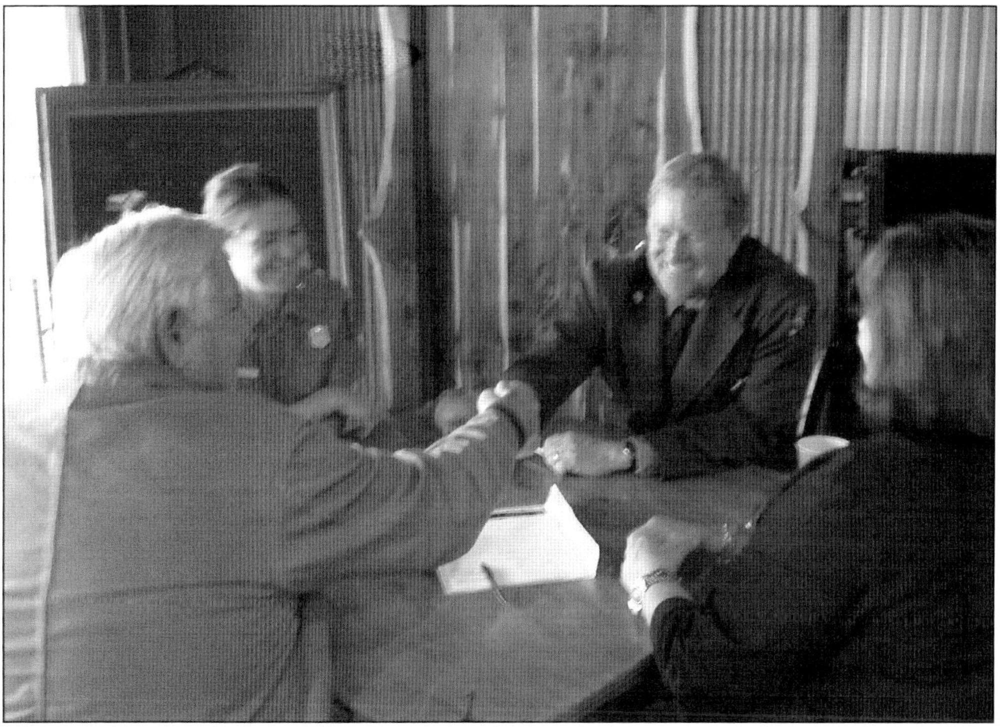

Pictured, from left to right, are Kit Worley, Kristin Van Fleet, Aaron Mahr of the National Park Service, and Linda Worley. This photograph documents the Worley family entering into a voluntary program run by the NPS–National Trails Intermountain Region. Known as a Landowner Certification Program, or LCP, it is an agreement between a property owner and the NPS stating that both entities will work together to protect trail resources. (Courtesy of Joy Graham.)

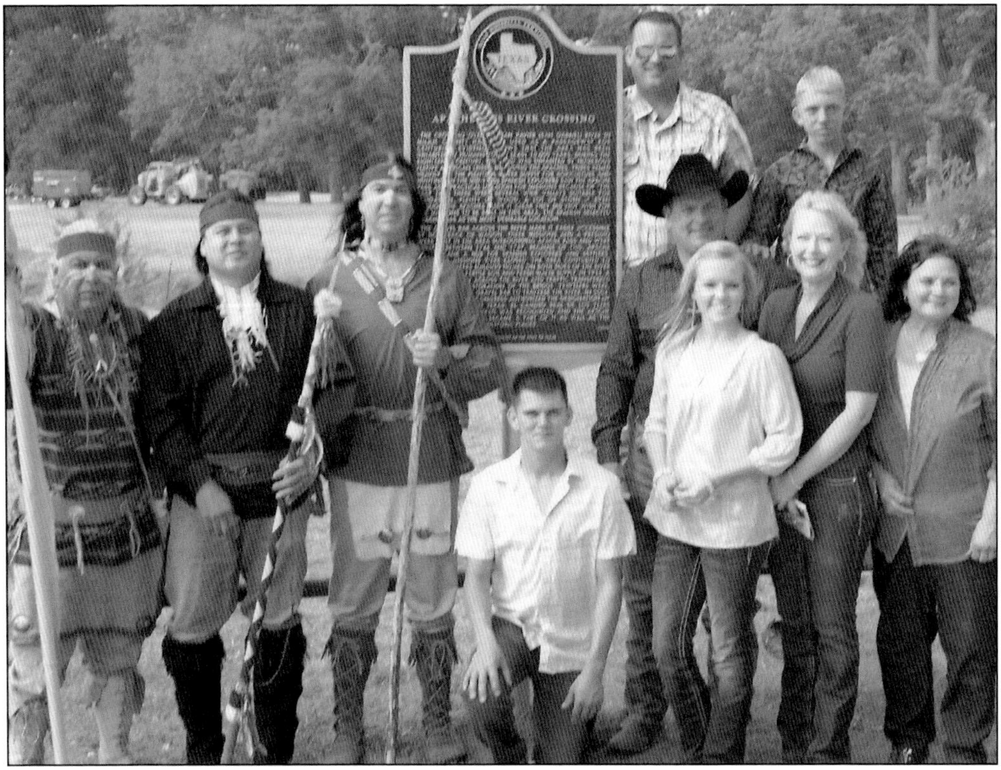

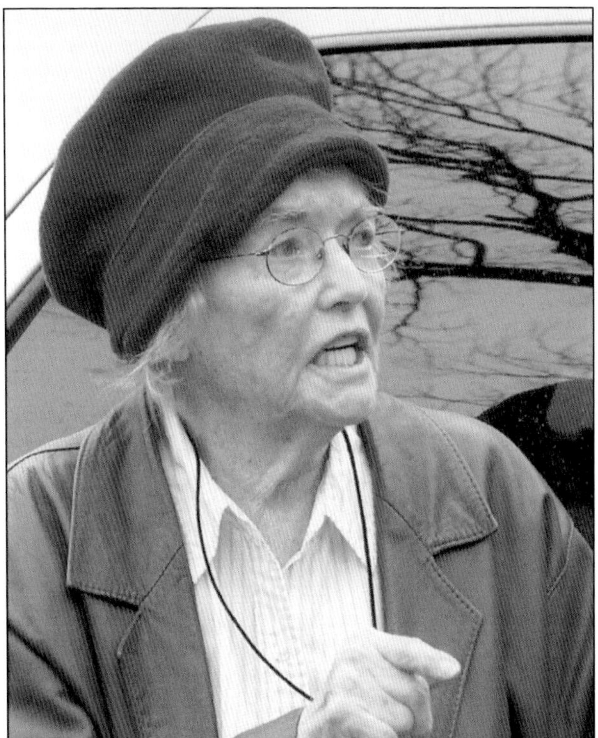

This photograph shows the dedication of the historical marker at Apache Pass on October 26, 2013. The Joe Ochoa family is on the left, and the Worley family is on the right. (Courtesy of Joy Graham.)

Archaeologist Dr. Kathleen Gilmore, pictured here, documented the history of the San Xavier Missions from 1969 to 2010. (Courtesy of Lucile Estell.)

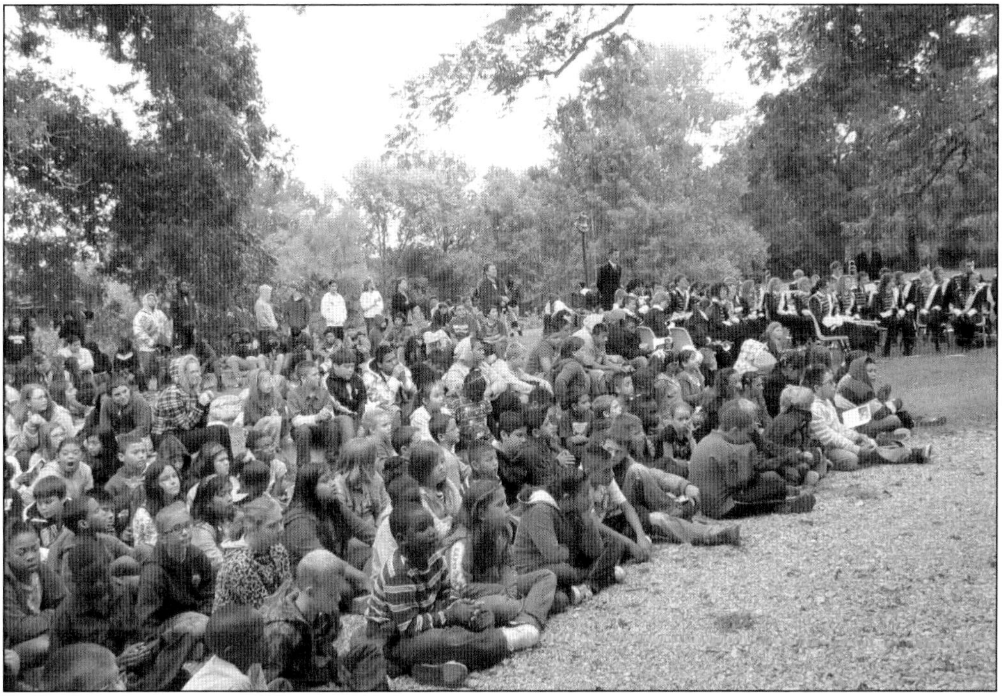

The dedication of National Historic Trail signage in Milam County was held on October 8, 2012. Local fourth- and seventh-grade students attended the dedication, and the Thorndale High School Band played for the event. An estimated 1,000 local guests, state officials, and National Park Service officials participated in the program. (Courtesy of Texas Historical Commission.)

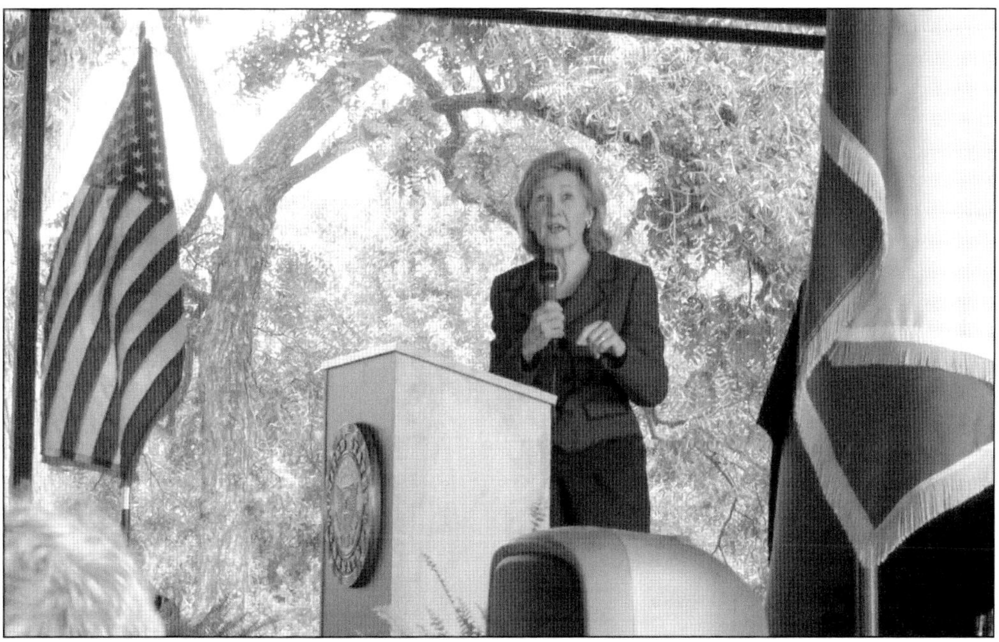

Sen. Kay Bailey Hutchison spoke at the dedication ceremony on October 8, 2012. In Washington, DC, she and US Congressman Ciro Rodriguez were the driving force behind getting the Camino Real recognized as a National Historic Trail. (Courtesy of the Texas Historical Commission.)

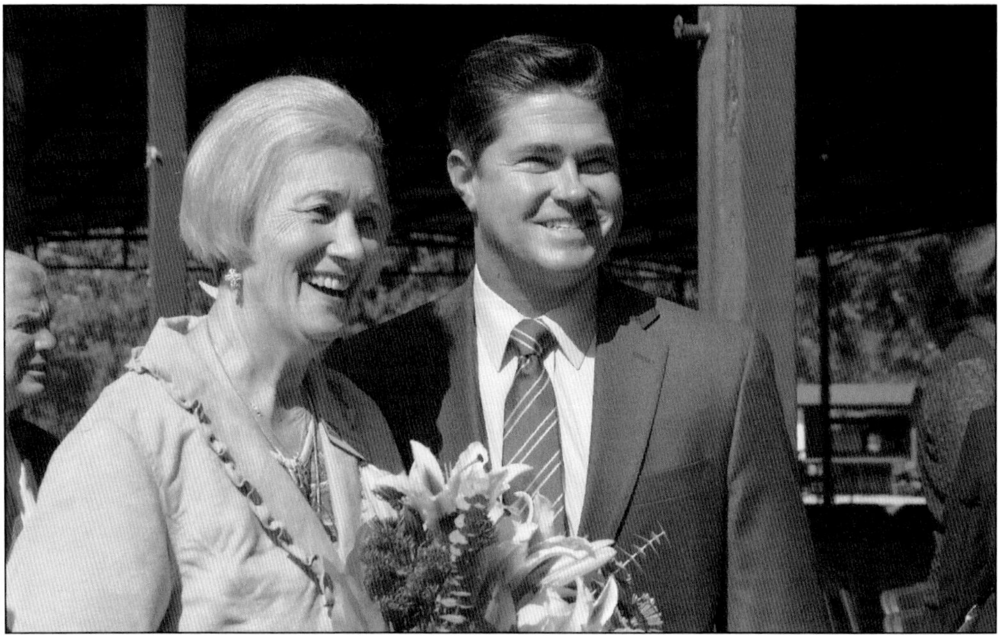

Joy Graham (left) and Carl Mica (right) are pictured here at the sign dedication ceremony. Carl has been on the trail's board of directors and served as president for the 2014 term. (Courtesy of Smokey Clark.)

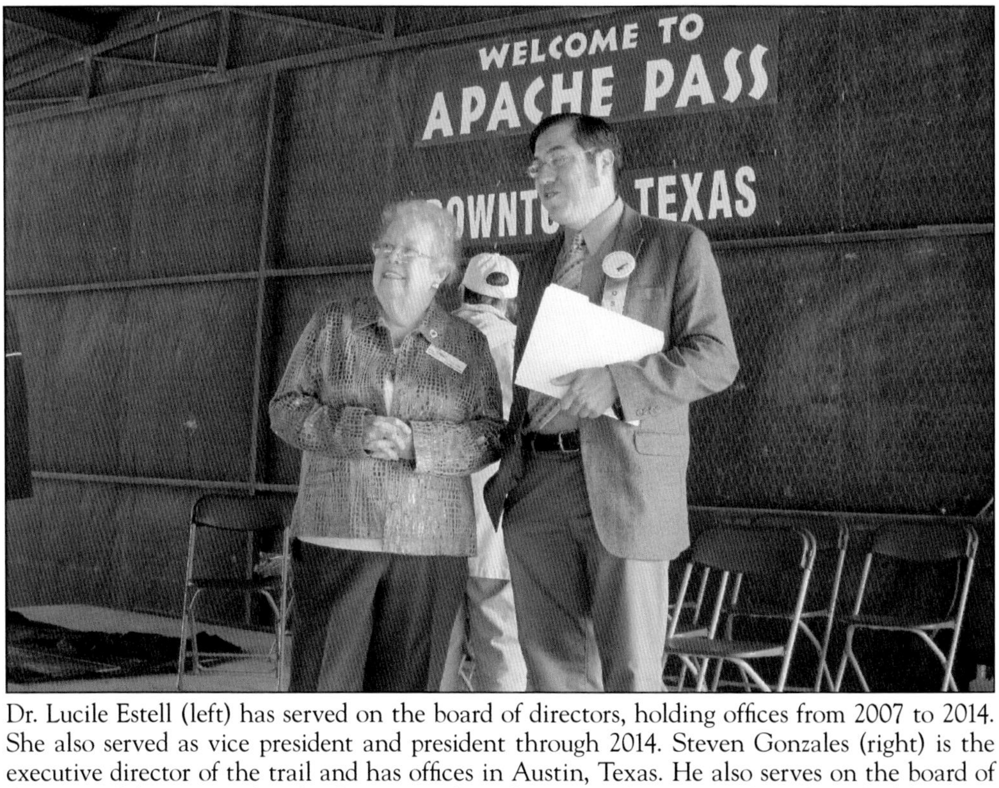


Dr. Lucile Estell (left) has served on the board of directors, holding offices from 2007 to 2014. She also served as vice president and president through 2014. Steven Gonzales (right) is the executive director of the trail and has offices in Austin, Texas. He also serves on the board of directors of the Partnership for the National Trails System. (Courtesy of Smokey Clark.)

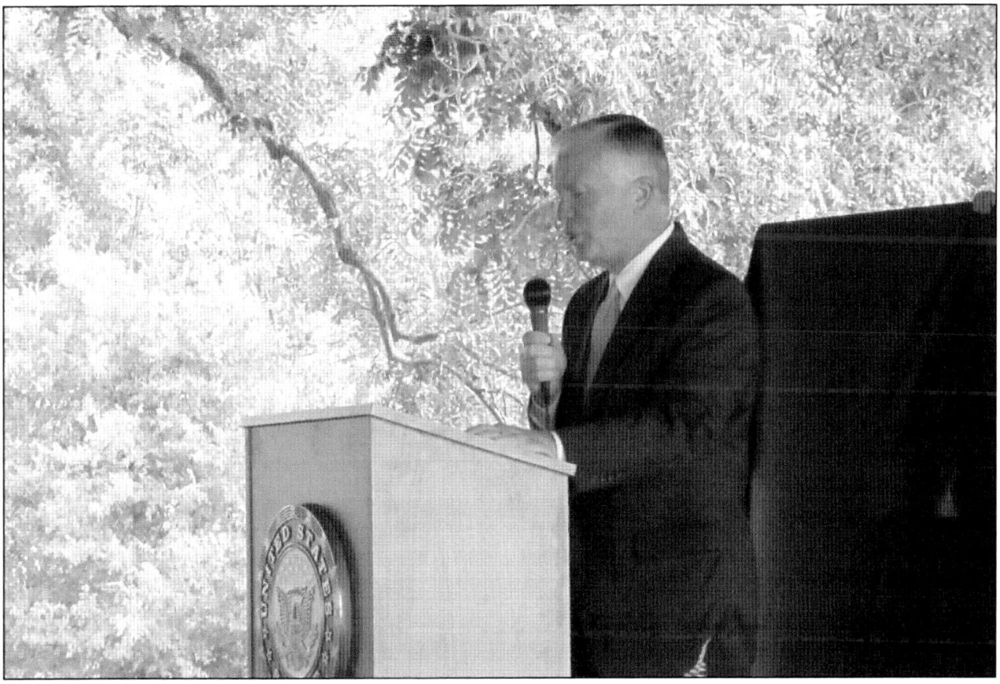

Terry Colley is the deputy executive director of the Texas Historical Commission. He served on the Signage Committee, which helped to pass legislation to allow NPS signage to be placed on roadways in Texas. (Courtesy of the Texas Historical Commission.)

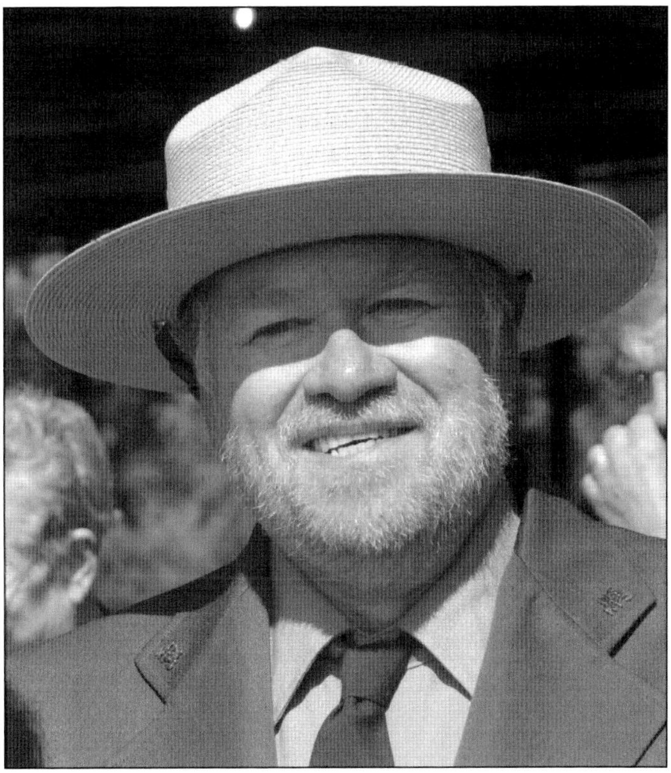

Aaron Mahr is superintendent of the National Trails Intermountain Region of the National Park Service, within the US Department of the Interior. As superintendent, he has the ultimate responsibility for the stewardship of the trail and implementation of its planning document, which is titled *El Camino Real de los Tejas National Historic Trail, Comprehensive Management Plan and Environmental Assessment.* (Courtesy of Smokey Clark.)

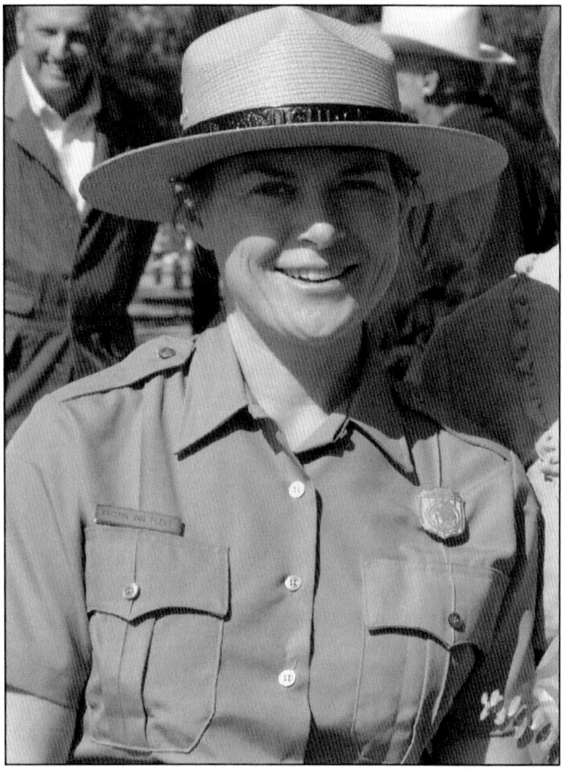

Kristin Van Fleet is a landscape architect with the National Park Service's Intermountain Region. She facilitated the creation of a signage plan for El Camino Real de los Tejas National Historic Trail. (Courtesy of Smokey Clark.)

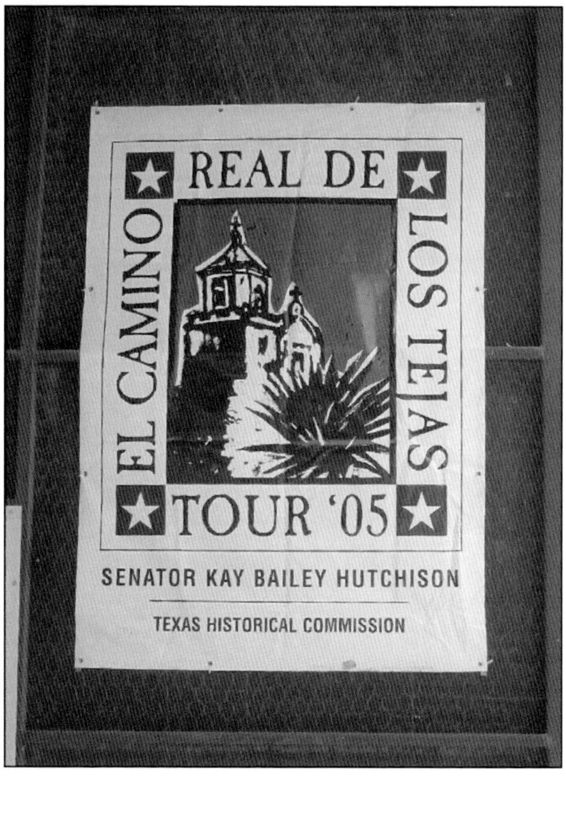


Sen. Kay Bailey Hutchison sponsored a tour of El Camino Real de los Tejas across Texas in 2005. Her assistant Carl Mica facilitated the five-bus travel tour from Milam to Eagle Pass. (Courtesy of Smokey Clark.)

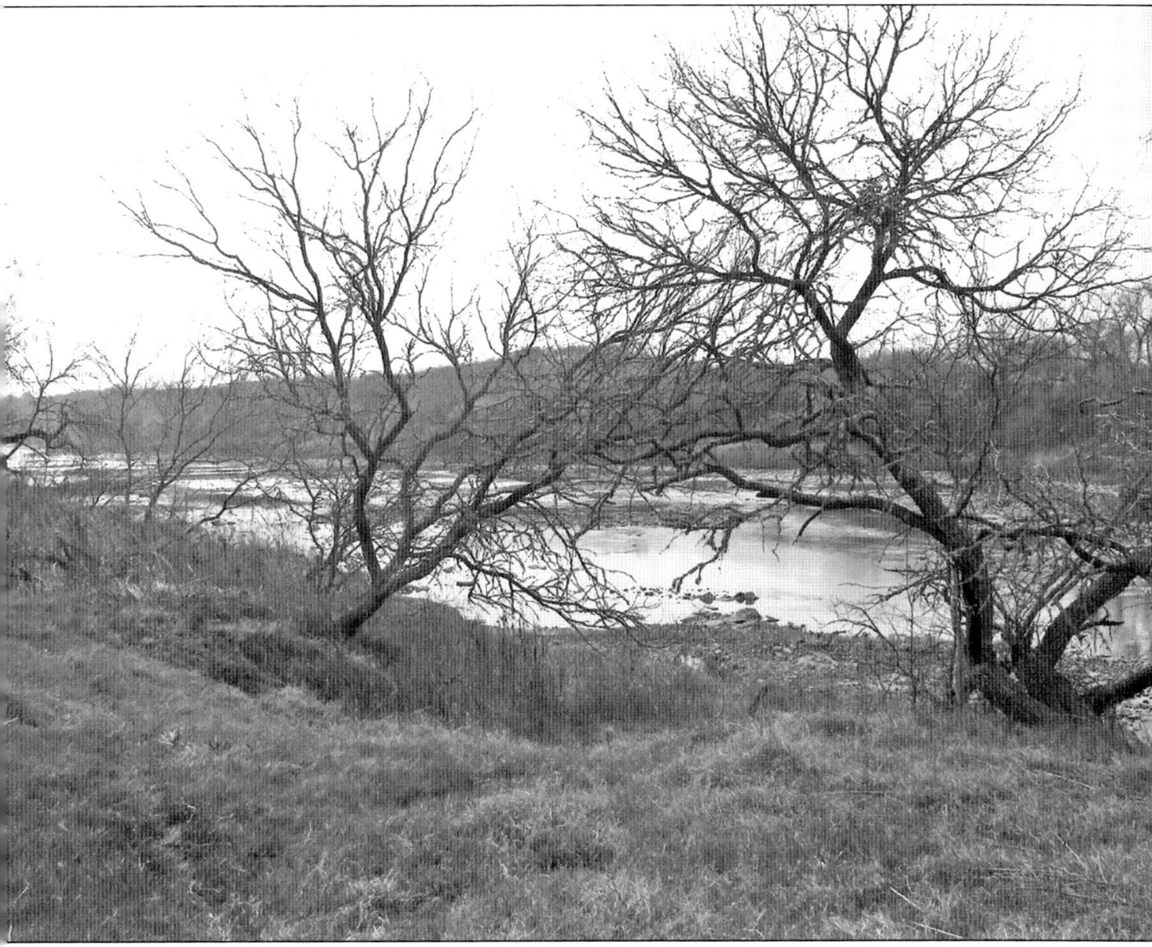

The Burnett Shoals are a shallow-water crossing of the Brazos River between Milam and Robertson Counties. A deep swale can be seen leading to the river between the two large trees in the foreground. (Courtesy of Joy Graham.)

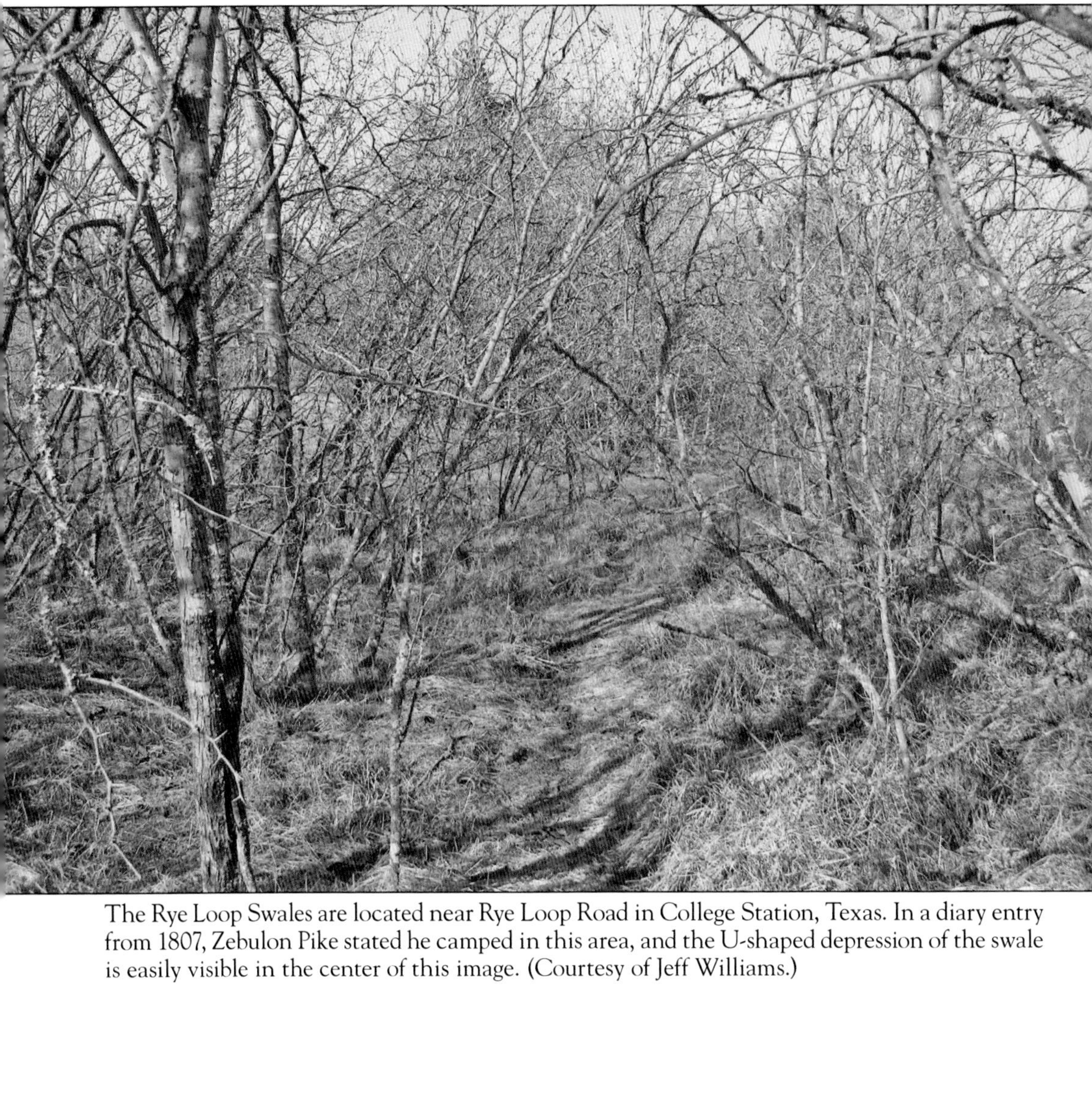

The Rye Loop Swales are located near Rye Loop Road in College Station, Texas. In a diary entry from 1807, Zebulon Pike stated he camped in this area, and the U-shaped depression of the swale is easily visible in the center of this image. (Courtesy of Jeff Williams.)

El Camino Real often served as a boundary between land grants, other types of properties, and in this case, counties. Notice how the Old San Antonio Road portion of Camino Real is the boundary between Brazos and Robertson Counties all the way from Highway 190 in the west to their eastern boundaries with Madison and Leon Counties. (Courtesy of El Camino Real de los Tejas National Historic Trail Association; map by Nathan Garza.)

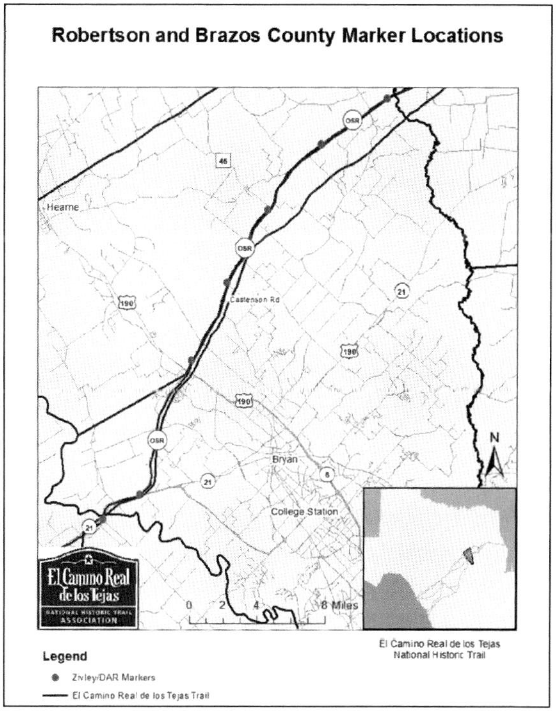


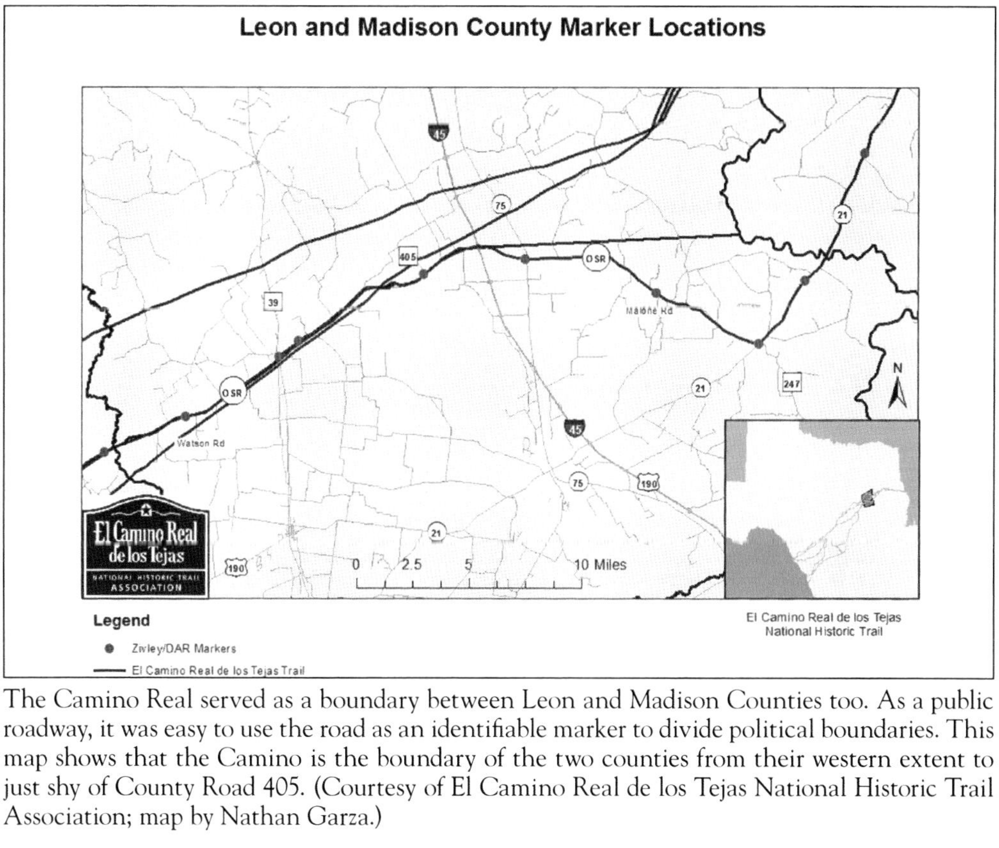


The Camino Real served as a boundary between Leon and Madison Counties too. As a public roadway, it was easy to use the road as an identifiable marker to divide political boundaries. This map shows that the Camino is the boundary of the two counties from their western extent to just shy of County Road 405. (Courtesy of El Camino Real de los Tejas National Historic Trail Association; map by Nathan Garza.)

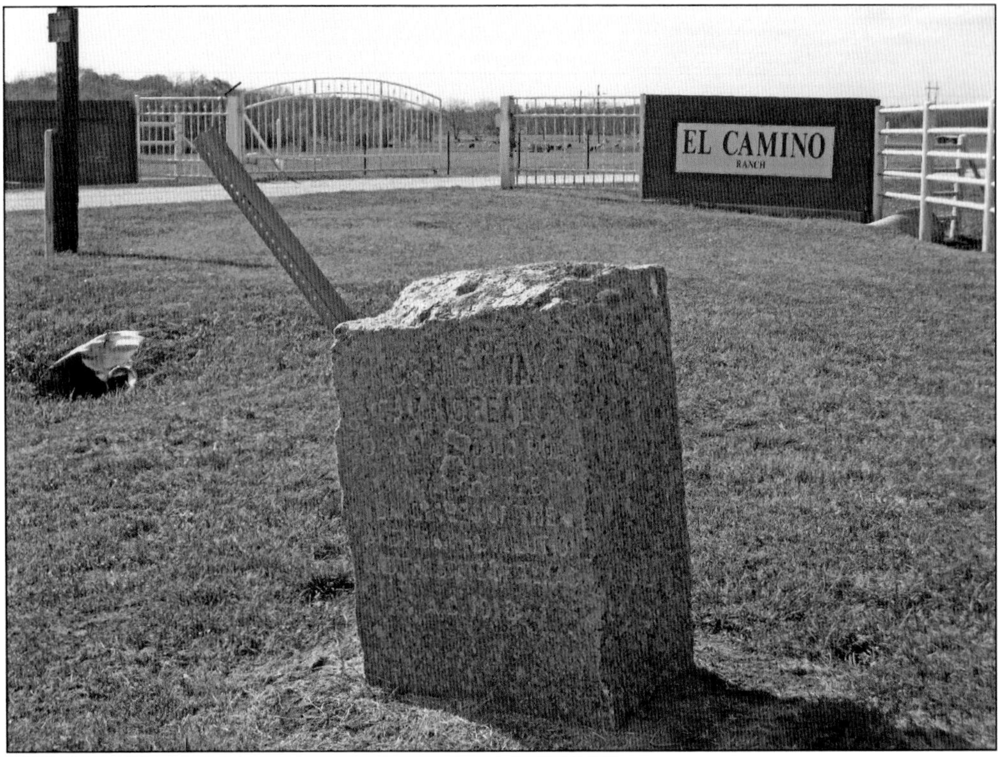


This DAR marker is on the Old San Antonio Road right in front of the El Camino Ranch. Landowners adjacent to the road are often aware of its significance and are proud of their place along it. (Courtesy of Steven Gonzales.)

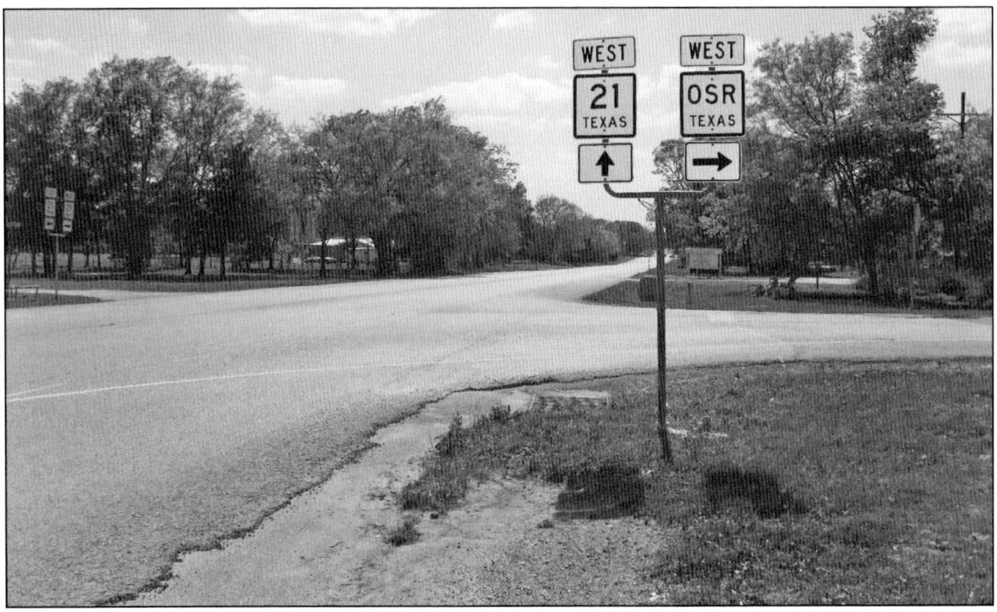


Breaking off of Highway 21 to travel the arc of the OSR, from just west of Bryan to Midway, may take a little longer, but the road ahead and the experience is well worth it. (Courtesy of Steven Gonzales.)

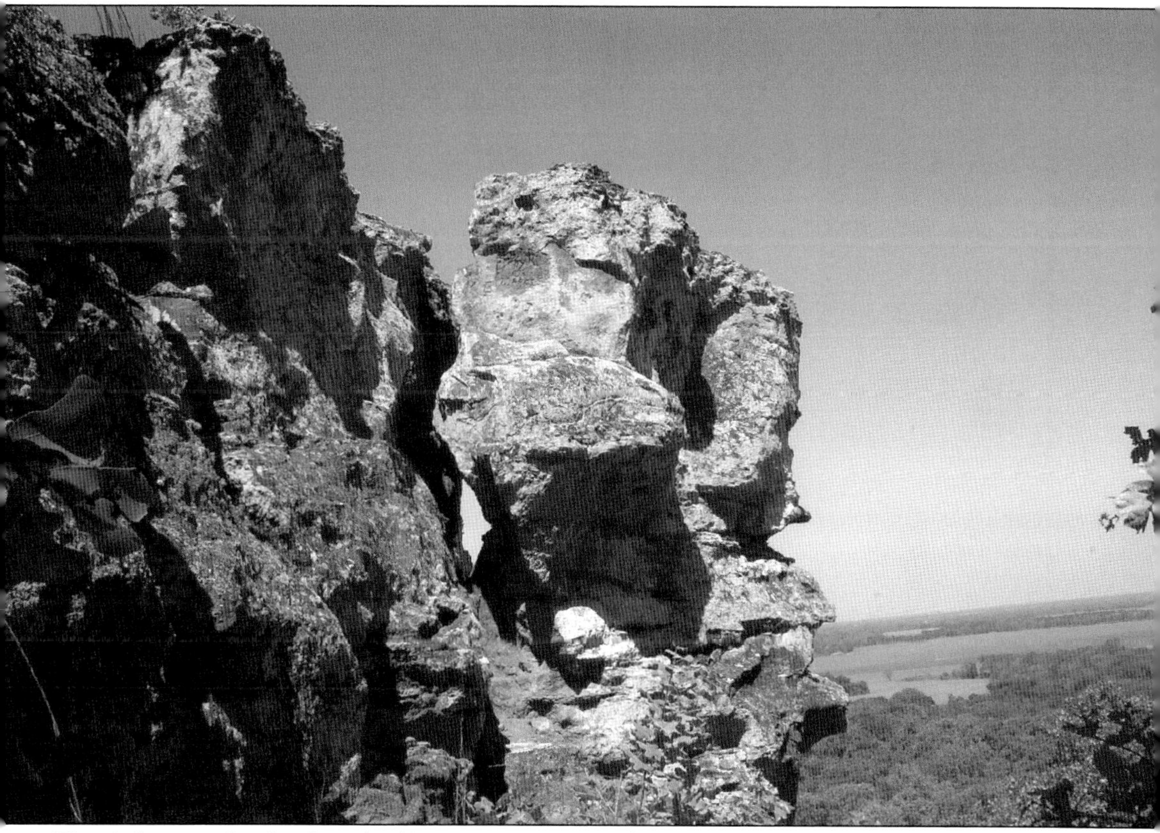

The dedication for the Sugarloaf Mountain THC marker was held on October 26, 2013. The mountain is located near the confluence of the Little and Brazos Rivers and is capped with red sandstone rock. The Ervipiame Indians, who were later joined by Tonkawa, Mayeye, and Yojuane tribes, inhabited the area. They used trails that marked an old road system known as the King's Highway, which is now El Camino Real de los Tejas National Historic Trail. (Courtesy of Lucile Estell.)

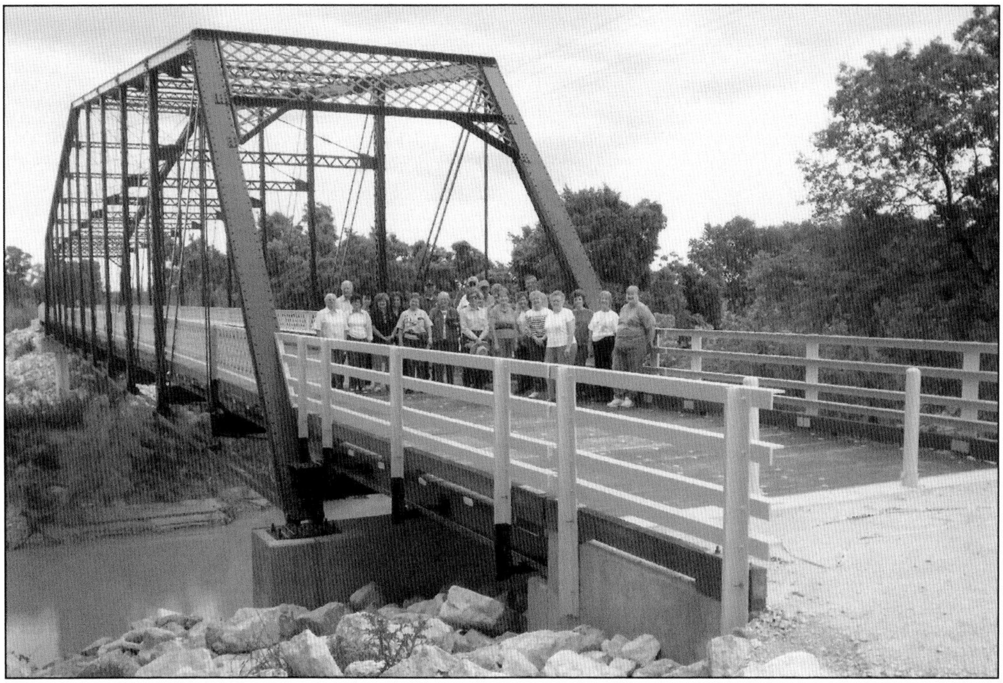

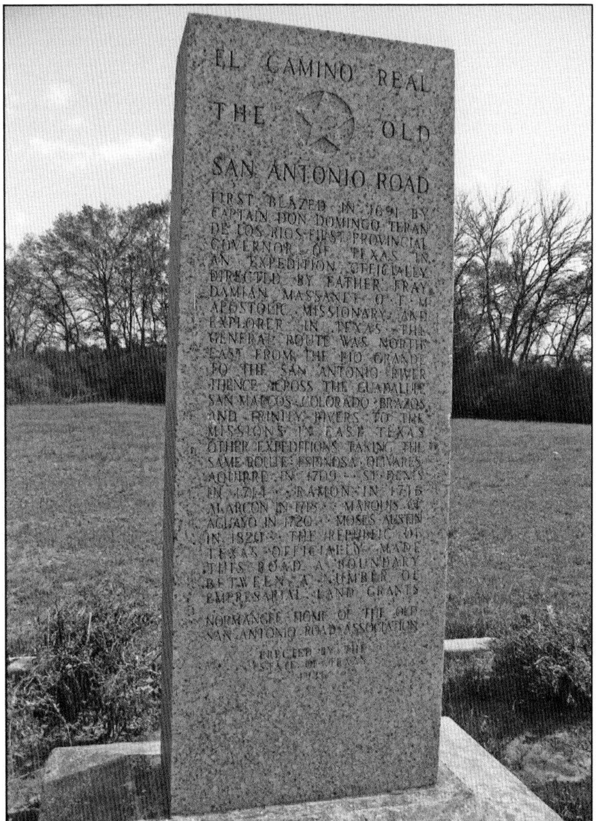


The Faubian Historic Bridge is recognized by a Texas Department of Transportation marker. It is open as a walking bridge and is a part of a small "Marker Park" recognizing the bridge and Sugarloaf Mountain. Members of the Milam County Historical Commission are pictured here, gathered on the bridge. (Courtesy of Joy Graham.)

This marker along the Camino Real is like no other. Its size and design are different than every other Camino marker across the trail. The reason for this is that the marker is in Normangee, Texas, which was the home of the Old San Antonio Road Association. At this writing, little is known of the OSR Association. The community of Normangee was incorporated in 1913, and the marker pictured was placed in 1936, so sometime between these dates, the OSR Association formed. At what point the OSR Association ceased to function remains to be researched. (Courtesy of Joy Graham.)

# *Four*

# EAST TEXAS AND CADDO REGION

El Camino Real de los Tejas National Historic Trail begins in the lush, green forests of two Louisiana parishes: Sabine and Natchitoches. The city of Natchitoches and its equally lovely sister city of Nacogdoches, Texas—located approximately 100 miles away—are integral parts of the history and heritage of those who forged the trail. Remnants of this history abound in the parishes and counties along the camino, while worthwhile experiences await visitors at forts, missions, and log homes and amid the cuts and swales of the trail itself. Fort Jesup, in Many, Louisiana; Fort St. Jean Baptiste, in Natchitoches, Louisiana; Los Adaes, near Robeline—which served as the capital of Texas for about 50 years—and the Old Stone Fort, in Nacogdoches, are just a few of the historic sites that reside along this segment of El Camino Real.

Moving along the trail, this history continues to be evident thanks to the presence of swales, the actual indentations that mark the route taken by the trail. One of the better-known swales in this region is Lobanillo Swales, near San Augustine. The board that governs El Camino Real has raised money to buy the four-acre tract of land on which these swales are located so that they might be protected and preserved.

Moving on toward the Brazos Region, history continues to manifest itself. The Caddoan Mounds and Mission Tejas are two prime examples of sites in this area, and both have interpretive centers to help visitors grasp the historic importance of these sites.

And consider the Adai Caddo Indian Nation—what a presence they have here! Their lovely cultural center, located near Robeline, Louisiana, and also near Los Adaes explains much of their history with an emphasis on the profound influence that these people have had in shaping American culture and in influencing the culture of both Texas and Louisiana. The Adai Caddo Indian Nation first appeared in the early 1500s and was among the first to be influenced by Spanish explorers who were exploring Texas at that time. The very name of the trail, El Camino Real de los Tejas, the Royal Road of the Tejas, emphasizes how strong the influence of these Native Americans was in the development of this Royal Road.

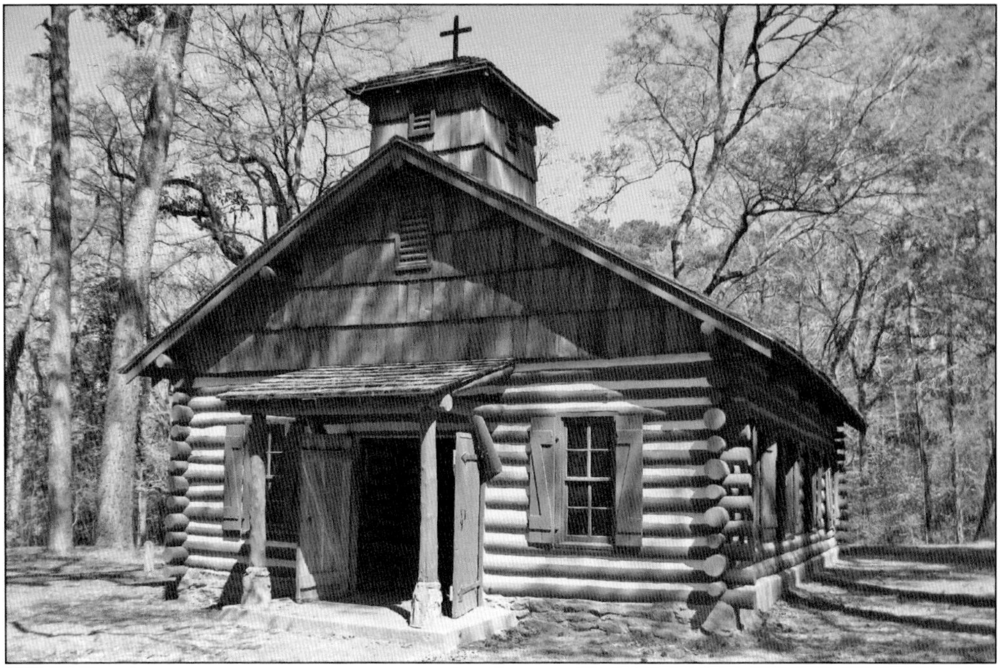

This image is from Mission Tejas State Park in Houston County. Originally established in 1690, this replica of Mission Tejas commemorates the site of Mission San Francisco de los Tejas, the first Spanish mission established in the province of Texas. Though the exact location of the original mission has yet to be discovered, physical remnants of the trail have been confirmed within the park in the form of swales and a Caddoan Indian village. (Courtesy of Steven Gonzales.)

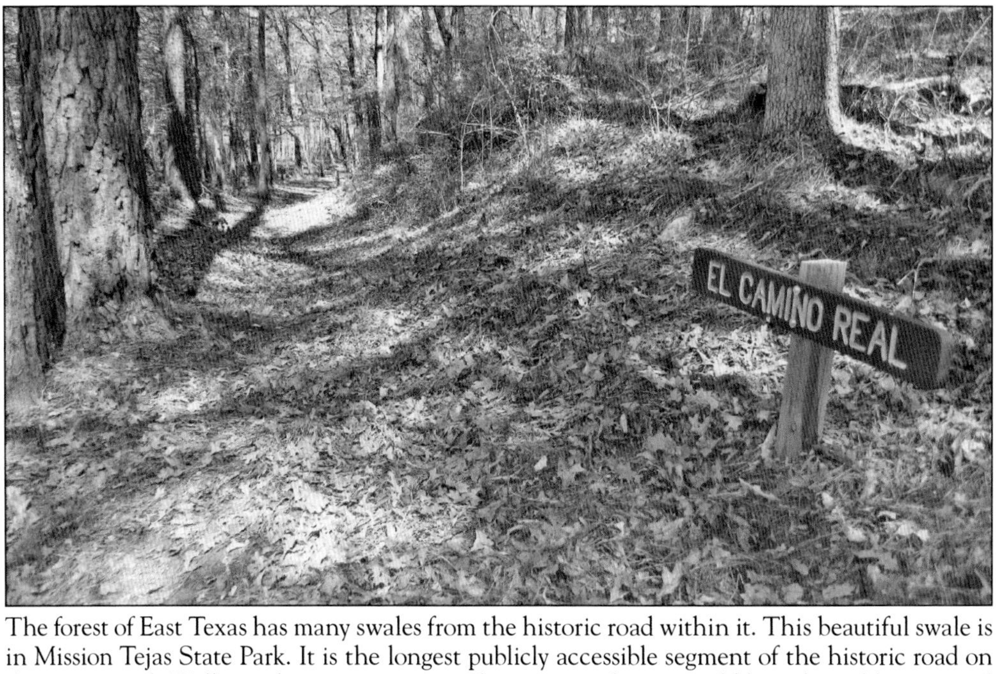


The forest of East Texas has many swales from the historic road within it. This beautiful swale is in Mission Tejas State Park. It is the longest publicly accessible segment of the historic road on the entire trail. Walking along it, one can truly imagine what it would have been like to travel the trail hundreds of years ago. (Courtesy of Steven Gonzales.)

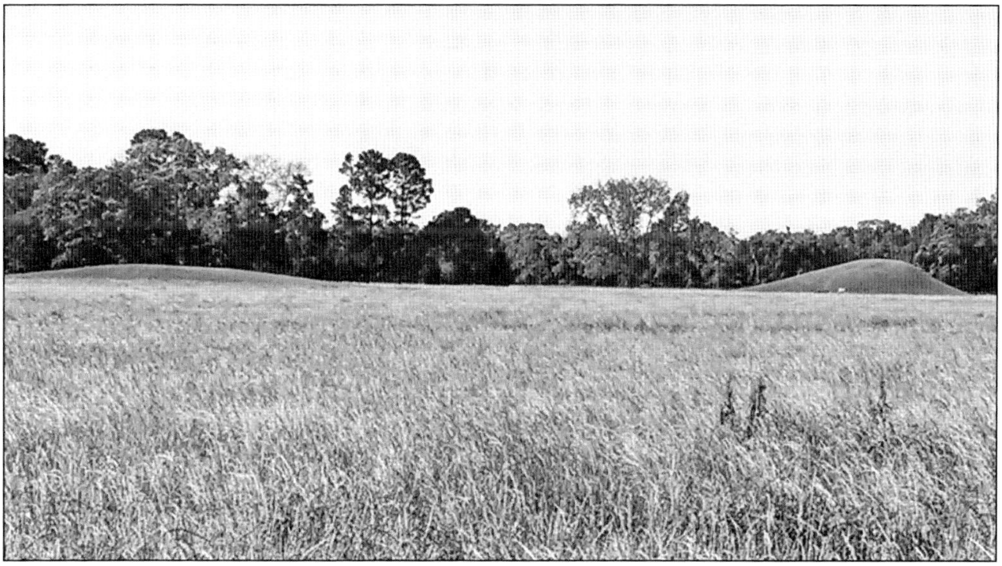

The 1806–1807 Juan Pedro Walker map clearly indicates the relationship of El Camino Real de los Tejas to the Caddo Mounds State Historic Site. The mounds and the trail's relationship to them are also discussed in primary Spanish documents. For example, in 1767, Nicolas de Lafora recorded passing just north of the mounds, stating, "We forded this river [the Neches] in shallow water and one league beyond we climbed a hill. On the summit is a mound which appears to be hand-made." (Courtesy of Steven Gonzales.)

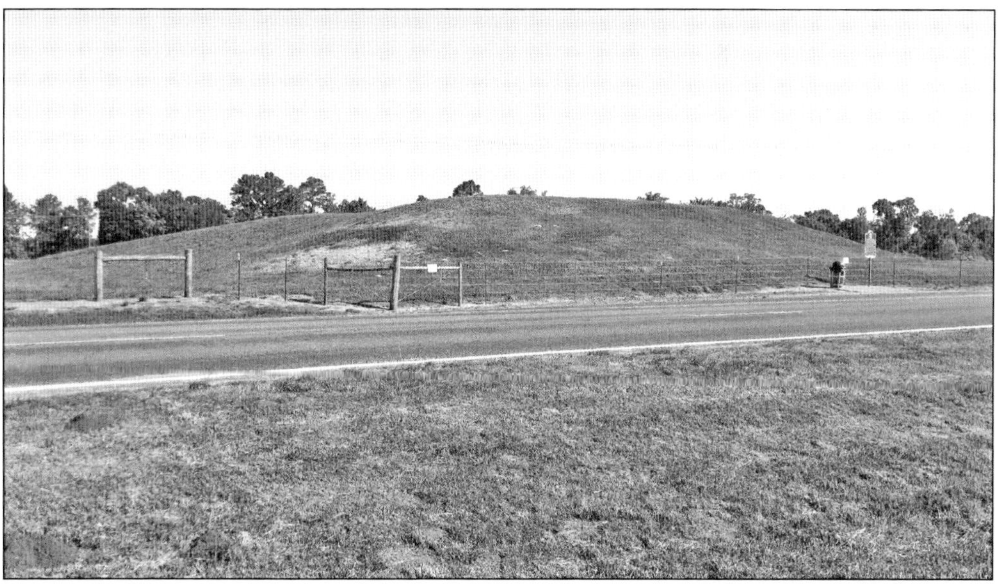

This is the largest mound at Caddo Mounds State Historic Site. It is situated across the street from the main site but is easily viewable from the pullout on the road and there is a historical marker with detailed history. (Courtesy of Steven Gonzales.)

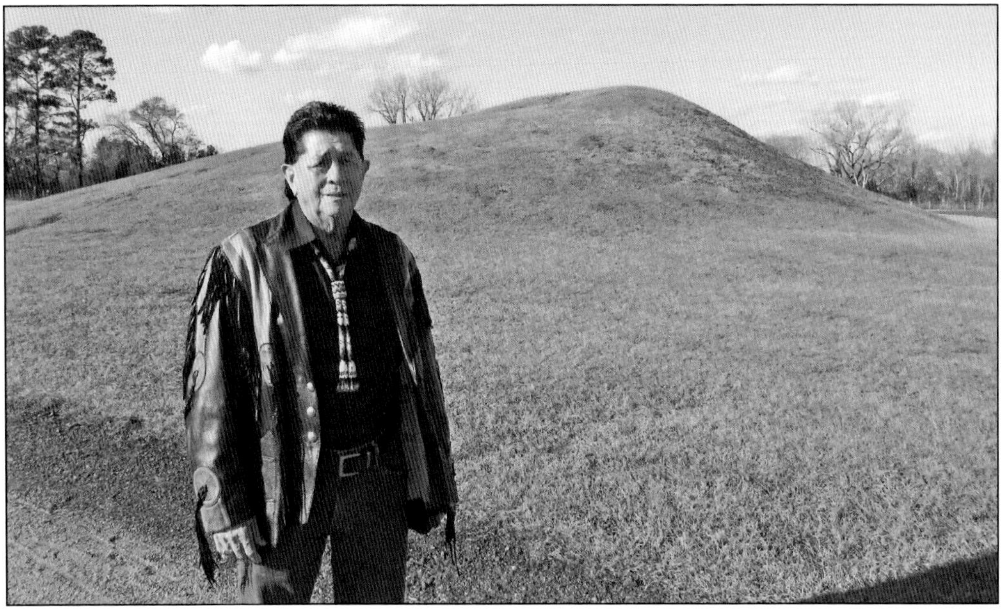

Rufus Davis is chief of the Adai Caddo Indian Nation and a board member of El Camino Real de los Tejas National Historic Trail Association. Chief Davis is pictured here at Caddo Mounds State Historic Site. As the name of the site indicates, it is part of the Adai's cultural homeland. (Courtesy of Steven Gonzales.)

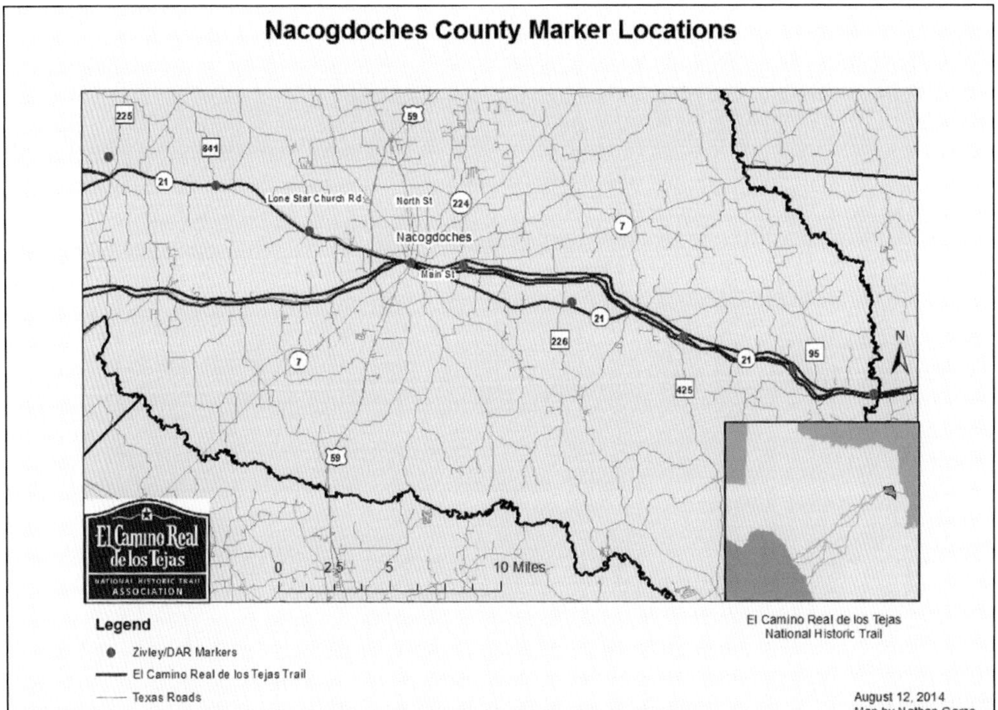


This map of DAR markers illustrates their location across Nacogdoches County. As can be seen on the map, and traveling the trail, Main Street in Nacogdoches is the Camino Real. (Courtesy of El Camino Real de los Tejas National Historic Trail Association; map by Nathan Garza.)

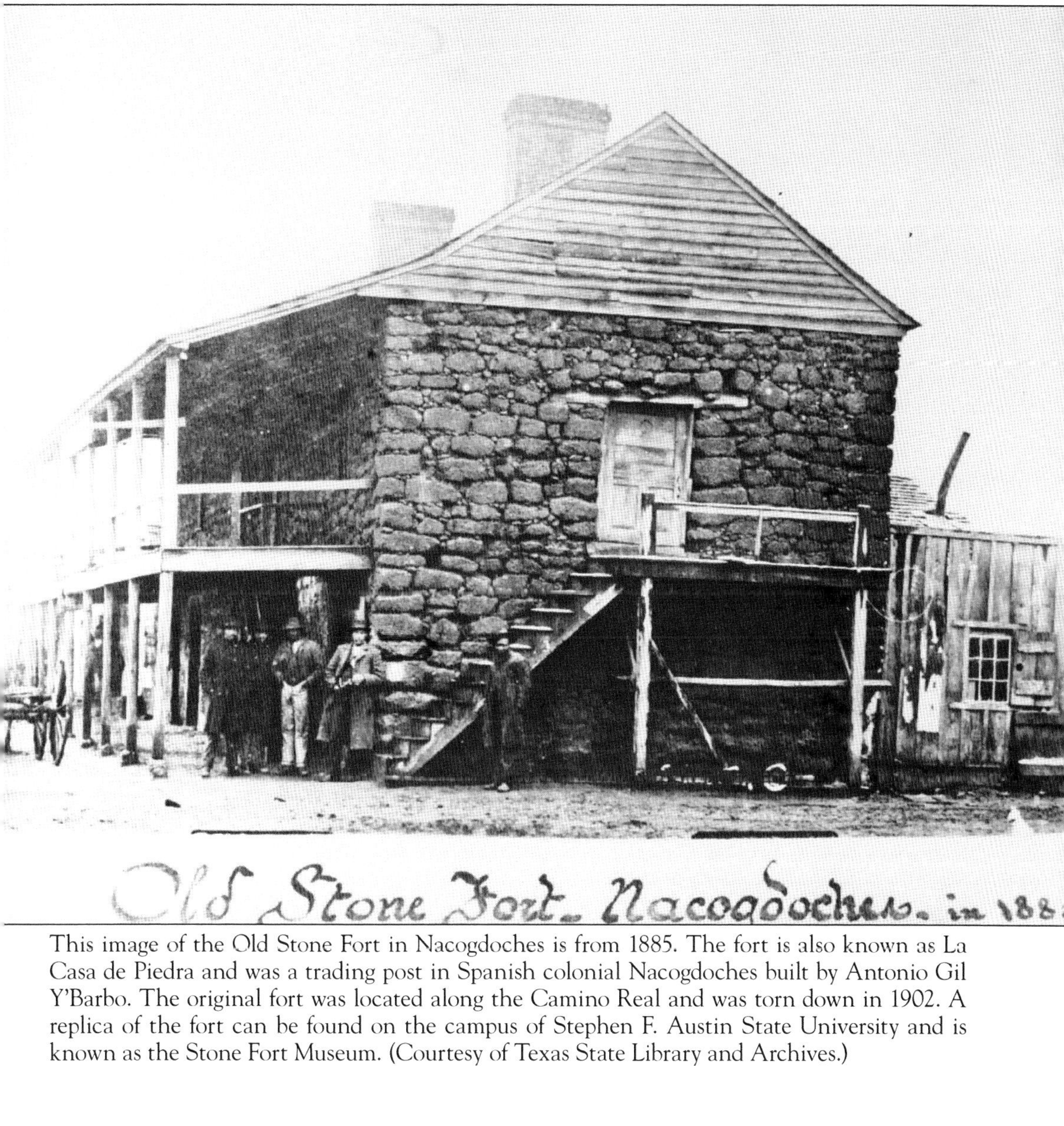


This image of the Old Stone Fort in Nacogdoches is from 1885. The fort is also known as La Casa de Piedra and was a trading post in Spanish colonial Nacogdoches built by Antonio Gil Y'Barbo. The original fort was located along the Camino Real and was torn down in 1902. A replica of the fort can be found on the campus of Stephen F. Austin State University and is known as the Stone Fort Museum. (Courtesy of Texas State Library and Archives.)

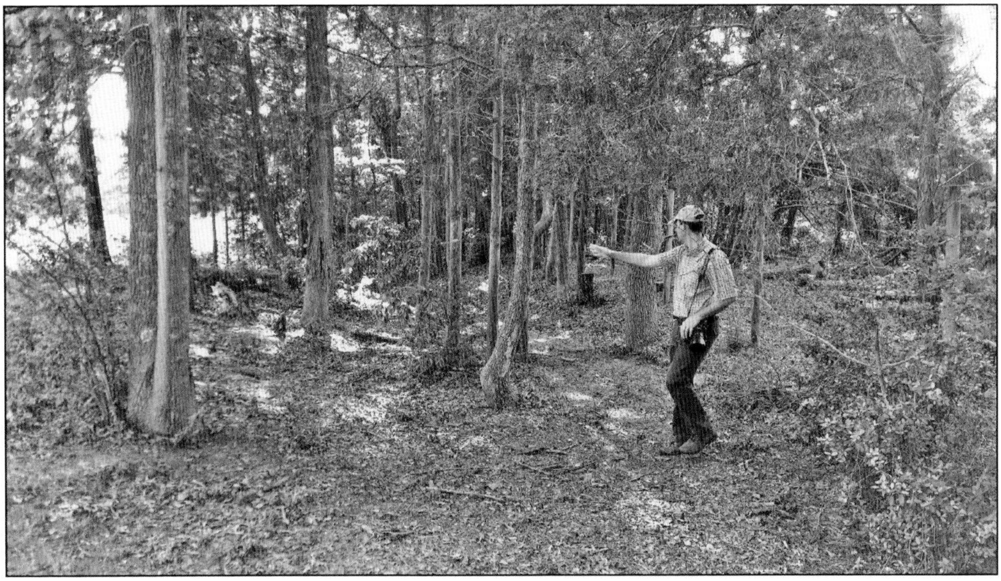

El Camino Real de los Tejas National Historic Trail Association board member Christopher Talbot is pictured here pointing out a Camino Real swale on his property in Nacogdoches County. As mentioned in an earlier chapter, the Camino Real often served as a boundary between properties. This is evident in this image, as one can see the barbed wire fence behind Christopher, running along the right bank of the swale. (Courtesy of Steven Gonzales.)

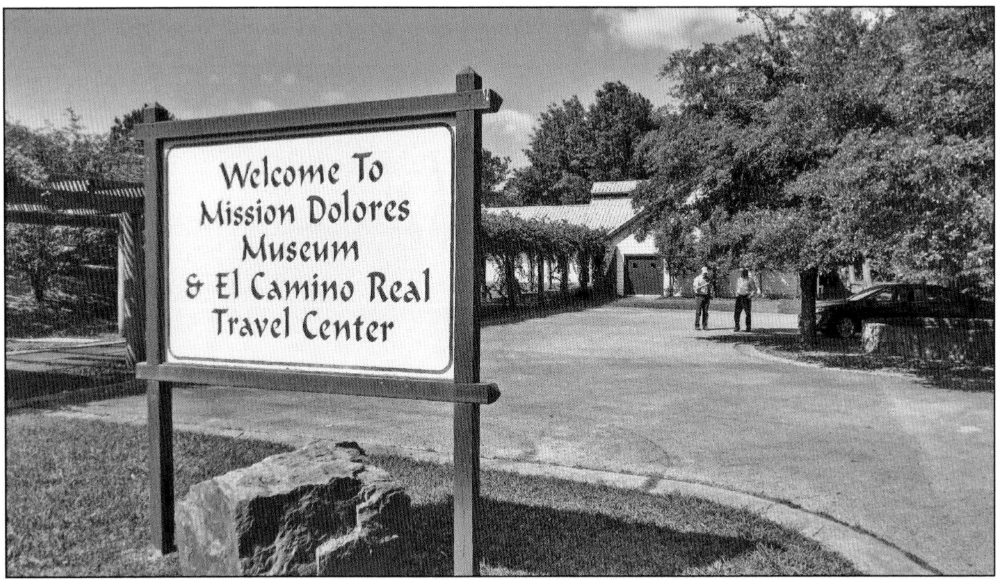


The Mission Dolores Museum and El Camino Real Travel Center is the only visitor center on the entire trail that is exclusively dedicated to El Camino Real. The site is located in San Augustine and is situated at the second site of Mission Nuestra Señora de los Dolores de los Ais. Stephen F. Austin State University also has an archaeological lab at the site where research of the trail is conducted. (Courtesy of Steven Gonzales.)

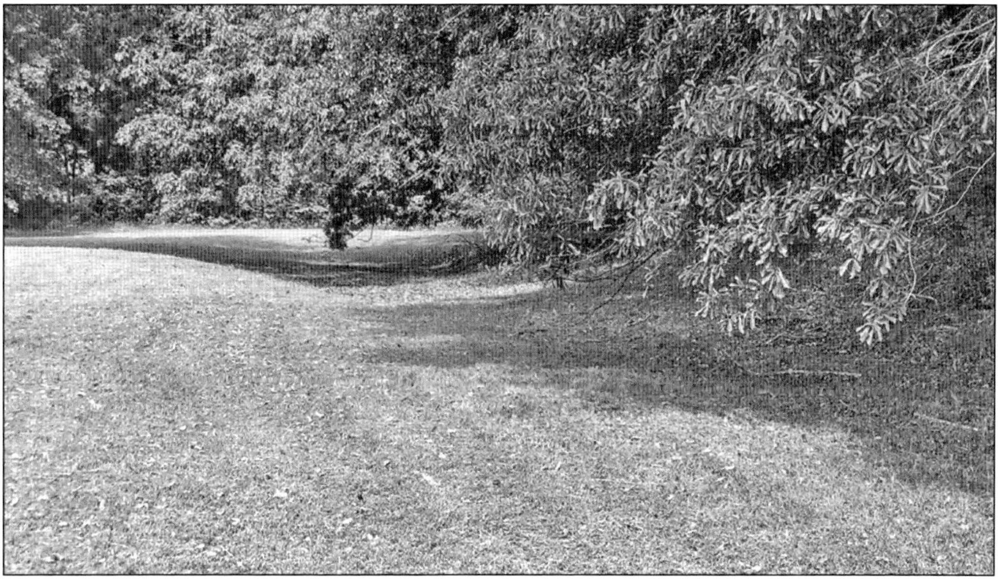

A swale can be seen across the street from Mission Dolores. A DAR marker and Texas Historical Commission marker are also nearby, and they tell the tale of the trail. (Courtesy of Steven Gonzales.)

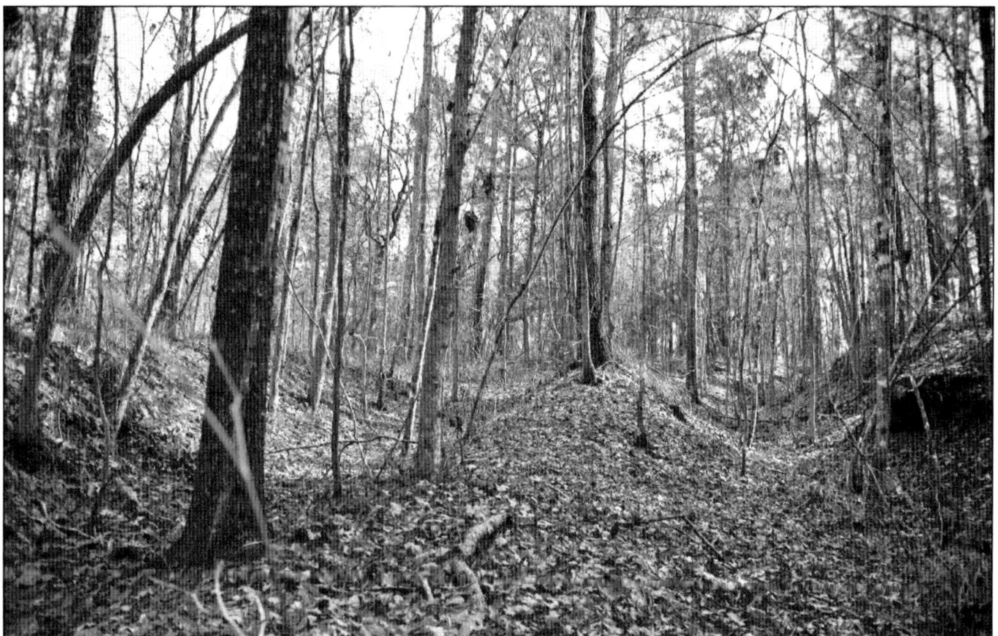

In far east Texas, there is a set of trail remnants that is unparalleled in its magnitude. Seven remnants of the Royal Road, as much as 20 feet deep and 12 feet wide, lie side-by-side as a sort of "superhighway." The site was recently acquired by El Camino Real de los Tejas National Historic Trail Association after a successful fundraising and publicity campaign run by Steven Gonzales. The association is developing a visitor use and stewardship plan for the site in conjunction with the National Park Service, and in the near future, it will be open to the public. (Courtesy of Steven Gonzales.)

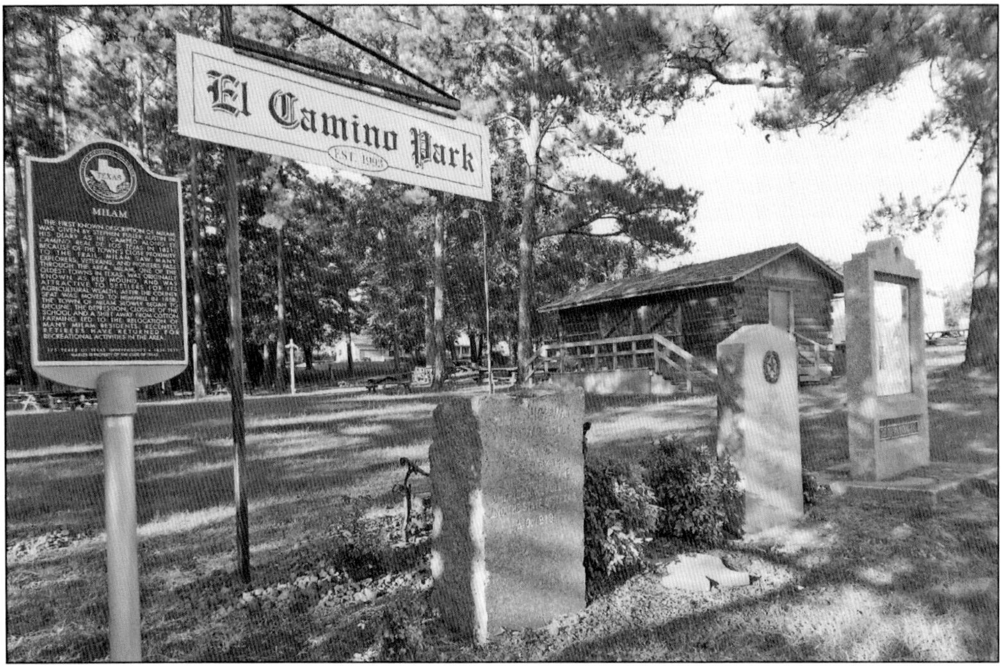


El Camino Park is located in Milam, Texas, just west of the junction of Highway 21 and Highway 87. It is a serene setting complete with a DAR marker and other historical markers about the trail and Milam. There is even a beautiful log cabin and picnic tables for a nice lunch underneath the pines. (Courtesy of Steven Gonzales.)

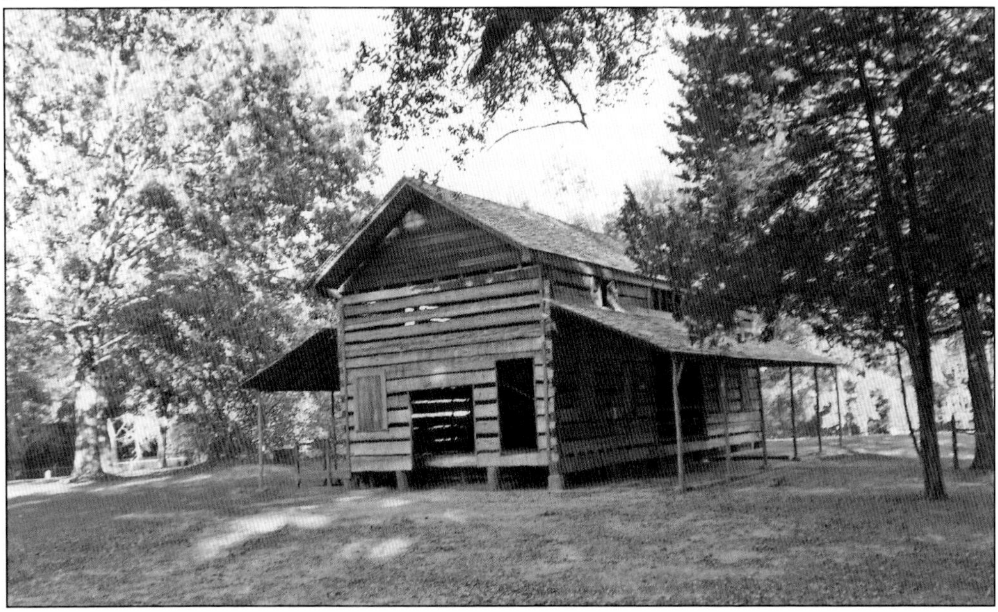

The Gaines-Oliphant House is one of the oldest pre-republic Anglo structures in Texas. Built around 1818 by James D. Taylor Gaines, the Oliphant House was situated near the strategic crossing of the Sabine River at what would become known as Gaines Ferry. The ferry was the main crossing of the Sabine, and as such, countless thousands of people crossed the river at this location while traveling the Camino Real. (Courtesy of Steven Gonzales.)

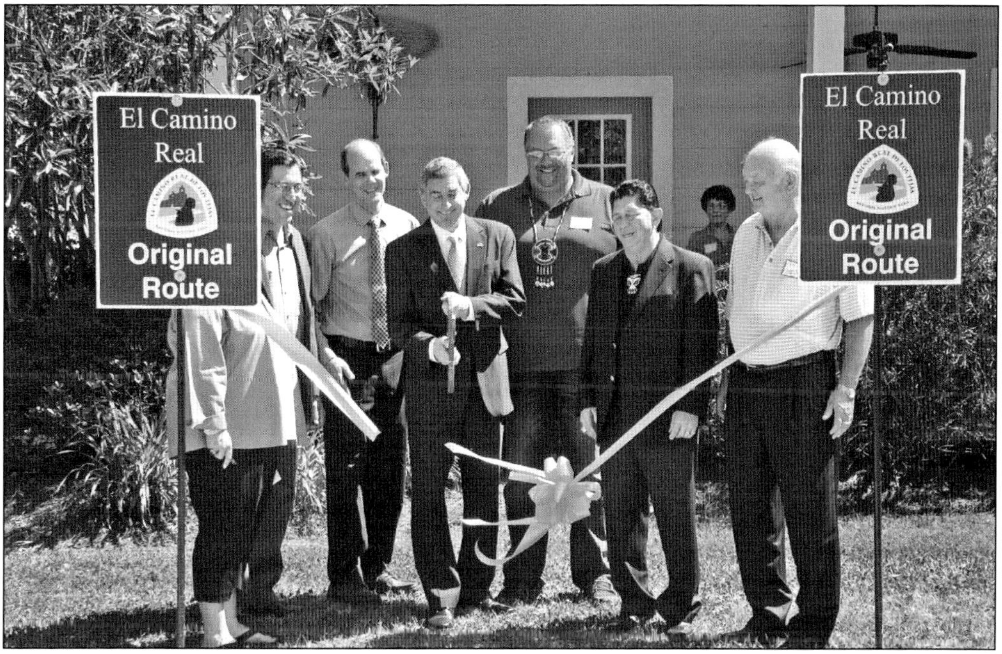


A ribbon cutting took place in Many, Louisiana, on May 6, 2014, to unveil over 40 miles of directional signage along the trail in the state. Association representatives, tribal leaders, and Louisiana lieutenant governor Jay Dardenne took part in the ceremony. Pictured from left to right are board member Linda Curtis-Sparks, executive director Steven Gonzales, board member Christopher Talbot, Lieutenant Governor Dardenne, Jack Rivers of the Choctaw Apache, board member and chief of the Adai Caddo Indian Nation Rufus Davis, and board member Duke Lyons. (Courtesy of Sabine Parish Tourist Commission.)

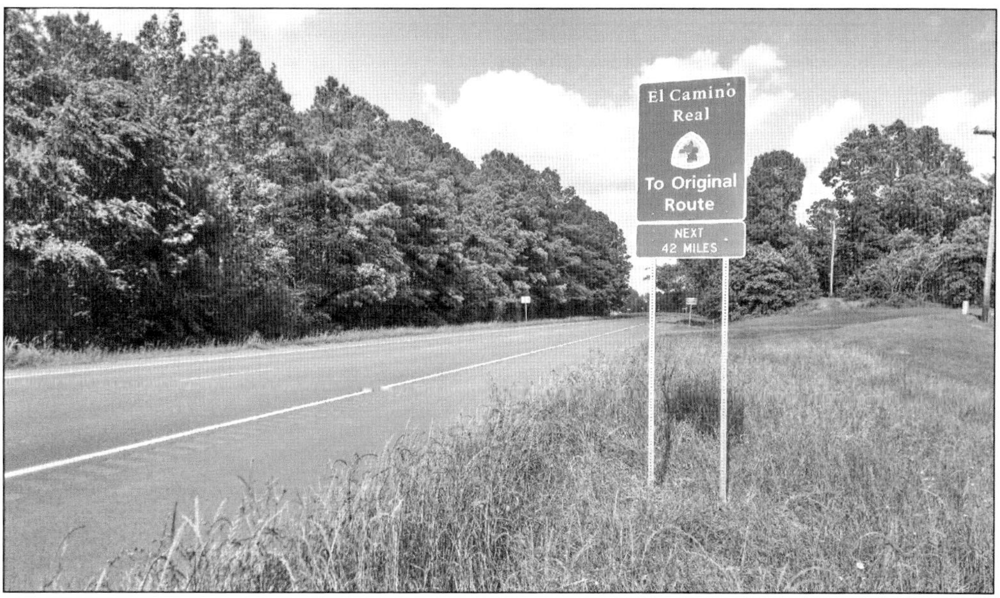


The state of Louisiana was the first place anywhere along the trail to have original route signage. Original route signs indicate to trail travelers that the modern roadway they are traveling is immediately on top of the historic route of the trail. (Courtesy of Steven Gonzales.)

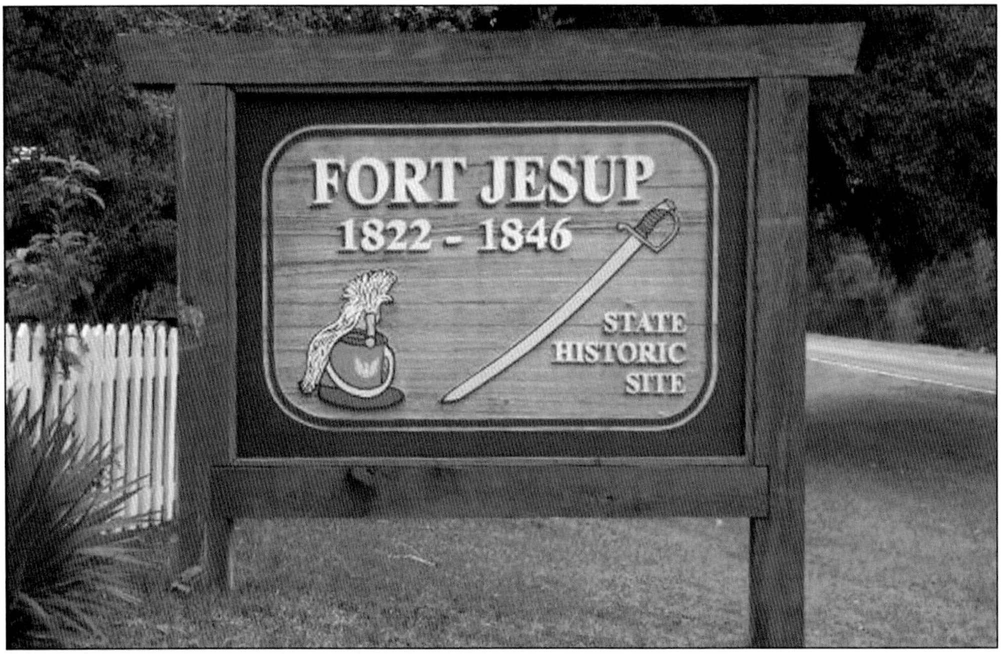


Fort Jesup was built in 1822 in an effort to bring law and order to the neutral ground that had flourished after the Louisiana Purchase failed to clearly establish boundaries. It operated as a fort for approximately 25 years and was abandoned in 1846. (Courtesy of the Sabine Parish Tourist Commission.)

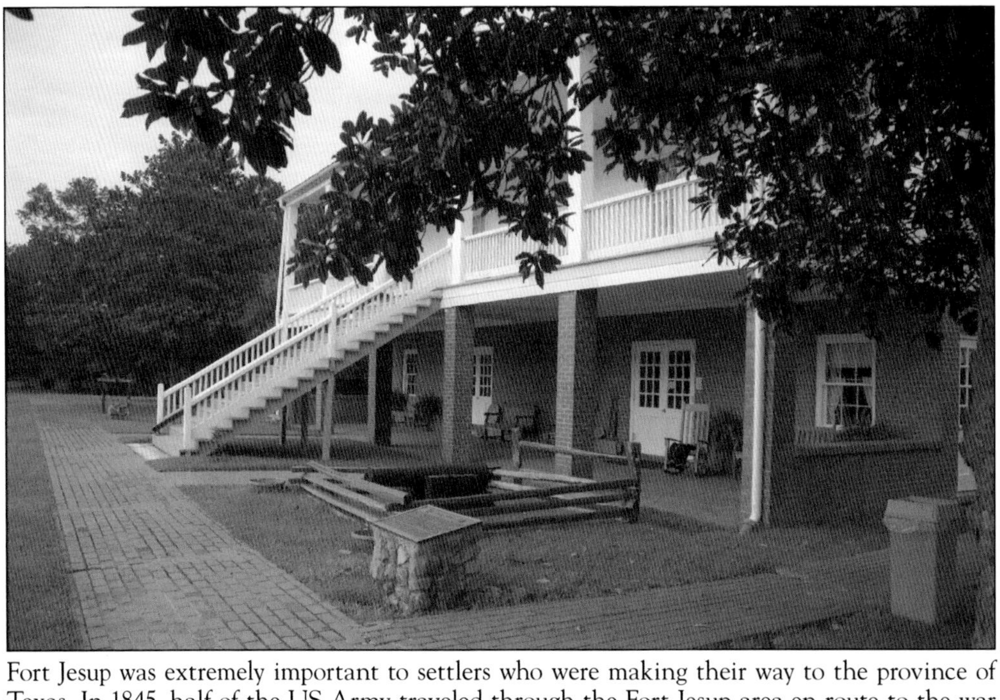

Fort Jesup was extremely important to settlers who were making their way to the province of Texas. In 1845, half of the US Army traveled through the Fort Jesup area en route to the war with Mexico. Located on El Camino Real, the fort once consisted of 82 structures. (Courtesy of the Sabine Parish Tourist Commission.)

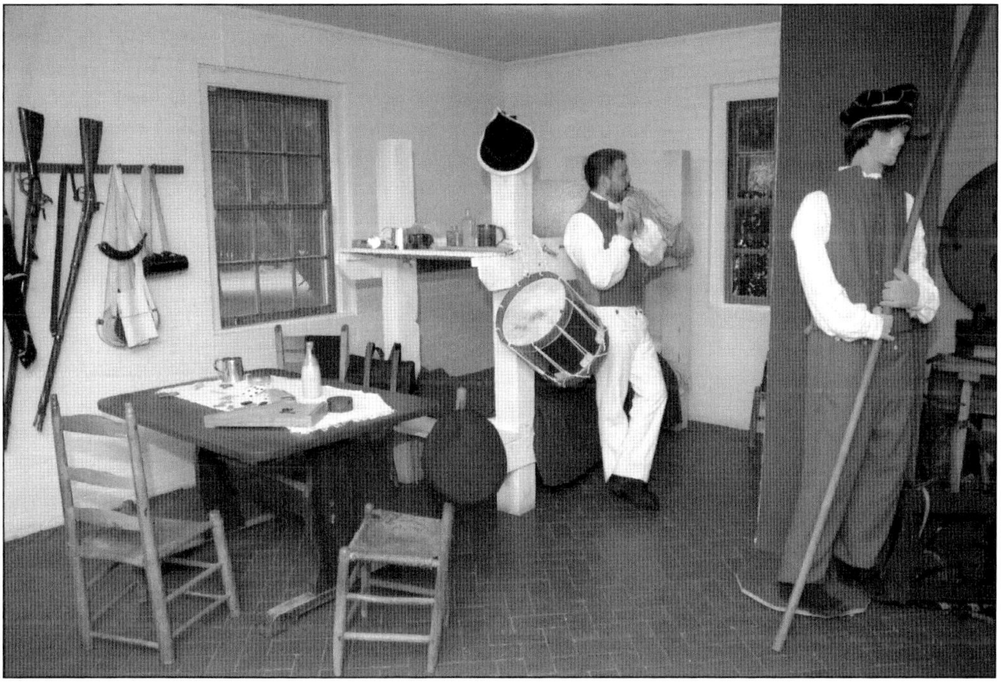

The replicas of the original structures are given life by people portraying the dress and activities of the time. (Courtesy of the Sabine Parish Tourist Commission.)

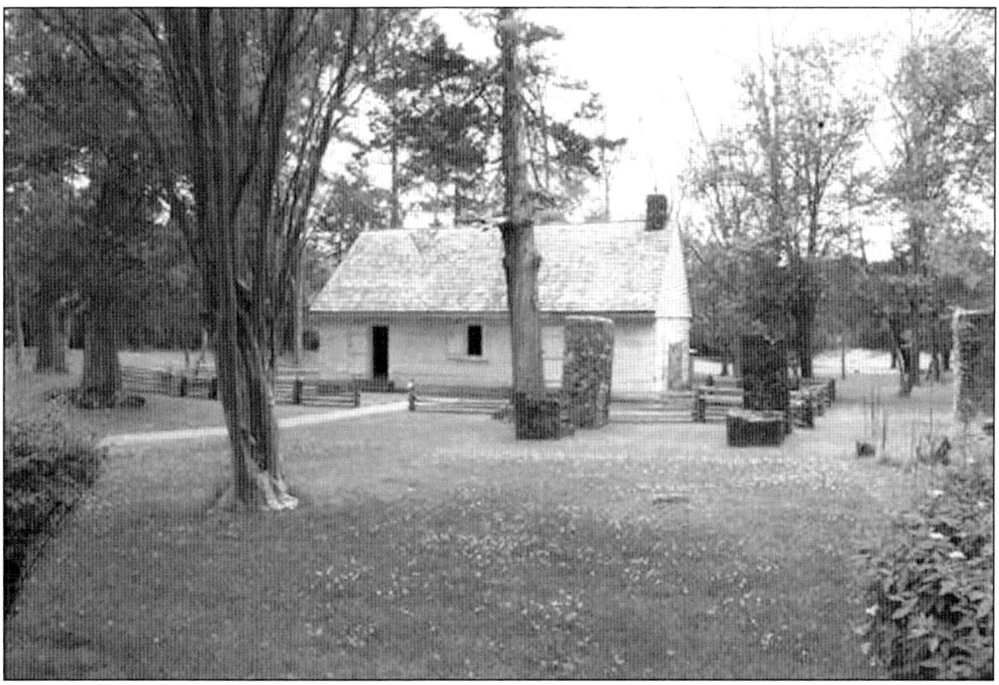

This is the kitchen of the original fort. It is the only original structure still standing. (Courtesy of the Sabine Parish Tourist Commission.)

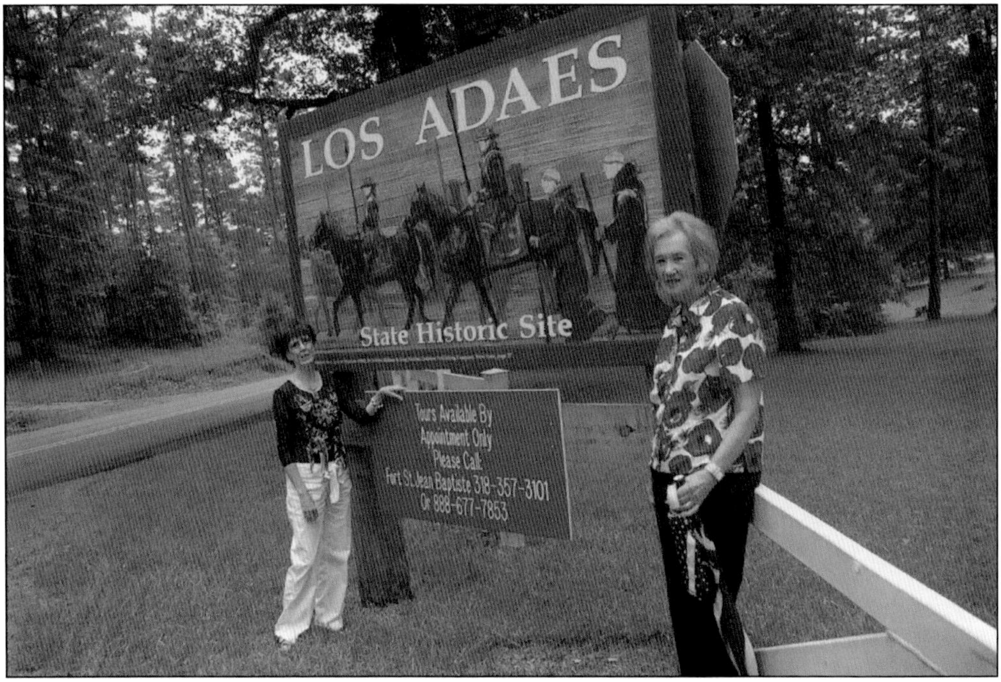


El Camino board members Maureen Winn (left) and Joy Graham (right) prepare to explore Los Adaes State Historic Site in Robeline, Louisiana. It is located on Louisiana State Highway 485, the same highway which leads to the present home of the Adai Caddo Indians. (Courtesy of Lucile Estell.)

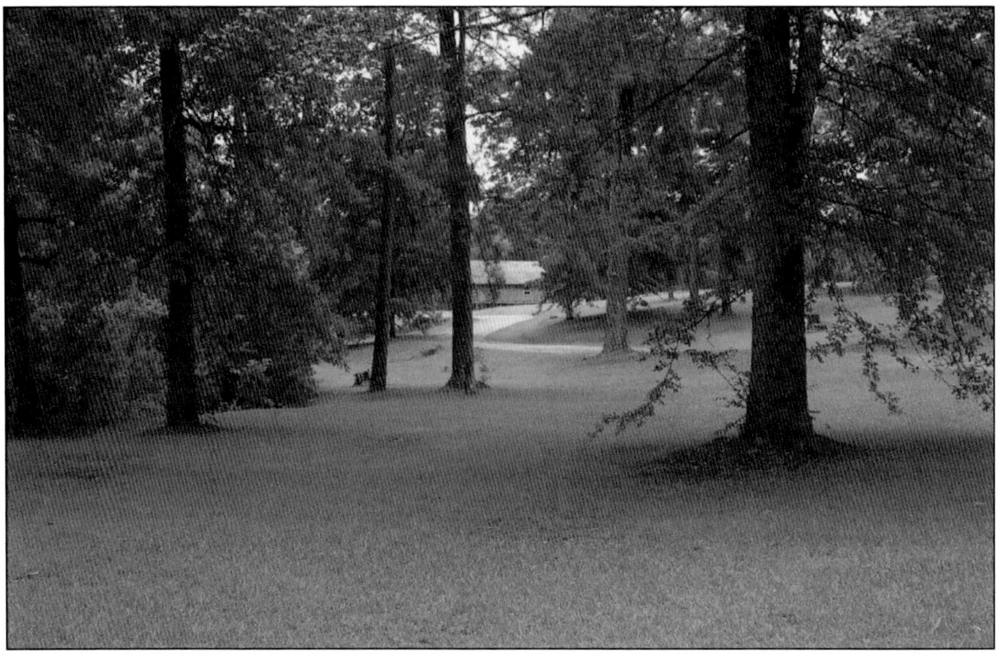

Today, a winding road leads to the main building at this location. Los Adaes dates back to the early 1700s, when a Franciscan missionary, Fr. Francisco Hidalgo, urged the French governor of Louisiana to establish a post near East Texas. (Courtesy of Lucile Estell.)

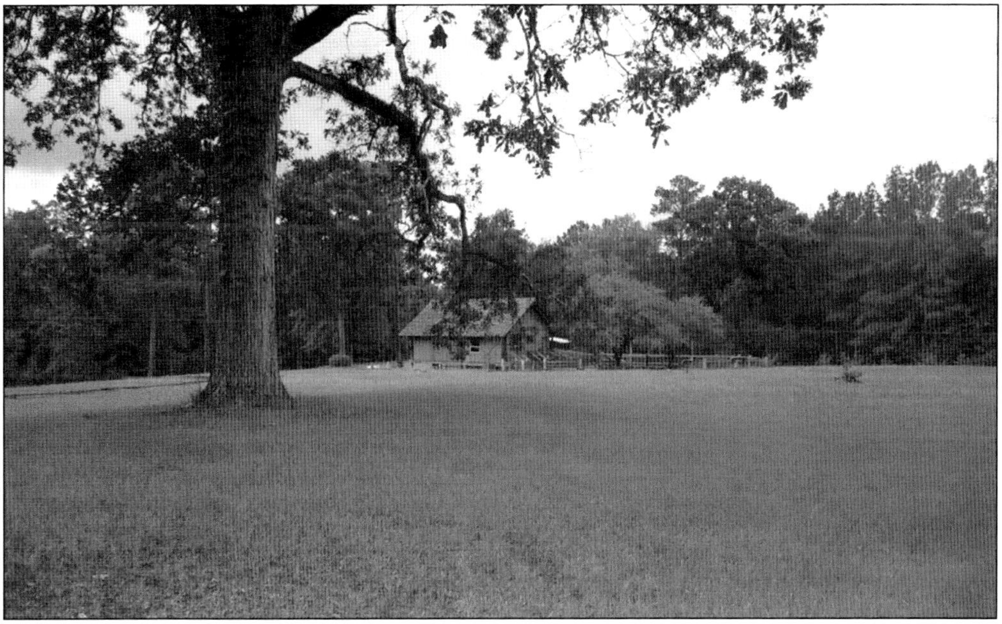

A new fort, the Presidio Nuestra Señora del Pilar de los Adaes (or, the Fort of Our Lady of Pilar at the Adaes) was built at Los Adaes. The fort was surrounded by a presidio in the shape of a hexagon. Interpretive signs show the location to today's visitors. In 1729, Spain designated Los Adaes as the capital of the Province of Texas. Los Adaes was the seat of government for the entire province for 44 years. (Courtesy of Lucile Estell.)

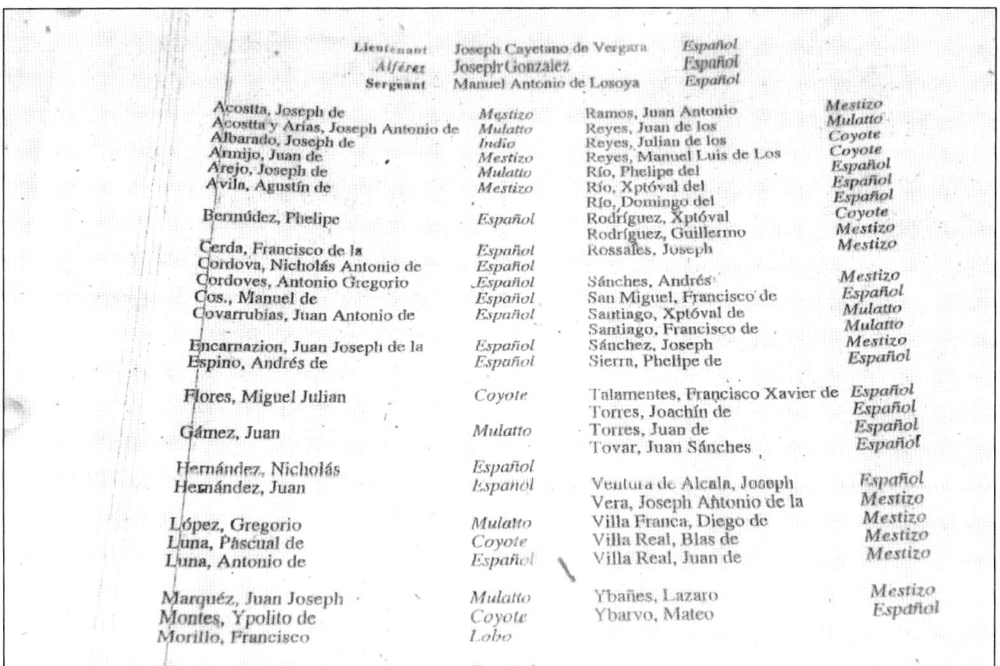

| | | |
|---|---|---|
| **Lieutenant** | Joseph Cayetano de Vergara | *Español* |
| *Alférez* | Joseph Gonzalez | *Español* |
| **Sergeant** | Manuel Antonio de Losoya | *Español* |

| | |
|---|---|
| Acostta, Joseph de | *Mestizo* |
| Acostta y Arias, Joseph Antonio de | *Mulatto* |
| Albarado, Joseph de | *Indio* |
| Armijo, Juan de | *Mestizo* |
| Arejo, Joseph de | *Mulatto* |
| Avila, Agustín de | *Mestizo* |
| Bermúdez, Phelipe | *Español* |
| Cerda, Francisco de la | *Español* |
| Cordova, Nicholás Antonio de | *Español* |
| Cordoves, Antonio Gregorio | *Español* |
| Cos., Manuel de | *Español* |
| Covarrubias, Juan Antonio de | *Español* |
| Encarnazion, Juan Joseph de la | *Español* |
| Espino, Andrés de | *Español* |
| Flores, Miguel Julian | *Coyote* |
| Gámez, Juan | *Mulatto* |
| Hernández, Nicholás | *Español* |
| Hernández, Juan | *Español* |
| López, Gregorio | *Mulatto* |
| Luna, Pàscual de | *Coyote* |
| Luna, Antonio de | *Español* |
| Marquéz, Juan Joseph | *Mulatto* |
| Montes, Ypolito de | *Coyote* |
| Morillo, Francisco | *Lobo* |
| Nápoles, Francisco de | *Español* |

| | |
|---|---|
| Ramos, Juan Antonio | *Mestizo* |
| Reyes, Juan de los | *Mulatto* |
| Reyes, Julian de los | *Coyote* |
| Reyes, Manuel Luis de Los | *Coyote* |
| Río, Phelipe del | *Español* |
| Río, Xptóval del | *Español* |
| Río, Domingo del | *Español* |
| Rodríguez, Xptóval | *Coyote* |
| Rodríguez, Guillermo | *Mestizo* |
| Rossales, Joseph | *Mestizo* |
| Sánches, Andrés | *Mestizo* |
| San Miguel, Francisco de | *Español* |
| Santiago, Xptóval de | *Mulatto* |
| Santiago, Francisco de | *Mulatto* |
| Sánchez, Joseph | *Mestizo* |
| Sierra, Phelipe de | *Español* |
| Talamentes, Francisco Xavier de | *Español* |
| Torres, Joachín de | *Español* |
| Torres, Juan de | *Español* |
| Tovar, Juan Sánches | *Español* |
| Ventura de Alcala, Joseph | *Español* |
| Vera, Joseph Antonio de la | *Mestizo* |
| Villa Franca, Diego de | *Mestizo* |
| Villa Real, Blas de | *Mestizo* |
| Villa Real, Juan de | *Mestizo* |
| Ybañes, Lazaro | *Mestizo* |
| Ybarvo, Mateo | *Español* |

Records on display at Los Adaes provide insight into how Los Adaes might have looked in its heyday. This listing provides information from the records that were kept about Los Adaes. (Courtesy of Lucile Estell.)

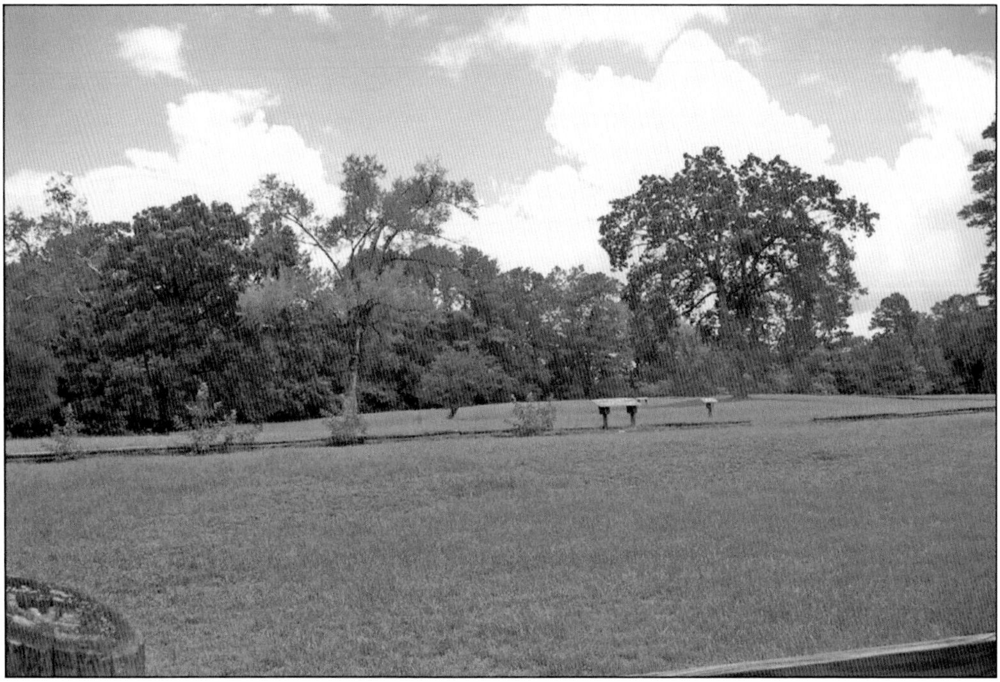

This peaceful scene does not convey how life really was at Los Adaes. The nearest supply post was 800 miles away, and supplies spoiled easily in the rainy weather. It was possible to trade with Natchitoches, but that was forbidden by Spain. (Courtesy of Lucile Estell.)

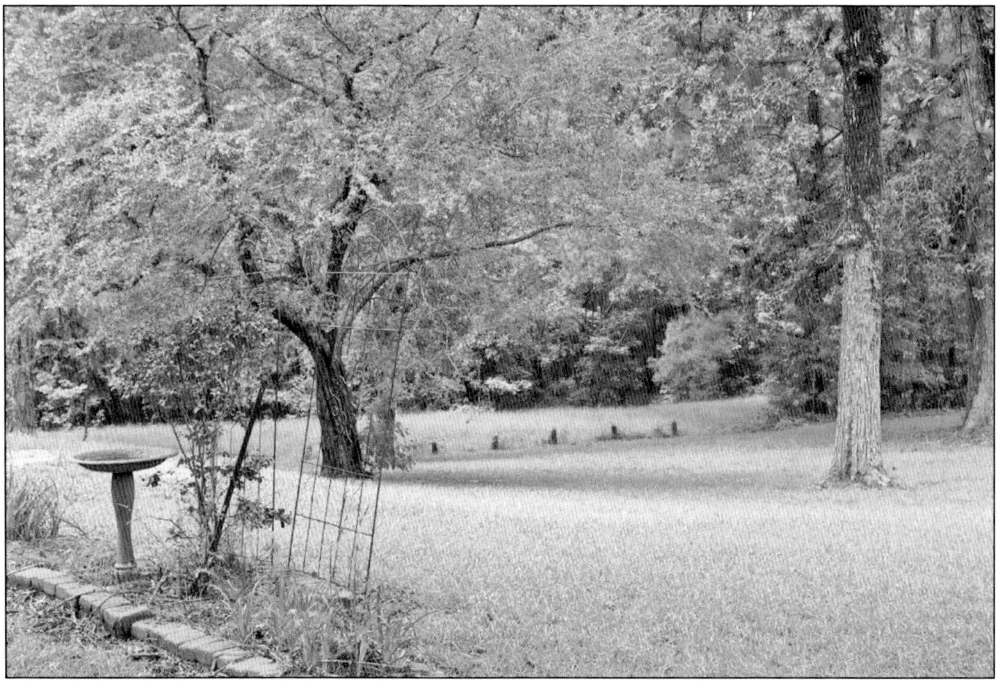

Los Adaes closed in 1772, and most of the people living there moved to San Antonio. Many later returned to Louisiana. (Courtesy of Lucile Estell.)

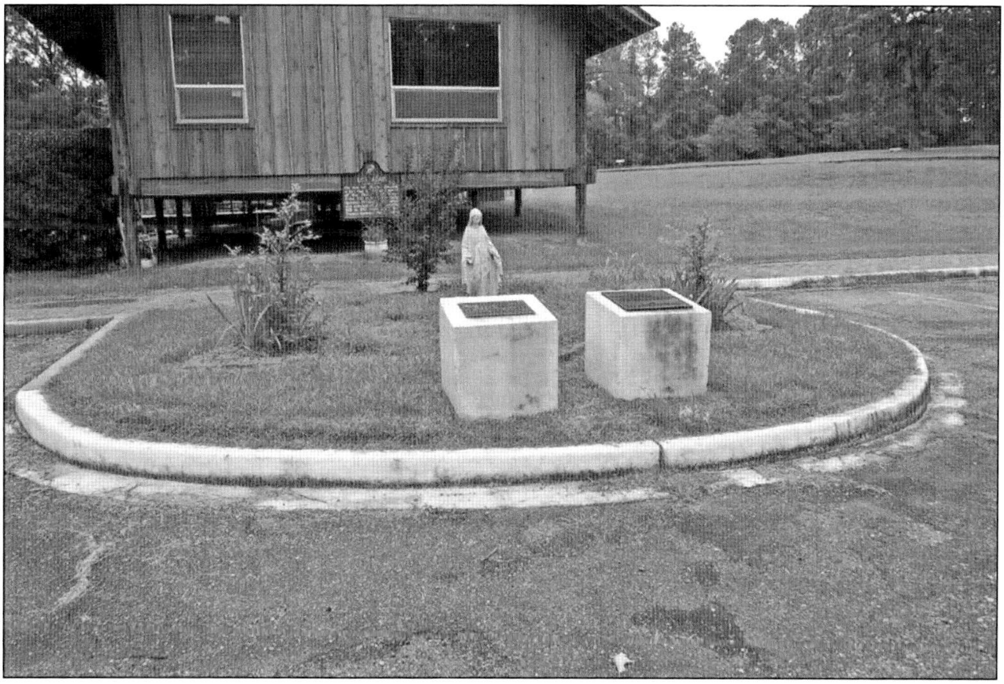

Today, Los Adaes is beautifully landscaped and arranged in such a way that visitors there can get a feeling for how life was along this important part of El Camino Real de los Tejas. (Courtesy of Lucile Estell.)

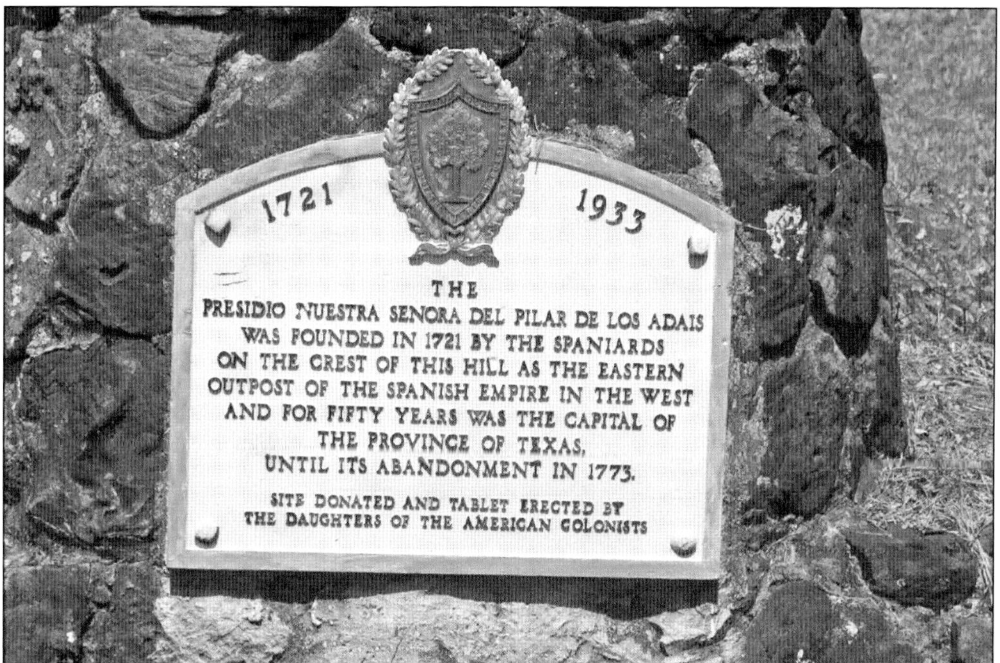


This plaque, located at the main building at Los Adaes, provides a summary of the importance of this vital link along El Camino Real. (Courtesy of Lucile Estell.)

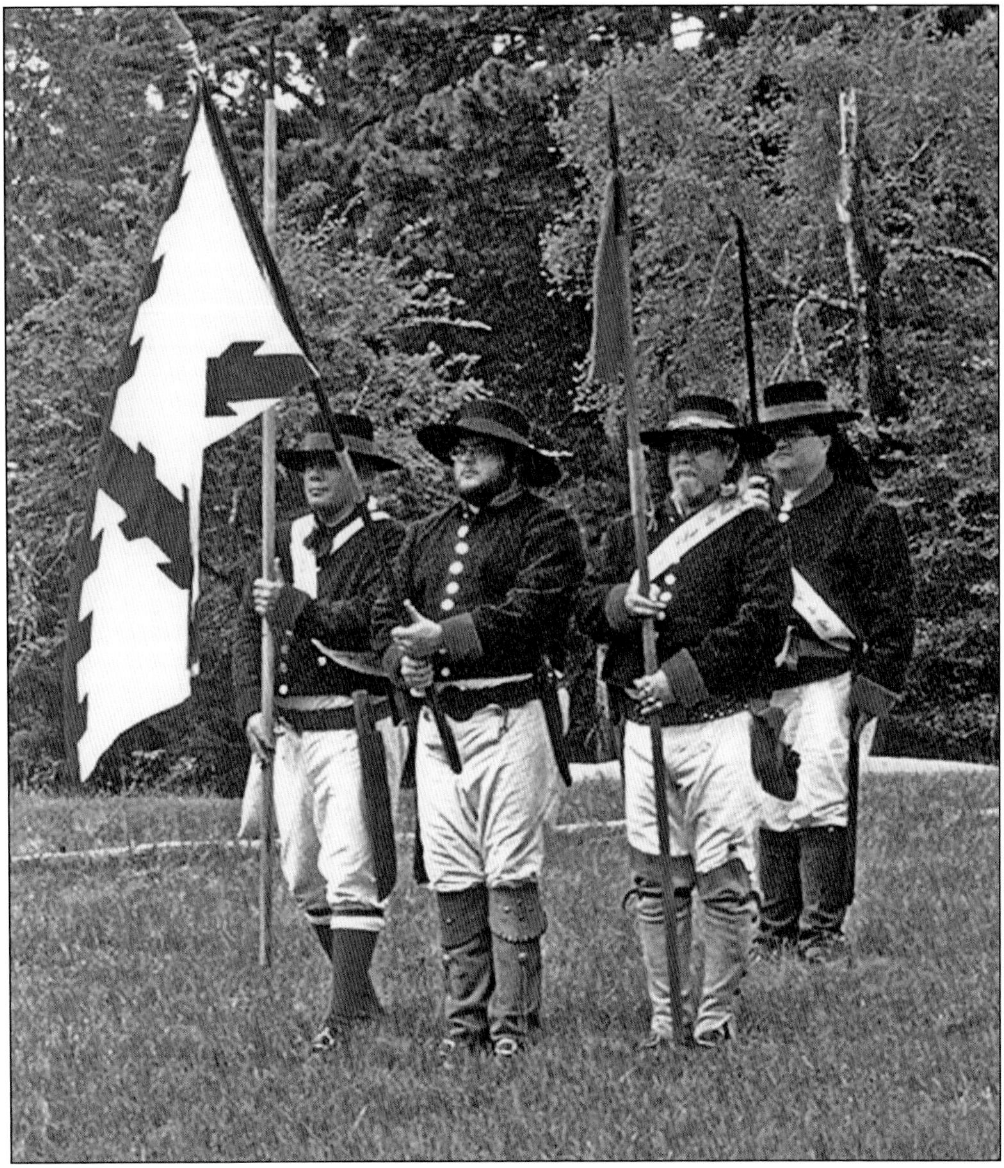

Los Adaes is truly one of the significant sites along El Camino Real de los Tejas National Historic Trail. The connection of Los Adaes to the Adai Caddo Indians and the proximity of this site to their cultural center (located a few miles from Los Adaes on Louisiana State Highway 485) make this area extremely important in the history of the trail. Pictured here are some of the reenactors who help preserve the site's legacy. (Courtesy of Jeff Williams.)

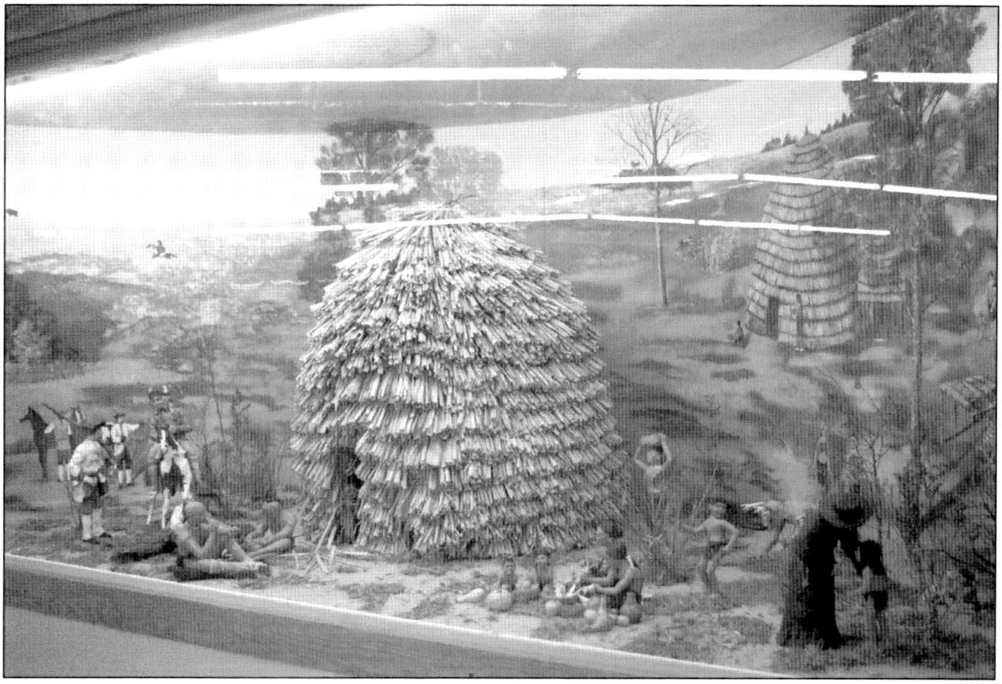

The Adai Caddo Indian Nation keeps a lovely cultural center (pictured above) near Robeline, Louisiana, and Los Adaes that explains much of their history while placing an emphasis on the profound influence that these people had in shaping American culture and in influencing the cultures of both Texas and Louisiana. The Adai Caddo Indian Nation was among the first native groups to be influenced by Spanish explorers in Texas in the early 1500s. An annual powwow is held at the Adai Caddo Cultural Center each October. The head of the Adai Caddo Indians is Chief Rufus Davis (at left in the picture to the right), who is also a member of the board of El Camino Real de los Tejas Historic Trail Association. Also pictured is Andrew Sansom, first president of El Camino Real de los Tejas National Historic Trail Association. (Both, courtesy of Lucile Estell.)

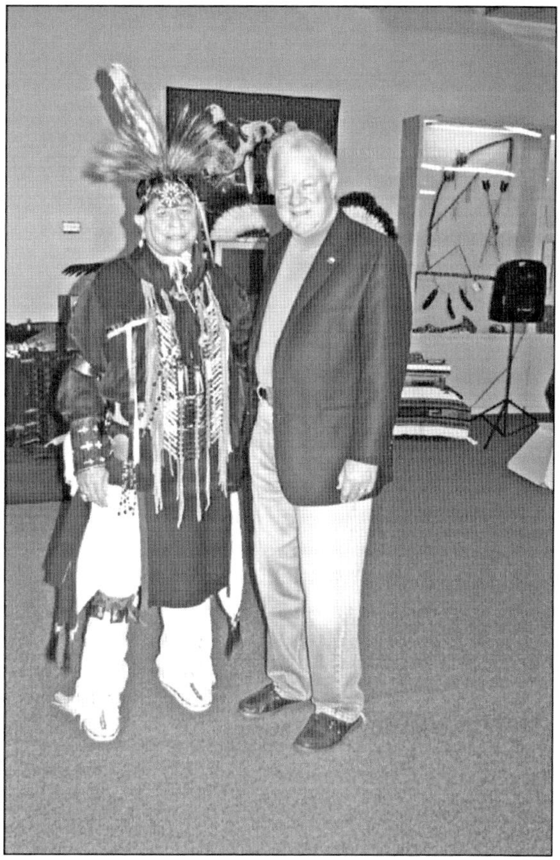

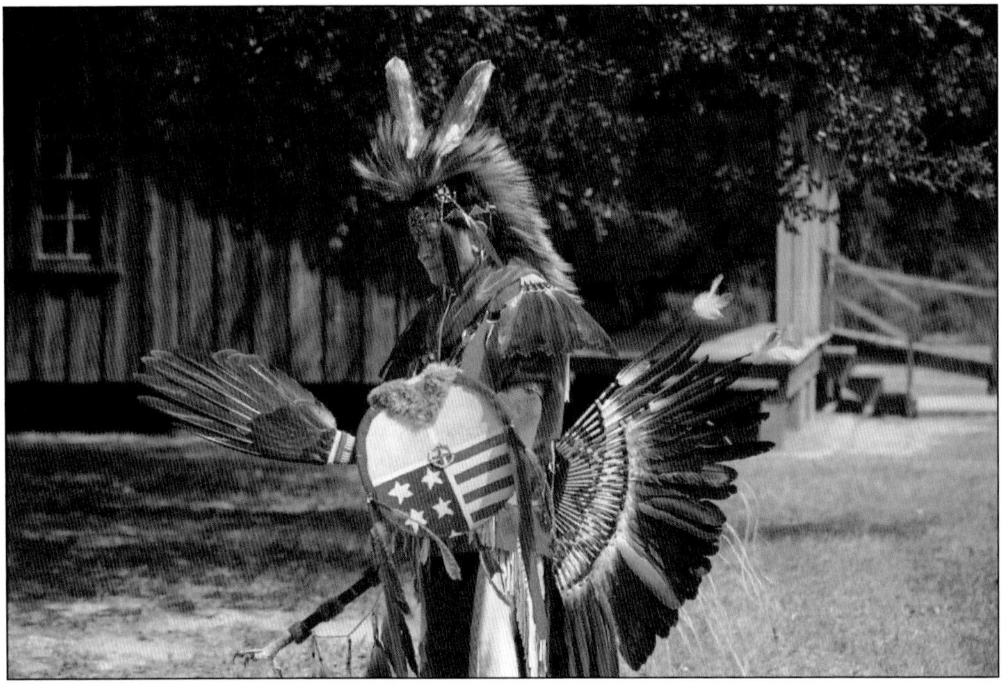

The Adai Caddo Indian Nation continues to play an important role in the development of El Camino Real de los Tejas National Historic Trail. Their chief, Rufus Davis, is an active member of El Camino Real's board of directors, and two of the annual meetings of the board have been held in conjunction with the annual powwow in Robeline. The very name of this trail, El Camino Real de los Tejas, the Royal Road of the Tejas, emphasizes how strong the influence of these Native Americans was in the development of this Royal Road. (Both, courtesy of Chief Rufus Davis.)

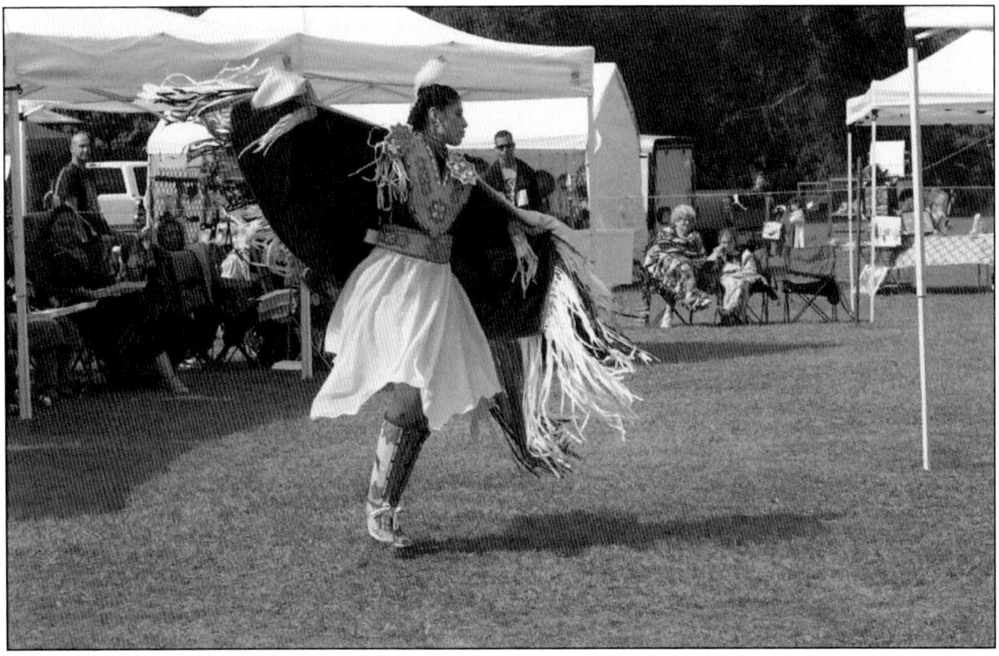

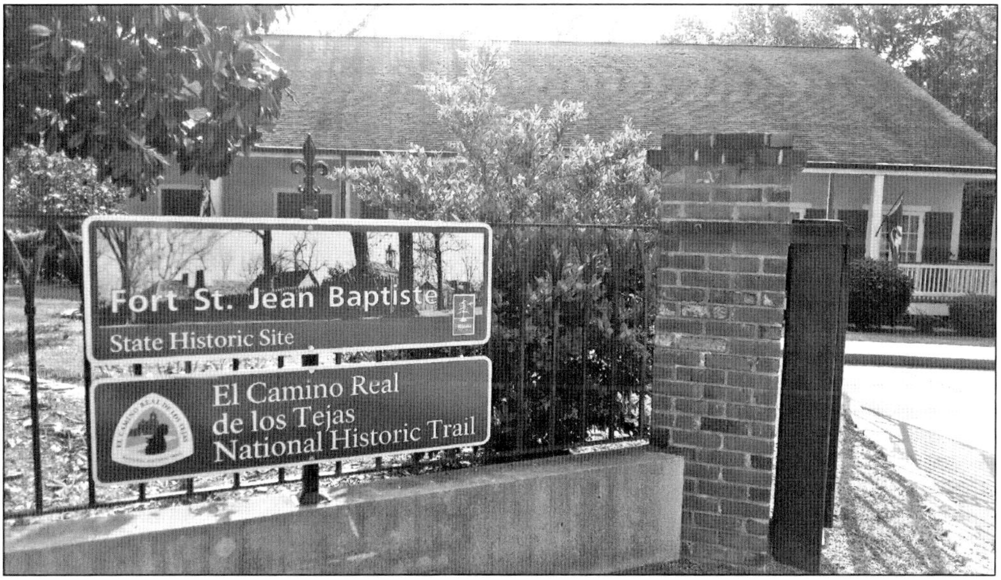

The Fort St. Jean Baptiste State Historic Site is located at 155 Jefferson Street in Natchitoches, Louisiana. The fort was built in an effort to stop the Spanish from advancing into French territory and served as a military outpost until 1762, when the Louisiana Colony was ceded to Spain. (Courtesy of the Sabine Parish Tourist Commission.)

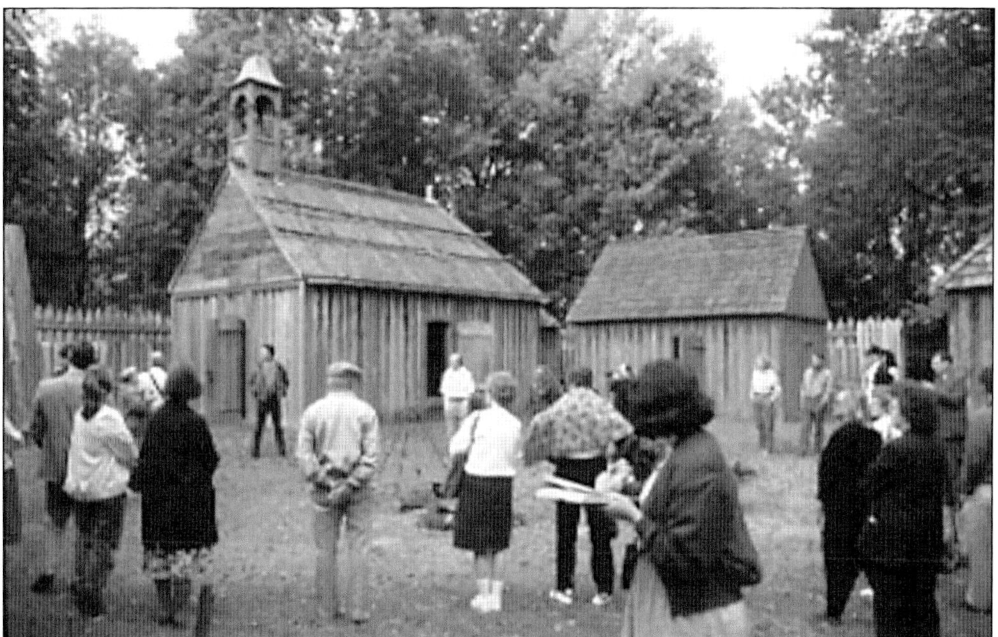
Construction of a replica of the fort began in 1979. It is located on the Cane River a few hundred yards from the original site. The replica was based on extensive archival research to ensure its authenticity. (Courtesy of Steven Gonzales.)

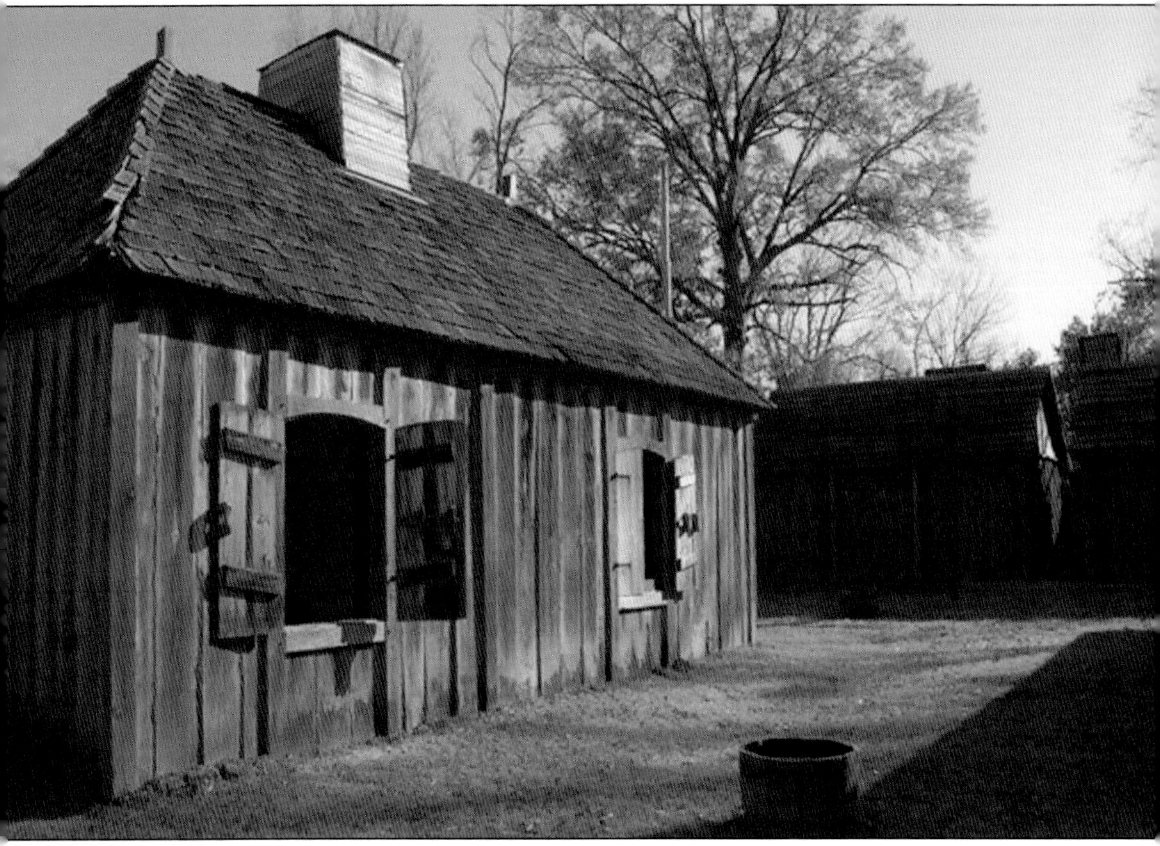

The replicas of buildings on this historic site are as authentic as possible. Nearly 2,000 treated pine logs and 250,000 feet of treated lumber went into their construction. Research continues today to ensure the authenticity of this replication. A trip to this site provides the visitor with insight as to what life was like along this portion of El Camino Real in the 18th century. (Courtesy of the Sabine Parish Tourist Commission.)

Visitors to this historic site have an opportunity to immerse themselves in the rich history of Natchitoches. Natchitoches was actually founded by a French Canadian, Louis Antoine Juchereau de St. Denis. (Courtesy of the Sabine Parish Tourist Commission.)

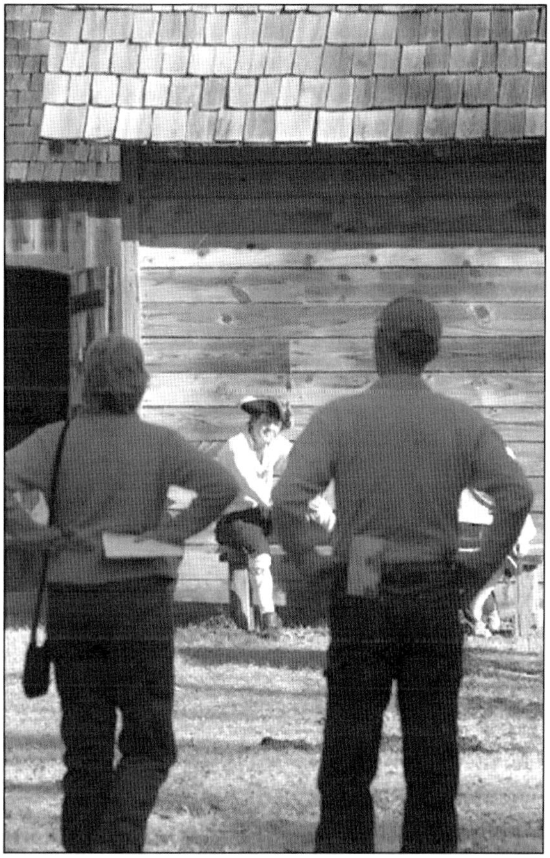

Visitors can also see how Fort St. Jean Baptiste was defended. The detailed replication of the fort makes a visit interesting for young and old alike. (Courtesy of the Sabine Parish Tourist Commission.)

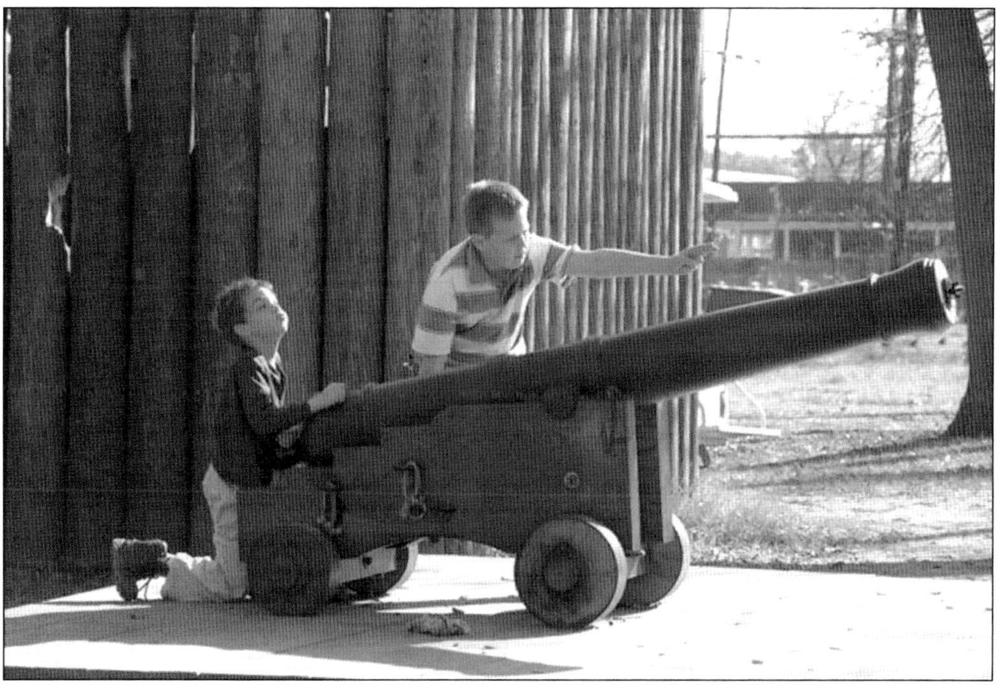

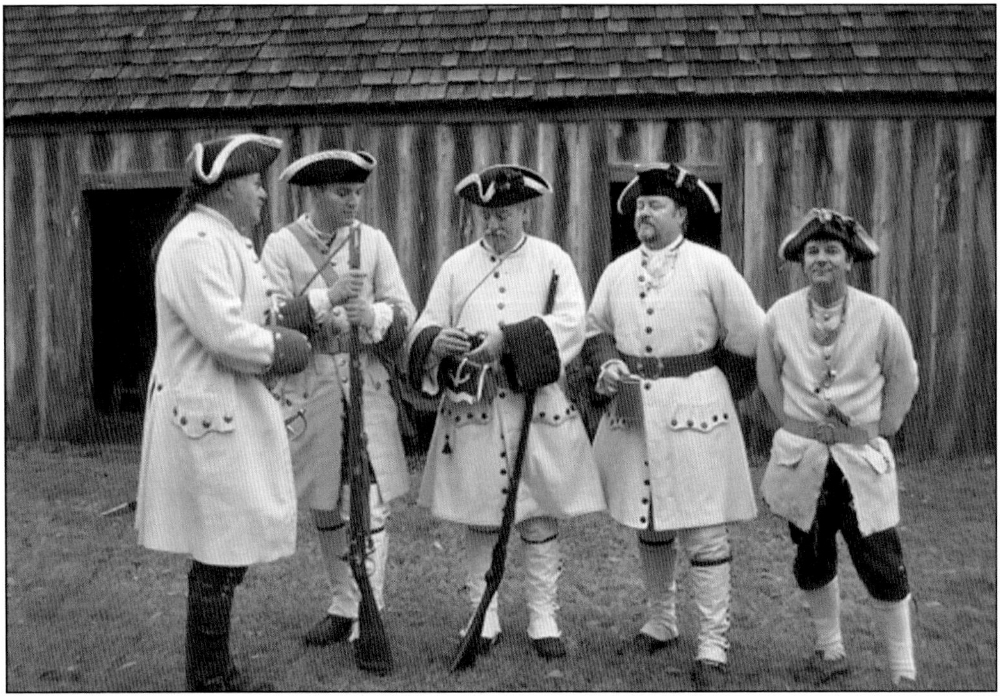

A living history program brings excitement and interest to this historic site. Authentic uniforms and well-researched reenactments contribute to the success of this program. (Courtesy of the Sabine Parish Tourist Commission.)

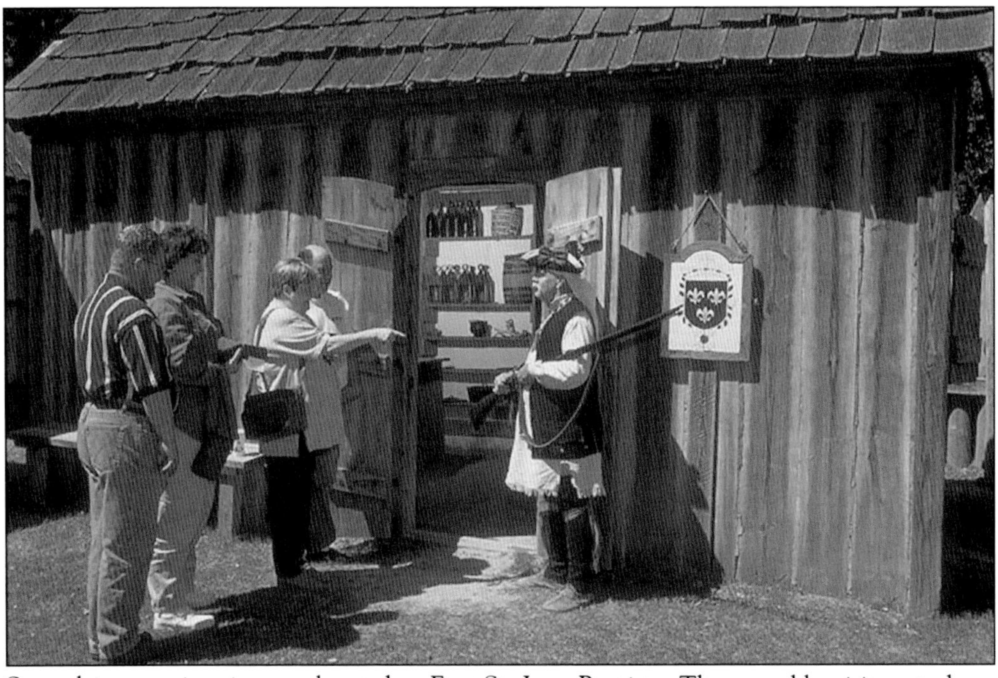

Several interpretive sites are located at Fort St. Jean Baptiste. These enable visitors to have hands-on experiences, which contribute to an understanding of what life was like in the days when the fort was in operation. (Courtesy of the Sabine Parish Tourist Commission.)

# *Five*

# Advocacy, Education, and the Future

It can be said that many a valiant person has traversed El Camino Real de los Tejas. From the time of de León to that of David Crockett and beyond, renowned figures have built the history of the Camino. Describing such a thing can be difficult, but Dr. J. Francisco de la Teja said it well when he stated, "How then to describe the camino real? First, it might almost be considered a living thing: ever changing its humors, taking on new roles and responsibilities, responding to the needs of a developing frontier province. The obstacles of travel on the road made the wayfarer respectful and fearful of it. Anyone wishing to go from Texas to the rest of the world had to be patient with the road, for it had a slow and evasive nature. Second, the caminos were the arteries that kept Texas alive."

What Dr. de la Teja said still applies to the Camino Real in modern times. The road is constantly taking on new roles and responsibilities as it is protected and developed. It still has a slow and evasive nature that is seen daily as association members work to develop signage, visitor use plans, and interpretive material for the trail. It all takes time, and time is something that El Camino Real has.

With that in mind, it is important to know that "el camino" means not only "the road" but also "the journey" and "the way." The association journeys on this road daily in an effort to protect it and raise awareness about its national significance. And so, it issues a call to join in its effort to protect a piece of irreplaceable history and ensure that the road that led to the founding of Texas is not forgotten.

Please visit www.elcaminorealdelostejas.org for more information or to donate to the effort to protect El Camino Real de los Tejas National Historic Trail. The Camino Real is a living, breathing artery in Texas, and, with readers' help, it can stay that way.

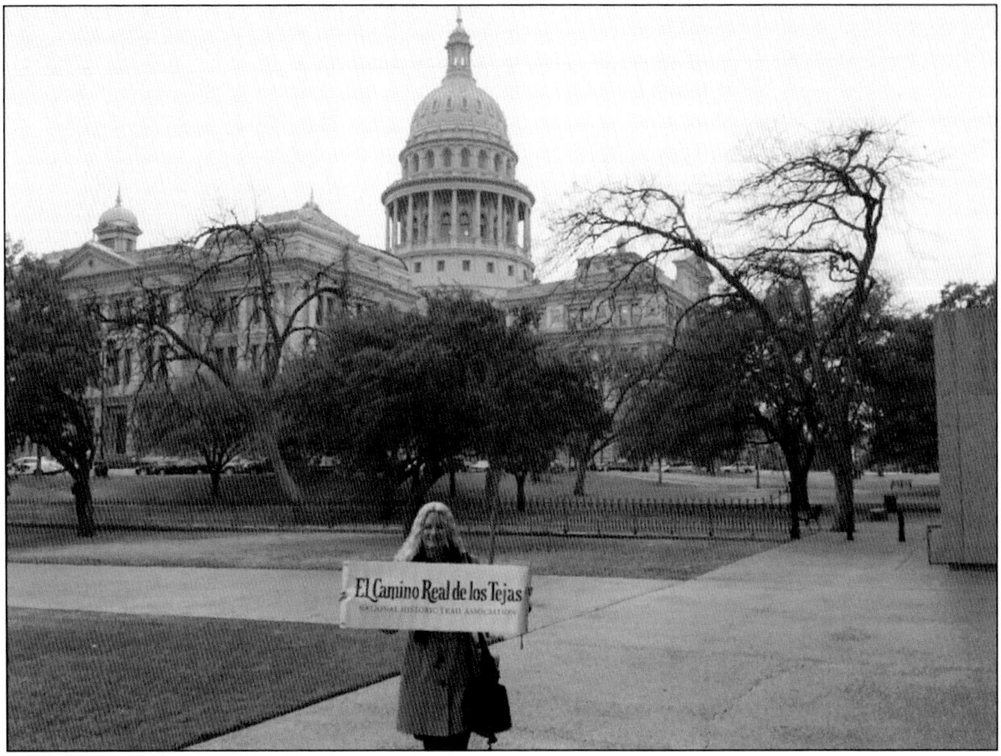


Here, Mo Brown is advocating for El Camino Real de los Tejas National Historic Trail at the Texas State Capitol in Austin in February 2013. (Courtesy of Steven Gonzales.)

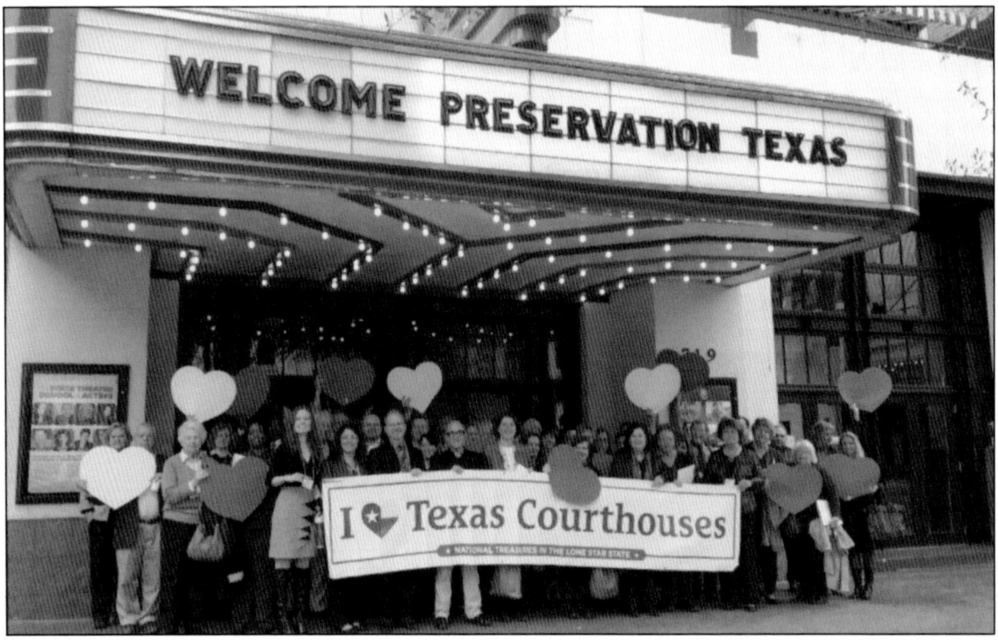


Mo Brown and Steven Gonzales advocated for El Camino Real by taking part in the 2013 Preservation Day in Austin along with preservationists from around the state. (Courtesy of Maureen Brown.)

Steven Gonzales and Mo Brown are in Washington, DC, in this photograph advocating for the funding of El Camino Real de los Tejas National Historic Trail. While there, they met with Congressional representatives from Texas and Lousiana. (Courtesy of Steven Gonzales.)

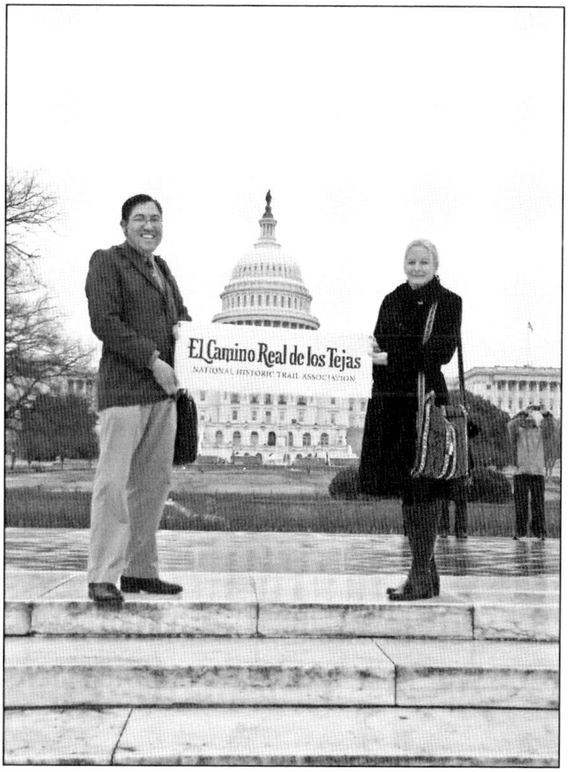


El Camino Real de los Tejas National Historic Trail Association's office is located in Austin, Texas. Executive director Steven Gonzales—under the direction of a 15-member board of directors—is responsible for the development of the association and working with the National Park Service. Jordan Mitchell (left) and Joel Schmitt (right) are interns at these offices. (Courtesy of Steven Gonzales.)

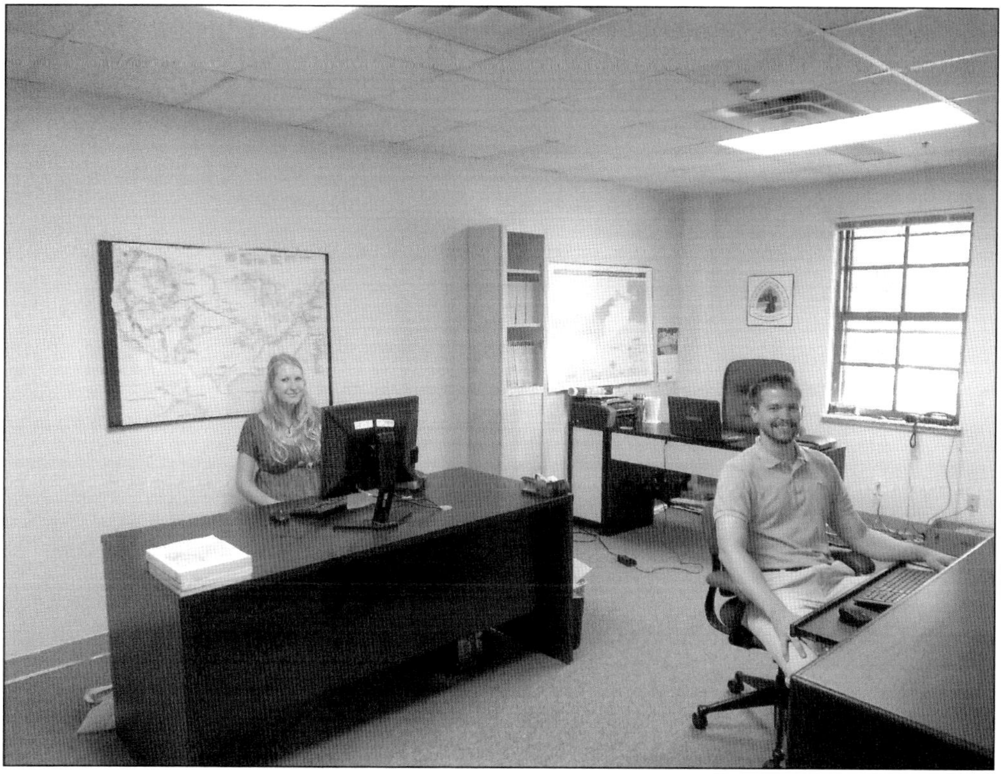

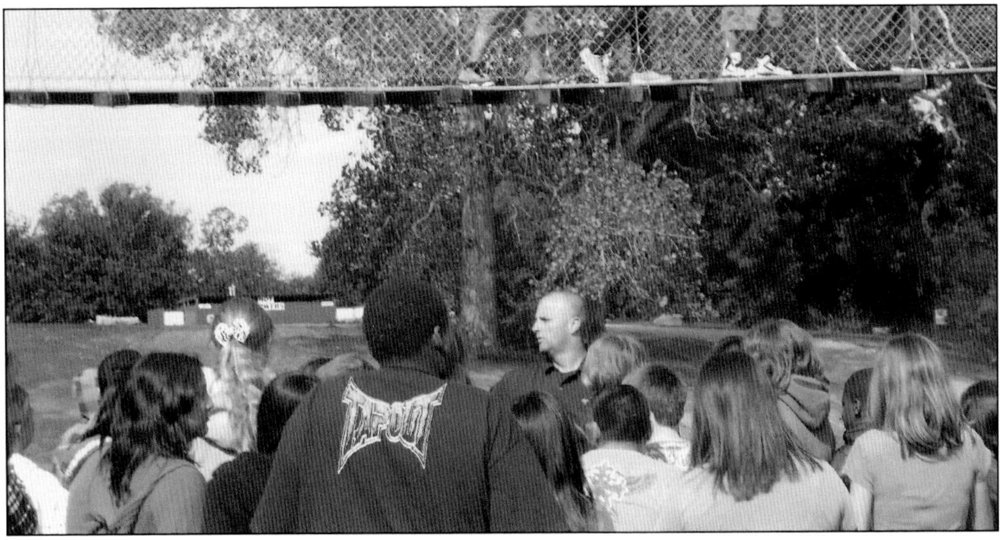


Educating children and teenagers about the importance of the trail is the most significant aspect of the trail's future. As the leaders of tomorrow, young people will determine what is important in their time and what they stand for. As such, it is essential that today's young people understand the importance of El Camino Real de los Tejas, because they will be the future stewards of the trail. Every year, the association hosts an annual statewide videoconference on El Camino Real for fourth- and seventh-grade Texas history students, reaching a growing number of children each year. By instilling the importance of the trail in them, the association can ensure that it will be taken care of for generations to come. (Courtesy of Steven Gonzales.)

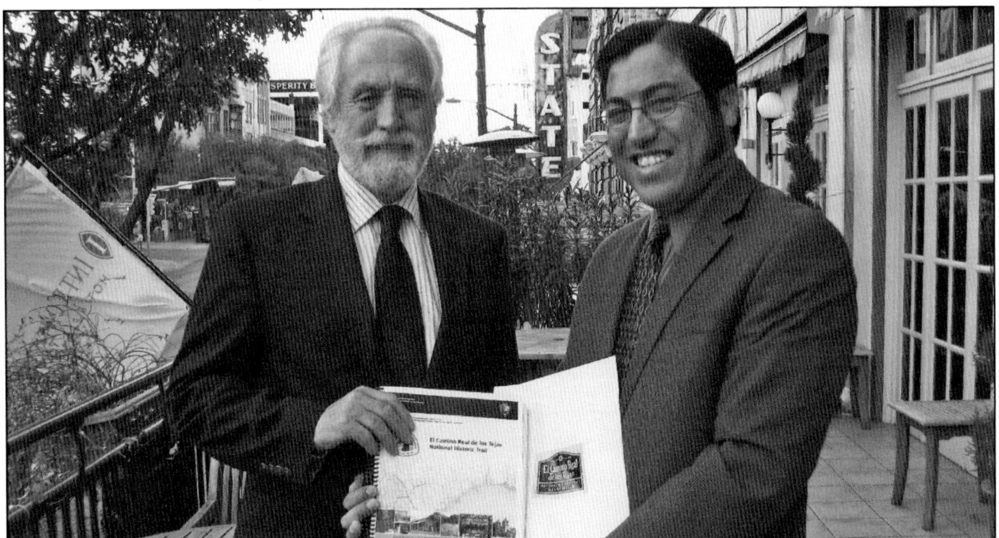


The future of El Camino Real de los Tejas National Historic Trail will be greatly enhanced by partnerships between El Camino Real de los Tejas National Historic Trail Association, the National Park Service, and other interested parties. An example of these collaborations can be seen in their partnership with the consul general of Spain, Miguel A. Fernández de Mazarambroz. The consul general (left) is pictured here with association executive director Steven Gonzales (right) as they plan for a symposium and exhibit on El Camino Real. (Courtesy of Steven Gonzales.)

The future of protecting and developing the trail also depends on signing the trail with official National Park Service signage. Placing signs along the trail will guide visitors to trail sites and allow the public to know where the trail is. Pictured from left to right are Russell Niemtschk, Billy Felfe, Jeremy Hoskins (in the bucket), Kelton Kroeger, and Precinct 4 commissioner Jeff Muegge. (Courtesy of Joy Graham.)

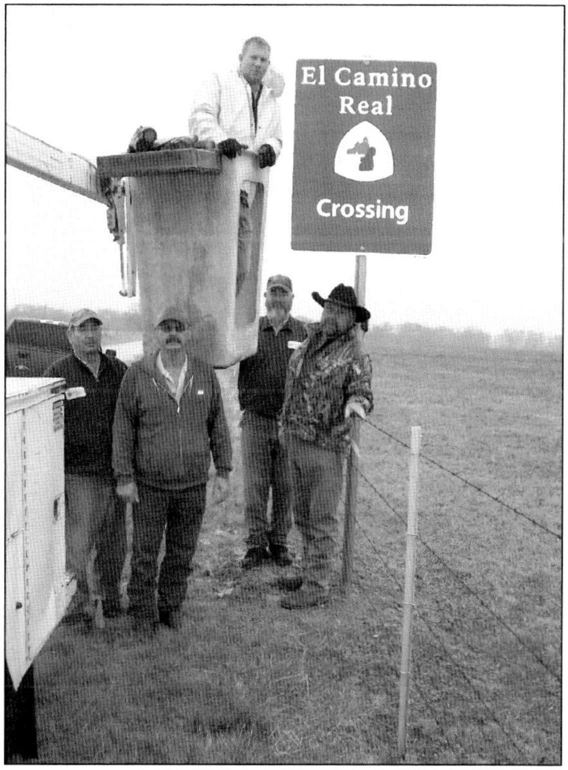


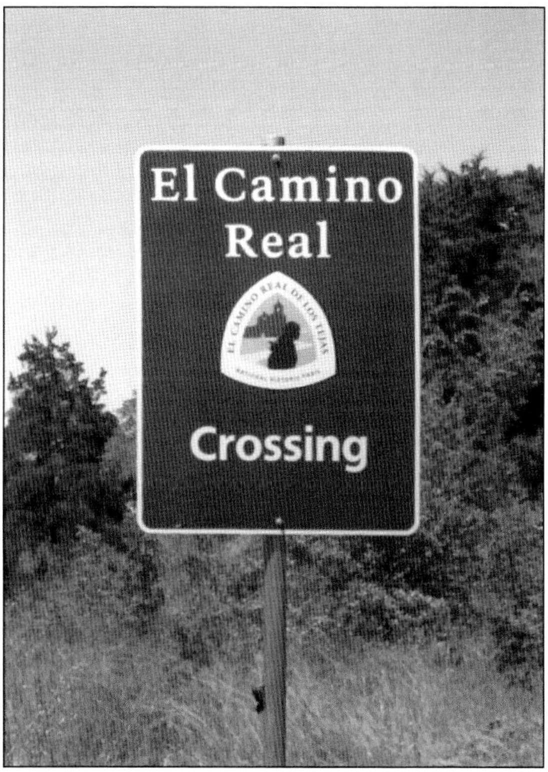


As one of the newest National Historic Trails in the nation, signage began going up along El Camino Real in early 2013. Placing signs along the trail will guide visitors to trail sites and allow the public to know where the trail is. By simply seeing the signs, visitors and passersby will hopefully become curious about it and want to know more. With this added awareness, there should be greater public support for protecting the trail. (Courtesy of Steven Gonzales.)

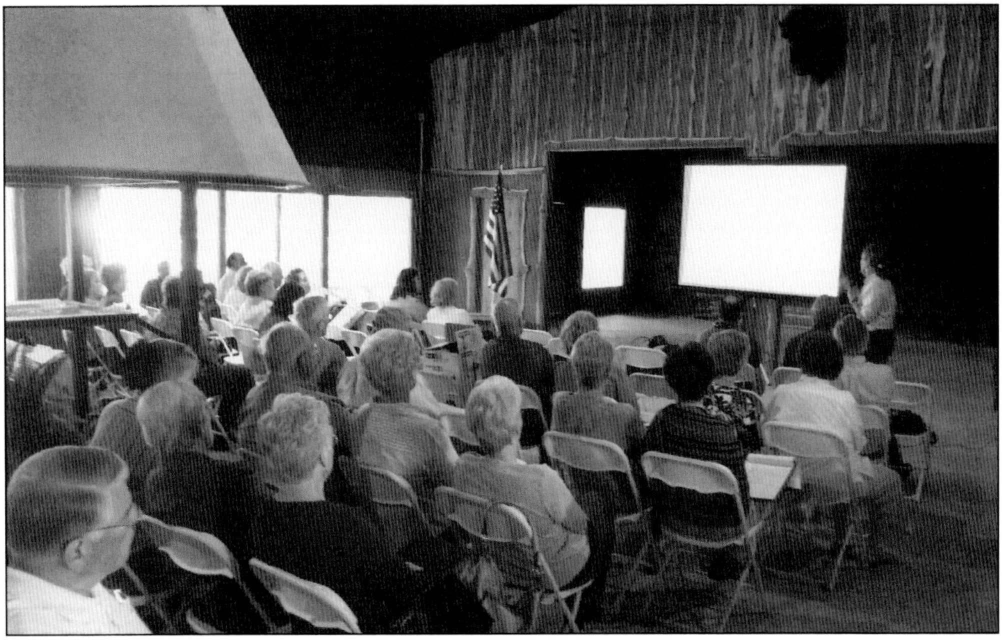

The association is also beginning a program known as the Model Trail Community (MTC). The MTC program will encourage communities to identify, protect, and develop trail resources in their area. In doing so, the trail will be protected and developed in perpetuity, and communities will benefit from heritage tourism generated by trail visitors. (Courtesy of Steven Gonzales.)

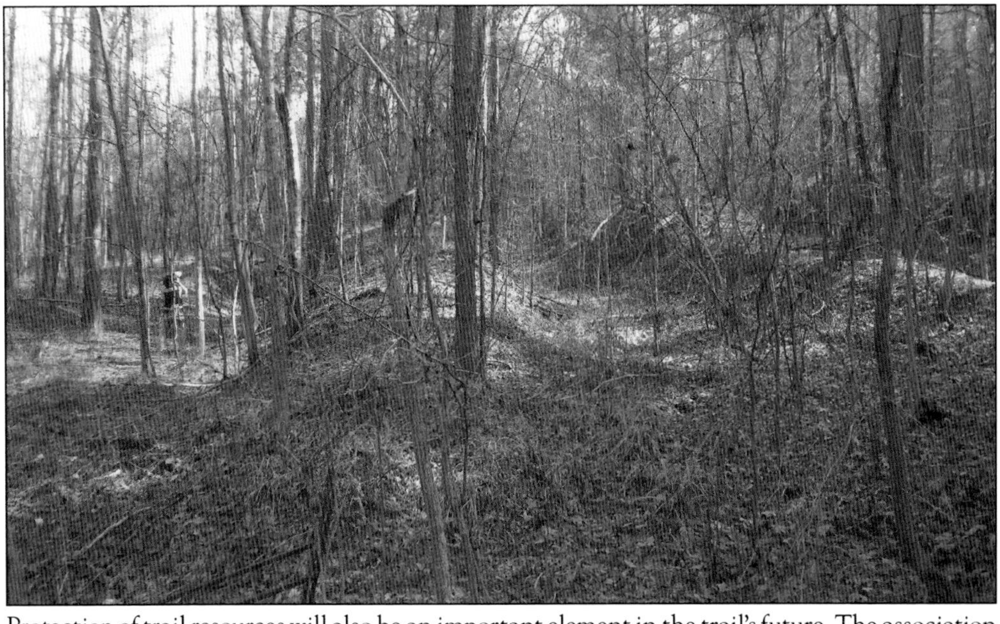

Protection of trail resources will also be an important element in the trail's future. The association has for the first time ever recently acquired and protected a piece of the trail. In September and October 2013, a fundraising effort was conducted to purchase an unparalleled portion of trail in East Texas. The property will be opened by early 2015 and will provide a vicarious experience of traveling the trail—just as explorers and settlers did hundreds of years ago. (Courtesy of Steven Gonzales.)

# Bibliography

*El Camino Real de los Tejas National Historic Trail, Comprehensive Management Plan and Environmental Assessment*. Santa Fe: National Park Service, US Department of the Interior, 2011.

Estell, Dr. Lucile. *Rockdale*. Charleston, SC: Arcadia Publishing, 2012.

Gilmore, Kathleen K. *San Xavier Missions: A Study in Historical Site Identification, Report No. 16, March 1969*. Austin: Texas Historical Commission, 1969.

Graham, M. Joy, and Dr. Lucile Estell. *Historic & Architectural Resources Survey of Milam County Texas*. Certified Local Government Survey, 2007.

McGraw, A. Joachim, John W. Clark Jr., and Elizabeth A. Robbins. A *Texas Legacy: The Old San Antonio Road and the Caminos Reales, a Tercentennial History, 1691–1991*. Austin: Texas Department of Highways and Public Transportation, 1991.

Thomas, Alston V., ed. "Native American Land Use in the Yegua Creek Basin and Vicinity: Ethnohistoric and Archaeological Records." *Reports of Investigations No. 5, Center for Ecological Archaeology, Texas A&M University, College Station* (2004): 35–48.

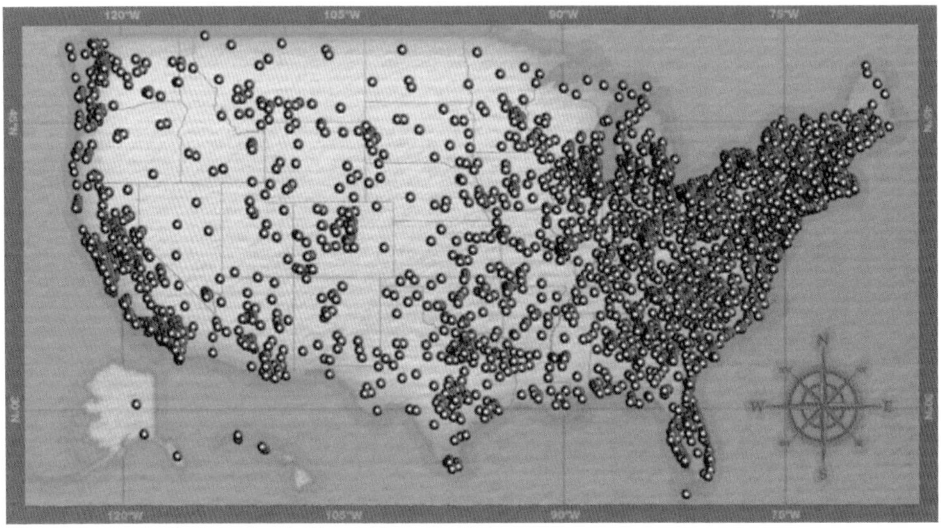




Consistent with our mission to preserve history on a local level, this book was printed in South Carolina on American-made paper and manufactured entirely in the United States. Products carrying the accredited Forest Stewardship Council (FSC) label are printed on 100 percent FSC-certified paper.

MADE IN THE USA